W9-AHH-600

MEANING-MAKING

Therapeutic Processes in

Adult Development

Mary Baird Carlsen

W • W • NORTON & COMPANY

NEW YORK • LONDON

A NORTON PROFESSIONAL BOOK

Published simultaneously in Canada by Penguin Books Canada Ltd.,
2801 John Street, Markham, Ontario L3R 1B4.

Printed in the United States of America.

First Edition

Library of Congress Cataloging-in-Publication Data

Carlsen, Mary Baird, 1928-
   Meaning-making: therapeutic processes in adult development.
   "A Norton professional book" — P. facing t.p.
   Bibliography: p.
   1. Psychotherapy.   2. Cognition.   3. Developmental
psychology.   I. Title.   [DNLM: 1. Cognition.   2. Human
Development.   3. Psychotherapy — methods.   WM 420 C284m]
RC480.5.C356   1988   616.89′14   87-31342

ISBN   0-393-70049-6

W. W. Norton & Company, Inc., 500 Fifth Avenue, New York, N.Y. 10110
W. W. Norton & Company Ltd., 37 Great Russell Street, London WC1B 3NU

1 2 3 4 5 6 7 8 9 0

To Jim, my partner in process

CONTENTS

SECTION I

An Overview of Theory

Metaphors of the "dark wood" and the "side of the mountain" provide a *leit motif* for the contrasts between the beginnings and endings of therapy. Many theories and therapies join in this meaning-making therapy — particularly those which honor the processes of growth and development in human life.

Difficult to define, "meaning" is a concept which psychology has tended to neglect. With new cognitive research and therapy, however, new alliances are being formed as "meaning" becomes the focus of multidisciplinary attention. The meanings of "meaning" range from the semantics of a single word to abstract philosophies of life in a hierarchy of systems. The systems perspective is very helpful in defining the difficult concept of meaning and for providing a base for meaning-making therapy.

The words "adult development" carry the contrasts of stability and change and give a conceptual frame for looking at theories of the life cycle. Schemata of life development often take the form of metaphors and models of life: the journey, the Way, the tapestry, the braid, for example. Ideas from ancient philosophy join the current thinking of researchers Erik Erikson, Robert Kegan and Michael Basseches.

SECTION II

A Bridge to Therapy

This chapter assembles the tacit assumptions for a therapy of meaning-making and illustrates how these assumptions influence the therapeutic process.

A brief pause in the forward motion of this book, this chapter uses a letter from Vicky to contemplate a few values questions.

SECTION III

A Meaning-Making Therapy

The focus of this chapter is the therapeutic sequence: establishment, data gathering, patterning and process, and termination. The behaviors, goals and results of therapy are considered through the windows of each of these stages.

Chosen to fit and facilitate the forward motion of this cognitive developmental therapy, these techniques pay particular attention to semantics, narrative form, creative written expression, historical data gathering, affective experience and imagery, the supportive dialogue of constructive contradiction, and the active, supportive use of teaching.

After introductory material which compares and contrasts short-term and long-term therapies, this chapter begins the stories of Jana, Jennifer, Nick, Sonny, and Vicky whose therapeutic experience illustrates the processes of meaning-making.

These client stories continue as the patterning and process of the middle stages of therapy gain complexity and momentum.

Building on the idea that growth and development never stop, this chapter reports on endings and new beginnings in the case histories recounted in these three illustrative chapters.

SECTION IV

Some Specific Therapies

Believing that the concept of career as "path" is a significant one for a meaning-making therapy, this chapter focuses more directly on a therapy of career development, and on the translations of some of its techniques into a more general psychotherapy.

With the theme of "partners in process" consideration is given to the evolving, overlapping growths of the individual partners who are joined within the evolving process called marriage. Not meant to be a definitive coverage of a complex therapeutic challenge, this chapter explores topics and introduces questions for further exploration and research.

Using models of successful aging from Siebert, McLeish, Selye, and others, this chapter formulates the later stages of life as the long view down the mountain. By articulating this long view the therapist is better able to teach and model "preventive maintenance" and proactive planning of successful aging.

ACKNOWLEDGMENTS

M̲EANINGS ARE MADE within contexts not only of private thought and event, but within the contexts of dialogues with those significant others who teach us, confirm us, challenge us, and contradict us. Certainly this book was forged out of such connection.

It is with a deep sense of appreciation, therefore, that I acknowledge those who have joined me in the writing of this book. I extend my thanks:

To Suzanne Rahn, Zola Ross, and Dorothy Bestor who have served as teachers and editors as they have nurtured and shaped my writing ability and helped me find my "voice." They guided the writing apprenticeship which brought me to a readiness for that chance meeting in Washington, D.C., when I first met Susan Barrows who was later to become my editor.

To the talented helpers who performed many of the tasks of sorting and transcribing: To Edith Summers who contributed a special wisdom to our joint efforts; to Cary Peterson whose fresh enthusiasm stimulated me; and to Bill Kauffman who helped me through the difficult details of final editing and revision.

To friends, colleagues and family members who have taken time to read my materials and to offer active feedback: Don Smith, James Mulligan, Joel Parks, Jan Lawry, David LaBerge, Barbara Walkover, Jo Blake, Robert

Goodman, Phil, Doug, Sue, Kris, Art, Mary, Paul, Charlotte, and James. And, particularly, I thank Jim who has always walked beside me, but who shared his expertise in a special way by editing my final materials.

To Michael Mahoney who graciously answered my letters as he responded with genuine dialogue. And to Al Siebert who took much time to critique and edit some early writings. Although we have never met he has treated me like a friend.

To the staff of the 1983 "Institute on Lifespan Clinical-Developmental Psychology" at Harvard, and of the Clinical-Developmental Institute in Belmont, Massachusetts—people who have taught and inspired me and urged me to continue my efforts. Certainly it was during those remarkable two weeks in the summer of 1983 that many of my ideas were both affirmed and clarified. (And, Robert Goodman, thank you for being among the first to encourage me to consider a book on developmental therapy.)

To Robert Kegan whose book *The Evolving Self* moved me to make connection with him. From that first meeting came my attendance at the Harvard institute, an emerging friendship, and an active dialogue with meaning-making. Bob has provided an intellectual "holding environment" (and you will meet those terms in Chapter 3), which has also provided confirmation and continuity; at the same time he has dared me to refine my thinking and create a focused direction for my book. It was through our dialogue that the title of this book emerged.

To my editor, Susan Barrows, who took time not only to read early materials but to encourage a book on developmental psychotherapy. Her support and her ready availability have sustained me in times of discouragement, and her editing has been sensitive to my style and my purposes.

Finally, to all my clients I give my deepest thanks. They have taught me, amazed me, dared me, confronted me, and moved me. Out of our joint meaning-makings I, too, have grown. They give evidence that no neat plan, prepared in advance, is ever going to touch the mystery of the unexpected in the therapeutic moment.

SECTION I

An Overview of Theory

Midway in our life's journey, I went astray from the straight road and woke to find myself alone in a dark wood. How shall I say what wood that was? I never saw so drear, so rank, so arduous a wilderness. Its very memory gives a shape to fear.

—Dante, *The Inferno**

. . . creating a new theory is like destroying an old barn and erecting a skyscraper in its place. It is rather like climbing a mountain, gaining new and wider views, discovering unexpected connections between our starting point and its rich environment. But the point from which we started out still exists and can be seen, although it appears smaller and forms a tiny part of our broad view gained by the mastery of the obstacles on our adventurous way up.

—Albert Einstein**

It is previous theory, more or less latent, that determines *what* we observe and *how* we observe, and it is from the imaginative leap of the mind rooted in previously established theories that our new theories come.

—James E. Loder, 1981, p. 22

CHAPTER 1

By Way of Introduction

Aₛ ᴀ ᴛʜᴇʀᴀᴘɪsᴛ I meet my clients when they are lost in their dark wood. Words such as, "It doesn't make sense," "I feel like I am in limbo," "I have an empty feeling within me," are signals that what made sense before, what held life together, what provided patterns of significance and intentionality, has broken apart thrusting these individuals into a transitional stage between the new and the old. This can be very frightening; after all, even though the old way is no longer working, at least it was known.

But therapy is more than a time of standing in the wood—it is a movement from the dark wood to new understandings, new experiences, and new meanings. With my clients I repeatedly encounter the chilling, poignant moment when together we look down the mountain. Something remarkable has happened to bring about a cognitive shift where the client no longer *is*

---

*I am indebted to Rollo May for the idea that this quote is a "marvelous statement of what people say in the first session of therapy." Interview by Susan Cunningham, "Rollo May: The case for love, beauty and the humanities," in the *APA Monitor*, May 1985, Vol. 16, #5, p. 17.
**This important quote has long influenced my thinking but its source has unfortunately long eluded me! I include it, nevertheless, because Einstein's beautiful words lead us so effectively into meaning-making.

the problem, but *has* the problem, thus is able to hold it, objectify it, and deal with it with a new construction of the reality of that problem. When this moment occurs I, as therapist, know that the client is arriving at a major transformation of thinking and interpretation—that he or she has moved from one way of cognitively shaping the world to another.

In their cognitive shifts clients who may never have explored themselves—and thus, never really known themselves—begin to understand the patterning and programs which have shaped their lives. Ordering and synthesizing this new information, they open their eyes to new possibilities and are often able to stand back with a new perspective on themselves. And, parallel to their cognitive understandings comes new awareness and recognition of the influence and meaning of their affective experience—not one without the other, but intertwining and developing in a dialectical synergy of life development.

The story of a developmental meaning-making therapy is the story of how the individual emerges from the wood to a place on the mountain. In this therapeutic process are the movements from crisis to resolution; from endings to new beginnings; from the unnamed to the named; from limbo to finding one's way; from the experience of being within the problem to standing outside the problem with new perspectives and understandings. This is the story, therefore, of the movement from meaninglessness to meaning.

To translate my intuitions about these movements of change into tangible statements of the how, the what, and the why of therapeutic happening I have searched client material, listened to transcripts, examined semantics, and identified the verbal forms, the visual images, the emotional expressions, and the new behaviors which give evidence of the transformational shifts. This book has been born of that search as I have sought to make sense of the orderings and reorderings of experience. The results of my search are in this articulation of an approach to therapy framed in the metaphorical language of human life development and meaning-making.

This developmental language uses many words which carry the prefix *pro*: *pro*active, *pro*cess, *pro*gressing, *pro*posing, *pro*creating, for example. This vocabulary reflects a paradigm of growth, of shifting designs and shifting purposes. This is in sharp contrast to the vocabulary of a reductionist, reactive, positivistic position. In the words of Gordon Allport:

The vocabulary emanating from this type of [positivistic] postulate is replete with terms like *reaction, response, reinforcement, reflex, respondent, reintegration*—all sorts of *re*-compounds. The reference is backward. What *has* been is more important than that which *will* be. Terms such as *proaction, progress, program, production, problem-solving,* or *propriate* are characteristically lacking. One would think that the client seated opposite would *pro*test, for the language of response negates the subject's immediate certainty that his life lies in the future. (1968, p. 70)

When I call this cognitive developmental therapy a "meaning-making therapy," therefore, I do so because it addresses proactive therapeutic passages and honors the evolving definitions of meaning in an individual's life, as well as the cognitive structuring of those meanings. In this therapy meaning is interpreted as both a process and an ideal, as a structure and a sequence, as possibility and constraint, as an achievement and an intending, and as both noun and verb as it forms and reforms through the ongoing stages of adult life.

I also call this a dialectical therapy as I build on the following definitions of *dialectic*:

Dialectical logic sees contradictions as fruitful collisions of ideas from which a higher truth may be reached by way of SYNTHESIS. (*Harper Dictionary of Modern Thought*, 1977, p. 170)

The ancient dialectic: "the art of conversation or debate, as used by *Zeno of Elea* (the inventor of dialectic according to *Aristotle*), Protagoras, Socrates, Plato, Aristotle, and the later Aristotelean scholastic philosophers of the Middle Ages. What links all of these is the understanding of dialectic as a 'method of seeking and sometimes arriving at the truth by reasoning'." (Tolman, 1983)

A current meaning: "it involves the following essential ingredients: movement from one state (ignorance, uncertainty, error) to a qualitatively different state (knowledge, certainty, truth) by means of a process (conversation, debate, dialogue) that is characterized by opposition (contradiction, refutation, negation) and governed by an internal necessity (logic, deduction)." (Tolman, 1983)

And, finally, from Michael Basseches:

Dialectic, defined as follows, ties together the concepts of change, wholeness, and internal relations. . . . Dialectic is *developmental transformation (i.e., developmental movement through forms) which occurs via constitutive and interactive relationships.* The phrase "movement *through* forms" is meant to distinguish such movement from movement *within* forms. (1984, p. 22)

By studying these definitions we can find many approaches to the processes of this therapy, particularly in the second definition from Tolman, which offers an excellent structure to follow in meeting the client and developing the therapeutic experience.

It is the search for meaning which is at the heart of this therapy. It appears the never-ending challenge for the person to create the orderings of experience as the mind works "incessantly to shape what otherwise would be inchoate fragments into patterns contributory to the goals it seeks" (Smith, 1965, p. 45). And, quoting Michael Mahoney, "As Hayek (1952) and others have noted, we seem to be neurologically 'wired' to classify our experiences and to transform the 'buzzing booming confusion' of sensation into some codified and dynamic representation of the world" (1982, p. 92). It is the drive to meaning—to making sense, to ordering one's experience, to finding some reference point for purpose and intent—that provides much of the motivation bringing the individual into therapy.

Accepting these premises brings the therapist to the hows, the whats, the whens, and the whys of the ordering experience. And with this attention, symptoms become signals but not primary focus as client and therapist jointly explore the patterns of life. There is no guarantee of success for this intangible process, this artificial relationship which Montalvo (1976) describes as an "interpersonal agreement to abrogate the usual rules that structure reality, in order to reshape reality." The variables of client motivation and courage, as well as the mesh between therapeutic posture and client need, create a wide range of result. But when the process *works*, the outcome can be the transformational, developmental experience which I am describing in these pages.

The writing of this book represents a miniature model of meaning-making. Sorting through my learnings and experiences, I have struggled to create a pattern, a form, which makes sense of a lot of material—a sense that makes sense to you as well as to me. In this process, my knowledge and expertise have grown into new cross-connections, new syntheses, new systems. I now can look back and see an emerging tapestry which grows increasingly complex, or, in the words of systems, I can see systems within systems within systems. I am struck by that fact that there has always been a developmental theme, one I didn't know at the time of its beginnings, but one, nevertheless, which has drawn to itself continuing accretions, acquisitions. Why this gathering around a common theme? I don't have an answer, but it is one of the questions I find particularly intriguing in the field of adult development. And it is one of the questions which has brought me to study my own transformational experiences to gain understanding of those tacit dimensions which have shaped and reformed the attitudes, outlooks, and knowledge which influence my therapy.

Thus, I take time here to sort and to acknowledge some of the theorists who have contributed to my evolving understandings. I consider this review a reminder and a reiteration that the processes of cognitive expansion and development include both a *what* and a *how*—both the contents of expanding knowledge which provide springboards and stimuli for new thinking, and the structurings of this knowledge in the evolving processing of experience. In describing these bits and pieces of theory I do not point to a simple aggregation—I point to a transformational process in my own intellectual and cognitive development.

In the early days of my training I discovered the work of Charlotte Buhler and Gordon Allport, whose concepts of goal-setting and "becoming" fit into my emerging sensitivity to the adult development process. Particularly, Allport's descriptor of the human being as "the being-in-the-process-of-becoming" (1962) has shaped my thinking in many ways. Next I found Carl Rogers, Abraham Maslow, and Rollo May who emphasize respect for the individuality and potential of the person. I was further enriched by the psychology of Andras Angyal (1965) with his conceptualization of the personality as a "temporal Gestalt," a pattern in which past, present, and future are firmly embedded. During this time I also came to appreciate the work of a variety of developmental theorists: Bernice Neugarten, Erik Erikson, Robert W. White, Daniel Levinson, Roger Gould, Jane Loevinger, George E. Vaillant, and Lawrence Kohlberg, among others.

Concepts of meaning and of the importance of personal coherence have been enriched by the work of Viktor Frankl, Leona Tyler, Anton Antonovsky, Hans and Shulamith Kreitler, and by Irving Janis and his research reports of post-trauma problem solving. I have also given attention to the more spiritual, philosophical perspectives of Michael Polanyi, Soren Kierkegaard, Maurice Friedman, Martin Buber, James Fowler, and Huston Smith. Their words have encouraged me to go beyond the concrete and the discrete to the abstract and the universal in human cognitive development.

At the present time my thinking is being stimulated by the research and wonderings of Robert Kegan, whose "constructive-developmental" theory has built upon the cognitive-developmental framework of Jean Piaget, as well as the work of Erik Erikson and Lawrence Kohlberg. Kegan describes his book *The Evolving Self* (1982, p. 15) as an "organized way of wondering what happens if the evolution of the activity of meaning is taken as the fundamental motion in personality." He considers the self in its developing social context throughout the lifecycle, and believes that psychology needs a "sophisticated understanding of the relationship between the psychological and social, between the past and the present, and between emotion and thought" (p. 15). I consider Kegan's attention to these overlapping systems and to the concept of meaning-making to be among his significant contributions to current thinking. He has provided a rich theory which I will explore in greater depth later in this book.

Another theorist whose work influences mine and which is complementary to the ideas of Kegan is George Kelly who wrote with seminal vision in *A Theory of Personality*, published in 1955. His theory started with the combination of two simple notions:

first, that man might be better understood if he were viewed in the perspective of the centuries rather than in the flicker of passing moments; and second, that each man contemplates in his own personal way the stream of events upon which he finds himself so swiftly borne. (Kelly, 1955, p. 3)

Building on such ideas he paid great attention to the human being as a personal *scientist* "ever seeking to predict and control the course of events with which he is involved" (Kelly, 1955, p. 5).

All these theorists pay attention to the meaning of the person within the long view of life and create an attitudinal framework for the actual practice of therapy. I combine their ideas with the therapeutic approaches of Carl Rogers, Andras Angyal, Rollo May, Aaron Beck, Richard Lazarus, Arnold Lazarus, Calvin Colarusso and Robert Nemiroff (whose assumptions about adult development therapy I will be synthesizing later), Bradford Keeney and cognitive behaviorist Michael Mahoney who also places great emphasis on concepts of meaning in the personal developmental process.

In his 1982 Master Lecture to the American Psychological Association Mahoney said, "Much of our moment-to-moment experience is imbued with "[a] contrast-laden quest for meaning." He also suggests that "Unless we appreciate the patterns by which individuals order their realities, we are unlikely to understand fully their requests for help." "The contexts by which an individual orders experience may well be one of the most challenging and promising targets of effective psychotherapy."

The most recent transformations in my thinking are being stimulated by Michael Basseches' *Dialectical Thinking and Adult Development*. Through the eyes of his dialectical schemata I am growing in my own dialectical structurings as I see enlarging questions in the formings and reformings of adult development. I am also appreciative of his concern for a values orientation in the field of adult development, a concern that we acknowledge and confront some of the implicit value systems which have already been built into the thinking of developmental models. In a critique of current popular models he writes:

What troubles me most about this sudden popularity is what seems to be happening to the idea of *development* in the process. Looking at the history of popular psychology from Adler to Laing, Russel Jacoby, in his book *Social Amnesia* (1975) documents a gradual movement in the direction of narcissistic preoccupation with subjective feelings and experience. The advocacy of ideal individual goals like self-actualization (Maslow, 1967), and techniques such as Gestalt Therapy (Perls et al., 1951), translated into a preoccupation with a kind of psychological self-aggrandizement. Phrases like becoming a "psychologically whole person" or an "expanded person" or "fully functioning and emotionally expanded" (Boy & Pine, 1971, p. 4) became popular. More recently, with books like *Looking Out For Number One* (Ringer, 1978), pop psychologists have become explicit prophets of universal selfishness. (1984, pp. 6–7)

For a profession that has so frequently exchewed values as a part of its theories, these are strong statements. But they provide a constructive contradiction for developmental theorists and therapists to ponder. They also join the ideas of Carol Gilligan and her colleagues who have challenged models of adult development which have placed strong emphasis on self-oriented developmental schemes of personal separateness and independence while either ignoring or downgrading the more feminine models of nurture, community, and care. Perhaps these challenges will help us transcend our old models of development into a human synthesis. Whatever the outcome, I am encouraged by this attention to values of human relationship in a dialectic of self and other.

As this book proceeds you will meet others. Among these others are Silvano Arieti, James Adams, Arthur Koestler, and Howard Gruber, whose work in creative thinking is a palette of ideas for a meaning-making therapist. I also allude to the work of Karl Pribram who is representative of contemporary scientists who are breaking apart our paradigms in leaps into new systems of thinking.

My own leaps from latent theory into new synthesis have brought me to a speculative model of development which I call "process and ideal." Many of its ideas were born in my career therapy where I work with clients to collect and sort personal descriptors of who and what they are. As these variables are collected clients are faced with an abundance of information but often do not have a way to order that information. If they have lost old organizing titles of "student" or "lawyer" or "mother," they don't have a means to make sense and to use this personal mass. What has to take place is the development of a new ordering system. What is needed is a goal, or a new title, or a new descriptor which can help the mind to catalog its information.

John, whom you will meet again in a later chapter, organized all of his life purposes under the ideal of meeting his father's expectations that he would become a political science professor. Everything he did and everything he believed about the meaning of life was categorized under this major guiding ideal. But one day, after several years of intensive search in the academic world, he realized that he would never make it into the ranks of academia. His ideal was shattered as a guiding model for his life. And thus, the systems of his life were also shattered, leaving the disparate elements of his being floating in limbo. When he came to see me he was in serious crisis, very depressed and upset. It took a close examination of his latent theories about himself, of his shattered ideal, and of his father's ideal, for him to rebuild his systems under a new ideal encompassing an independent role as author, consultant and scholar. It all made such good sense when the pieces fell into place. But until he saw the new ideal his personal processes were interrupted without an organizing design for the future.

In the cognitive world of ideas, images, ideals, and ideology we have our dependencies — old conceptualizations, old central images, old belief systems, old emotional expression, old habits, old paradigms — and it is this set of dependencies which is shaken at the moment of cognitive/affective rebirth. At the moment of this rebirth a dramatic reordering of the bases for experience can cause a kind of existential terror. Although the old ways are painful they are known ways, and the resistances of therapy can reflect the fear and confusion which comes with the breakup of a meaning system. Any resistance which occurs, therefore, can represent a protection of the old system as the client seeks to maintain its integrity and continuity. But it is in the breakup of the old meaning that we find the "dangerous opportunity" of crisis which is an impetus for continuing change.

In this cognitive reordering the therapist can play an important role as facilitator and supporter. And the therapist can provide both confirmation and the novelty of creative contradiction in stimulating the client to conceptualize his realities in new ways. This therapeutic role is central in a meaning-making therapy. To move us forward towards understanding of that therapy I turn now to questions of change and development.

One day in a therapy session my client, Nick, turned to me and with great intensity asked the following questions:

NICK There's a part of me that wants to change but doesn't know how. I ask myself so many questions about change. *Change what*?

THERAPIST Change what?

NICK I could change the way I came here this morning. Is that a change? You know. I could change some of the things that start my morning . . . I could reverse them all. I ask myself — is this change? This week I'm taking the days off . . . is that change? Then I ask myself, have I changed? And I look maybe where I was six months ago and I needed to make a change about my house . . . there was something to do there and I kept putting it off, putting it off. And that was a change. I realized I needed to do something about it. And I made that change. I made those changes because inside I wanted to be [more in charge of] what I was going to live with. I didn't want to be dependent. Like on the job . . . I could say "I need out" and "I can survive somehow." But I need to make a change in order for me to make that change. It is not going to be an easy transition. I may go through some basic financial hardships. . . maybe I will have to wait on tables a lot . . . but maybe I will be happier . . . I know I can survive . . . you know . . .

THERAPIST So you contemplate the different kinds of changes you could make?

NICK I know I could change. I know I have a car now and don't have car payments, I know I have a house I could rent. And I could live without a job because I don't have any balloon payments that I would have to deal with. I could live with that.

THERAPIST And I guess you know you could change to another job and stay at this job until you find the other job to change to. . . . In other words there are different ways to do this [i.e., job change].

NICK But would that change be good? Maybe I need a different perspective.

THERAPIST All right. The different perspective would be one way to change?

NICK Maybe I need to free up my thinking . . . because . . . the routine! Uh . . . I wrote something down here this morning — in going through change we experiment with ourselves and our lives. And that kind of clicked. I wrote it down here and I wrote it above my desk at home.

THERAPIST Good. Say that again so I can hear it again.

NICK It is only through change that we can continue to experiment with ourselves and our lives.

Nick's questionings have taken him from the concrete to the abstract as he has moved from simple evidence to new ways of thinking. Moving outside himself he has started comparing tangible behaviors with the intangibles of a change of thought — a change of perspective on the problems of change. He has also widened his questions opening cognitive doors to new ways of viewing his own motivations and his own purposes and meanings. What he arrived at at the end of this brief sequence was a new perspective on change, a new structuring of the concept and its relationship to his life, and some new more encompassing approaches to facilitating his own change.

For Nick this little sequence was a part of a major thrust forward. He was widening his circle of questioning, and each question came back upon itself to open new forms of questioning. This was remarkable for this client because when he first came for therapy he could not express himself, did not know his own feelings, and sat mute when I asked him questions. He did not like my questioning because it pushed him to the edge of his thinking and knowing. He felt inadequate. But little by little he began to open his mind to new ideas, and gradually he, too, began to question.

So here is one illustration of change: the change brought about by questioning which raises new issues which lead to new questions which raise new questions — a cybernetic looping of question and answer. As each question leads to a larger version of the same question new perspectives are opened on the problem at hand.

Here is another client's effort at addressing the questions of change. Sonny did not consider himself a poet, but this was what emerged after a brainstorming session with his computer.

Can we articulate the change? How do I translate from the complex back to the simple? What process lets me recover my youth? I was a child once. I was frightened once. I understand how I felt where I was and how I thought I had it down pat. But now I know I did not and never will. Faith in the possibility of growth, change and spiritual evolution. A true reincarnation of a personal mysticism waiting to be set free. I was caged once. A cage of my own making. Scared of what turns out to be beauty. Scared that I might not understand the complexity, scared that there may be too much gray, scared that life is difficult. Living in a world of laws but not of men.

And further:

An old reality now perceived in all its complexity. The "interconnectedness" of everything. I now stand in relation to other people as well as ideas and values. I now have the strength to recognize the separateness of each of us; yet I feel that I can love enough to overcome the separation — maybe only in small ways. I need to overcome the separation. I was scared once of the hard truths that would require of me; now I feel more confident. . . . Before I was a breakwall against an inevitable sea of reality. Now I accept — and sometimes it is so hard to accept. To live to see beauty rather than fight the ugly.

Sonny's words came at a time of marital separation, a time when all the concrete structures of home and relationship were changing. But what was remarkable here was that he was *developing* in the middle of the painful happenings in his life. As his words demonstrate, he began to think and feel in entirely new ways and, in spite of (or because of) his pain, he was able to stand outside himself to see how he was assimilating and accommodating these new feelings and experiences in his life.

Sonny and Nick are among those clients who do become different in some fairly significant ways: in outlook, in knowledge, in attitude, in the learning of tools which will serve them the rest of their life, and in central premises about self. But with Nick, Sonny and these others I don't see this change as serving them once and for all. Development seems to have a life of its own which I, as therapist, foster, encourage, negotiate, and facilitate, but the developmental life of the person means that certain forms of readiness lead the person to particular kinds of change in the contexts of particular moments in time. Because of this I keep the therapy door open to my clients so that they can come for what I whimsically call "tune-ups." My clients like that term. It puts therapy on a different basis than pathology. With that term therapy becomes a learning experience, a preventive maintenance, a supportive environment, a shot in the arm, or a push to completion— whatever it is the client feels is needed.

Because I keep the door to the therapy room open, it becomes even more necessary that I stay open to varying forms of change process. I find I can no longer depend on one set model for every meeting or one set body of techniques that will work every time. I end up being very flexible, putting a great deal of the choice in the hands of my client, particularly during later stages of the therapeutic learning process. Even my language has to change in dealing with my clients in the kinds of process ways I am describing.

What is very satisfying to me in the long-term relationships which I maintain is that when my clients have new concerns they come back to therapy at new levels of development. They have not gone back to square one; they are in a new square. Because of this they are able to move forward from a new position rather than the old. In this way therapy becomes a lifelong learning experience, each step building on those which have already been achieved. Once old systems are broken they will not return in the same form.

When we are talking about change we must order it along a continuum from external, superficial change to that which we call development, when cognitive structures and structurings are changed. It is a movement from the observable externals to the intangible abstractions of internal cognitive process.

Development is a transformational shift which occurs as a person moves from one system of structuring the world to another. In sorting this through I am struck by the similarities between James Loder's (1981) description of transformational experience and the transitional meaning-making therapy I am describing. First there is conflict; then comes the search for new data; out of this comes the "aha" of the new insight; next there is a surging of energy as the individual, freeing self from the original conflict, moves to the final stage of a new integration of the old with the new. It is not a simple cumulative process but a transformational one. With increasing complexity of thought and self-knowledge comes increasing capacity to achieve personal creative solutions and new forms of knowing.

A very significant part of the developmental sequence is in the final stage of reordering — of creating a new synthesis of the new and the old which is a reconciliation with and not an abandonment of what was known before. Again, the metaphor of the place on the side of the mountain is important — one can see what was not seen before. To illustrate: In writing this book I shared Nick's transcript with him. He told me that when he read his words about change he wept. Why? Because he felt a certain sadness in looking back on some of his old ways of looking at the world. It was a brief moment of grief, but he said he found new hope in that sadness as he realized how far he had come. It was a moment of comparing and contrasting, and then, of moving on. That same process of comparison and contrast was in Sonny's statement above.

In addressing the role of the therapist in facilitating transformational development I have developed a sequence for therapy consisting of four stages: (1) the establishment stage when the therapist creates a relationship with the client and begins to define the problems; (2) the data gathering stage when the therapist and client work together to assemble the historical data which feed into this moment in time; (3) the active work to find and reshape the patterns of personal experience; and (4) the resolutions which take the client to a new level of personal development.

In recognizing and naming this sequence in my therapy I have looked around for complementary models. Not only do I find Loder's model a great help in naming the process, but I also find much that is helpful in Bradford Keeney's book, *The Aesthetics of Change*. He draws distinctions in the stages of therapy:

First of all, there is the drawing of primary distinctions which the therapist uses to discern what can be called his "raw data". . . .

Given that first order of distinction, the therapist then jumps a level of abstraction and draws distinctions that organize his raw data. Here the therapist attempts to draw patterns that connect his data.

And finally, once the therapist has drawn distinctions that carve out his data and patterns that organize these data, he can step back and examine what he has done. (1983, p. 28)

Keeney's sequencing is very similar to my own, but I do not put as much emphasis on the therapist's role in the process. I prefer to accentuate the client's role as well as client variables which interact with my work in shaping the process. Thus, I teach my client to assemble the data, examine the patterns, and then to step back and organize what she or he has done. The reason I emphasize the teaching aspect of these steps is that I think this sequence is a very helpful tool for the client in times of future crisis and transition.

Gregory Bateson also delineated a change sequence which he felt would be part of a clinical epistemology—a sequence he described as the "weaving of three levels of abstraction":

the first, a concrete level of ethnographic data; the second, more abstract level, the arrangement of data to create "various pictures of the culture"; and the third, most abstract level, a "self-conscious discussion of the procedures by which the pieces of the jigsaw are put together" (1958, p. 281).

Bateson says that "teasing apart the levels inherent in one's attempt to understand a phenomenon constitutes an epistemological method applicable to the therapeutic setting."

Pertinent to these cognitive developmental processes is another domain of interest for developmental psychologists. Researcher Robert Glaser is one of those who is pondering the influence of new knowledge on personal knowing:

Developmental psychologists until recently devoted almost no attention to changes in children's knowledge of specific content. . . . Recently, however, researchers have suggested that knowledge of specific content domains is a crucial dimension of development in its own right and that changes in such knowledge may underlie other changes previously attributed to the growth of capabilities and strategies. (1984, p. 98)

He then quotes Minsky and Papert (1974, p. 59), who state that the "*knowledge* strategy sees progress as coming from better ways to express, recognize, and use diverse and particular forms of knowledge."

Attention to the contexts of knowledge is another dimension of a therapy of meaning-making. A therapist is a teacher in many ways: through modeling, through the sharing of insights, through the active teaching of all sorts of things—coping techniques, thinking tools, autobiographical exercises, models of relationship and even of values, though the therapist must be cautious not to instill values which are in opposition to client values.

All this affirms my belief that a new piece of information, a new understanding, a new awareness, a new attitude, can create a ripple effect through the tacit dimensions of personal knowing—a ripple effect like that created when a pebble is dropped into a quiet pool. New knowledge can challenge and interrupt the placid surface of personal knowing to create the transformational experience of development.

What is experienced in sequential progressions of development is what Michael Polanyi (1975) calls the "from-to" progression of personal knowledge—the movement from the simple to the complex in the development of structures of knowing and in the assimilation of new knowledge and new information. What appears to happen is the movement from patterns of black/white, dualistic thinking, from closed system perspectives, from formal thinking to dialectical, open systems forms of thinking. This is a movement through new forms of dialectical thinking which are more complex than those previously defined by Piaget and others.

The progressive movements of development are not neat and tidy. Sometimes they never take place either because motivation is lacking or because the cognitive structuring is so set in old patterns that nothing seems to jar it loose. Minds (including ours!) *do* get going in simplistic, adaptive, habit channels. The old folk metaphors are intuitively wise as they refer to minds which are *hardheaded, rigid, narrow, channeled, black/white, yes/no, either/or.* But when these channels do break, when the individual shakes the old system into forming the new, when old structures of processing information become replaced by those which are more complex, dialectical forms of thinking—then we see the evidence of genuine development.

Here I have introduced you to some of my language, my latent theory, my thinking, and my approaches to therapy. It is now time to attend to the developmental movements of this book.

In the ordering of this writing, I start with broad perspectives and gradually narrow the focus to specific examples and applications of theory in practice. The movement of the book, therefore, is from the general to the particular, from the theoretical to the practical. Consistent with this progression the book is divided into four major sections. In shaping these I have made an effort to follow a developmental sequence in the ordering of the material, starting with the theoretical chapters which form the foundation for the more pragmatic applications of therapy. Although the reader could gain from the applied sections alone, I feel the developmental, dialectical language and posture must be understood if this therapy is to find its contextual meaning. I encourage the reader, therefore, to follow the chapters as I have arranged them.

SECTION I: AN OVERVIEW OF THEORY

Chapter 1: Here I have introduced you to the theories, language, and thinking which form structural backbones for this book. I have also introduced you to some concepts about therapeutic ordering using two of my clients to suggest what this business of change and development is all about.

Chapter 2: "Questions of Meaning." Cherry calls "meaning" a "harlot among words"—slippery, elusive, impossible to anchor, difficult to pin to a conceptual ground. Because of these complexities, I take you on an exploratory walk around the concept to look in on it from varying perspectives. This is a walk in the manner of the blind men and the elephant; or of the portrait painter who takes many miniature snapshots of her subject in order to arrive at the sense of the whole. A valuable result of viewing meaning from these varying perspectives is the opening of the therapeutic viewpoint to the different ways that clients make meaning. In the process of all this I hope to stimulate you to arrive at your own translations and constructions of the meanings of meaning. I also introduce you to a bit of my style, which gathers data from a number of perspectives and then asks, "How can we pattern this? How can we think about this, and our thinking about our thinking about this?"

Chapter 3: "Languages and Models in Adult Development." Because of the burgeoning mass of material in the field of adult development, it is necessary to narrow the focus quite sharply. Accepting this I have chosen to focus on the languages and theories of adult development as found within these categories of material: (1) adult development as stability and change, (2) metaphors and models which shape developmental language and theory, (3) shifting perspectives in developmental theory, and (4) the featured theories of Erik Erikson, Robert Kegan, and Michael Basseches.

SECTION II: A BRIDGE TO THERAPY

Chapter 4: "Ties Between Theory and Therapy." This chapter assembles the tacit assumptions for a therapy of meaning-making and illustrates how these assumptions influence the therapeutic process. These assumptions are organized into three categories: (1) goals for a meaning-making therapy, (2) beliefs about the client as person, and (3) adult development as a cognitive system for conceptualizing both therapy and client.

Chapter 5: "A Bridge to Therapy." This chapter provides a brief pause in the forward motion of the book to contemplate a few values questions. A letter from my client, Vicky, as well as some of her comments on therapy, provide stimulus material for these contemplations.

SECTION III: A MEANING-MAKING THERAPY

Chapter 6: "Steps to Meaning-Making." The focus of this chapter is the theraputic sequence: establishment, data gathering, patterning and process, and termination. The behaviors, goals and results of therapy are considered through the windows of each of these stages.

Chapter 7: "Techniques of Therapy." Techniques for a meaning-making therapy are chosen to fit and facilitate the forward motion of cognitive development. In these techniques I pay particular attention to semantics, to creative written expression, to affective experience and imagery, and to the supportive dialogue of constructive contradiction—a contradiction which can stimulate client thinking through novelty and cognitive interruption. Case material is used to illustrate these varying techniques.

Chapter 8: "Beginnings." Introducing you to Sonny, Jennifer, Nick, Vicky, and Jana, I start to track their journeys through therapy. I also consider contrasts between short-term and long-term clients.

Chapters 9 and 10: "In Process" and "The Revolving Door." These chapters track the processes and the terminations of therapies of the clients introduced to you in Chapter 8. Included are quotations from their writings and from their therapy sessions which illustrate dilemmas and resolutions which provided the momentum for our work together.

SECTION IV: SOME SPECIFIC THERAPIES

Chapter 11: "Career Development as Meaning-Making." My experience in career development has fed many of the streams of this meaning-making therapy. In this I use the metaphorical concept of "career" as *path,* demonstrating how this more overarching concept enlarges the career process into a meaning-making process. Included will be some discussion of career development sequences, and illustration from the case of John who made a dramatic cognitive leap in the course of his career therapy. His was definitely a *therapy* of career development, a point I will clarify in comparing and contrasting career therapy with career counseling.

Chapter 12: "Marital Meaning-Making." This concerns a topic which is very important in therapeutic work — the evolving, overlapping growths of the separate individuals who are joined in the union called marriage. Not meant to be a definitive coverage of this therapeutic challenge, this chapter raises topics and questions pertinent to the meaning-making therapist.

Chapter 13: "Creative Aging." Enlarging the idea of a values orientation in development, this chapter challenges the therapist to consider health models which are guides for creative aging. Using research on positive aging, this chapter also ties some of these findings with the suggested "better ways" of developmental theory. Other topics which counterbalance this optimism are: human needs in creative aging, challenges, the "double-edged sword" of aging, dilemmas and tasks, and the role of the therapist in facilitating creative aging.

. . . beyond the specific goals to be achieved the person has the broader motivation of shaping his life into a coherent meaningful whole. The course of life is comparable to a work of art which one creates, shapes, and perfects by living it . . .

— Andras Angyal 1965, pp. 63–64

. . . it is not that a person makes meaning, as much as that the activity of being a person is the activity of meaning-making. There is thus no feeling, no experience, thought, no perception, independent of a meaning-making context in which it *becomes* a feeling, an experience, a thought, a perception, because we *are* the meaning-making context.

— Robert Kegan, 1982, p.11

We are language-related, symbol-borne and story-sustained creatures. We do not live long or well without meaning. . . . We live by forming and being formed in images and dispositions toward the ultimate conditions of our existence.

— James Fowler, 1984, p. 50

CHAPTER 2

Questions of Meaning

To STUDY MEANING is to discover the slippery, elusive nature of its concepts as it fulfills its reputation as a "harlot among words" (Cherry, 1961). To study meaning is also to discover its role in creating significance, in structuring reality, in serving as a kind of superordinate principle which orders disparate elements into synergistic systems. But, even more, to study meaning is to find oneself drawn into its dialectic of content and process, of noun and verb, of meaning and meaning-making.

This chapter comes from my journey into the meanings of meaning. The fact that I keep cycling back upon the word itself demonstrates how quickly it slips from cognitive understanding. And I don't think we can pin the word down—at least not yet—with our current understanding of cognitive functioning. But I think we are coming closer as we give greater respect to the word and its significance in the ordering of things.

In the spirit of the blind men and the elephant, therefore, I share my thinking and my data gathering. I have not tried to make this a tightly reasoned whole, preferring to let you share this search as I also teach you vocabularies and concepts which will wander in and out of the pages ahead. This is preparatory knowledge so that you will understand the tacit dimensions of words and theory which influence and shape a meaning-making therapy: synergy, hierarchies of systems, systematic pluralism and eclecticism, open systems, the "idealized model," *meaning* and *mean-ing*, emotions as barometers of meaning. These are among the ideas I offer here. I share them in the spirit and form of preliminary "data gathering," with a challenge to you to put them together in your own ways.

PSYCHOLOGY AND MEANING

So often in the history of psychology we have relegated the mediating variable — the stuff in the little black box — to the realm of the unknowable. When this has happened, much that constitutes the human being has been left to the philosopher and ignored by psychology. In this neglect the rich complexity of the concept of *meaning* has frequently been omitted from both therapeutic practice and psychological research. We have neglected basic human wisdom and wisdoms, and we have forgotten that "a person's behavior, in general, becomes meaningful only when integrated into a whole mind" (Polanyi, 1975, p. 48).

In his own focus on the more atomistic qualities of the human being, behaviorist James Watson (1925) was one of those who chose to eliminate the word *meaning* from his psychological vocabulary:

If you are willing to agree that "meaning" is just a way of saying that out of all the ways the individual has of reacting to this object at any one time, he reacts in only one of these ways, then I find no quarrel with meaning. . . . In other words, when we find the genesis of all forms of a person's behavior, know the varieties of his organization, can arrange or manipulate the various situations that will call out one or another form of his organization, then we no longer need such a term as meaning. Meaning is just one way of telling what the individual is doing. So the behaviorist can turn the tables on his critics. They cannot give an explanation. He can, but he does not believe the word is needed or that it is useful except as a literary expression. (pp. 200–201)

Writing in 1966 Marjorie Creelman addressed this neglect of the concept of *meaning* in her review of psychology's experimental approaches to the investigation of meaning:

the relegation to the never-never land of intervening variable — a land which need not be explored or mapped — of all phenomena defying explanation in terms of a simple model or presenting methodological problems with respect to observation, may allow us to cling to an oversimplified theory long after it has served its usefulness, at the expense of moving on to more fruitful models and methods. (pp. 212-213)

It is clear that the basic building blocks of psychological theory and analysis — human reflexes, motor action, drives, conditioning, learning theories — have often resulted in placing cognition, and thus meaning, in a secondary role. It is also a fact that humanistic psychologies have frequently pushed to the other extreme of ignoring these very building blocks which are important elements in the systems of the human being. The tensions between these two ways of viewing the human being—the atomistic and the holistic—reflect the reality of psychology's two cultures, cultures which have been and often continue to be at odds with each other. Out of his 1984 survey of the field, Kimble (cited in Wittig, 1985) named these two disparate groups the "tough-minded" and the "tender-minded," groups who disagree in three important areas: scientific versus humanistic values; objectivism versus intuition as sources of basic knowledge; and nomothetic versus idiographic approaches to the study of behavior.

What is needed is a dialectic approach with a broader conceptualization of the human being which appreciates and accepts the tension between these so-called opposites. With such an attitude psychology approaches the potential which Einstein described as "the uniting of two truths within a larger truth." What is gained is a perspective much akin to that of Eastern philosophies. In the words of Michael Mahoney (1982):

Where Western notions of truth require the absence of self-contradictory assertions, some Eastern perspectives define truth as the harmonic assimilation of opposites. In these systems, the contrast between truth and untruth is more frequently expressed as a contrast between whole and part rather than consistency and contradiction. (p. 82)

Part and whole. Within a systems perspective the parts are not lost but are subsumed within a larger system. It is not an either-or, but a both-and. I am an individual. I have many subsystems, and I am a part of groups subsumed by other groups. My individuality is relative to the varying systems of which I am a part. This is a way of thinking which Gordon Allport (1968) adopted in his proposal for *systematic pluralism:*

The goal of systematic pluralism is to fashion a conception of the human person that will exclude nothing that is valid, and yet at the same time preserve our ideal of rational consistency. It will allow for what is neural and what is mental; for what is conscious and what is unconscious; for what is determined and what is free; for what is stable and what is variable; for what is normal and what is abnormal; for what is general and what is unique. All these, and many other, paradoxes are actually resident in the human frame. All represent verifiable capacities and none can be ruled out of consideration in our theory-building.

In defining each man as a system, therefore, we should include all (and not simply a few) of the features intrinsic to this system. In doing so we shall neither rest content with reductionist theory nor deny the truth that lies therein. We shall not have to settle for arbitrary eclecticism, or for pragmatic pluralism, *we shall have defined our subject matter in such a way that any and all valid data and all verified processes can be woven into our central conception of man as an open system.* Even though no single psychologist will be able to discern the totality he will fit his own specialty into a larger and more hospitable theoretical edifice. In this way we shall, I hope, reconstruct psychology so that it will be a more openminded and also a more coherent science than it is at present. (pp. 116–117)

Allport's conceptualization gives challenge for therapeutic approaches which combine a systematic pluralism of theory with what he calls a "systematic eclecticism" of therapeutic practice. By embracing enlarging systems of psychological theory and practice, psychology advances in its own sequences of meaning-making.

In the fields of cognitive behavioral psychology and cognitive developmental psychology I find numerous examples of the transcendence of opposites in the enlargement of systems of thinking and practice. Representative theorists from these fields include Michael Mahoney and Robert Kegan whom I will acknowledge repeatedly throughout this book. I respect their comprehensive approaches to studying the human being — approaches which attend to the human being as meaning-maker. They are not ignoring traditional psychology but are incorporating its bodies of theory into more overarching conceptualizations of human growth and process. Kegan (1982) emphasizes the challenge: "Any metapsychology that does arise will have to be more than psychological, as the term implies; it will have to be explicitly attuned to the biological and the philosophical, as well as the psychological" (pp. 14–15).

An operational synthesis of stimulus-response theory with cognitive theory is occurring in the research and writing of Hans and Shulamith Kreitler (1976). In their book *Cognitive Orientation and Behavior* they write, ". . . the limitations of the conception of an organism controlled solely by its drives or the environment became so obvious that a new concept for explaining form and direction of behavior had to be looked for" (p. 3). They have arrived at the conclusion that *meaning* is such a concept.

The Kreitlers do not ignore traditional stimulus-response theory; in fact, they find support for some of of their interpretations of meaning within its early literature:

Remembering that Sokolov and others showed the orienting reflex to be the first reaction to every new or significant stimulus, we were struck by the sudden insight that the orienting reflex not only leads to the cognitive act of orienting but is itself elicited by the cognitive act of recognizing a stimulus as being new or significant. Hence there is no gap between the "higher" mental processes of cognition and the "lower" physiological processes like the orienting reflex and Sokolov's defensive responses, since the former are involved in the elicitation of the latter. (p. vi)

Developing their lines of logic, the Kreitlers describe meaning as a "cognitive orientation" which "characterizes the basic striving of humans to attain, preserve, and widen external and internal orientation on a cognitive level . . . [and] designates a particular matrix of beliefs that predisposes the formation of specific behavioral intents" (p. 12). Summarizing, they state that meaning is a "highly complex phenomenon" and that "the complex structure of meaning must be flexible enough to allow, at the very least, for influences of context and bonding with other meaning structures . . ." (p. 24).

What is being emphasized here is the complexity of meaning systems and the difficulty of definition. In Creelman's words:

What has emerged with considerable clarity is that the word "meaning" refers to so many different concepts, constructs, functional systems, processes, and areas of "experience" that it requires the flexibility of a mountain goat to leap from level to level. (1966, p. 209)

Entering systems of meaning is our task. But what systems of meaning? My articulation of this is from three perspectives on meaning: that of the parts, that of the process, and that of the whole. These are artificial separations, for the systems of meaning overlap, forming and reforming within systems of ever increasing complexity, but acknowledging these divisions can give us greater understanding of the meaning of "meaning."

MEANING AND MEANING-MAKING

At the elemental level of dictionary definition, "meaning" can be defined as "intention, purpose, or that which a speaker or writer intends to express." But what gives us our intent or our purpose? What leads us to what we have in mind, what we have to express? The Kreitlers would answer that meaning is always tied to some referent or source of meaning. They list these as ranging from an "object, a word, an abstraction, or an event, to a process, an activity, a sentence, a theme, or a whole present, past, or future situation, period, and so on" (p. 31). Eric Klinger (1977) showed that personal relationship, career, and an experience of personal growth were the primary sources of meaning in the subjects he interviewed. I would add to these tangible categories the more abstract realms of life purpose, of universal "truths," of personal patterns of significance. One of the arguments I am developing is that our systems of meaning move up and down ladders of abstraction from the concrete to the abstract. I also argue that the broader and more inclusive our referents of meaning, the less vulnerable we are to loss, say, of a relationship, a job, or a specific area of personal growth and intention.

Another point must be emphasized here. In any discussion of meaning and its referents emotional factors must be taken into consideration. Meaning-making is not just a detached, analytical, intellectual enterprise; it involves our excitements, our griefs, our passions as well. Richard Lazarus and Susan Folkman (1984) incorporate this feeling dimension in their considerations of meaning:

As we have argued, humans are meaning-oriented, meaning-building creatures who are constantly evaluating everything that happens, which is a constructionist rather than positivist position. These evaluations are guided by cognitive structures that orient the person with respect to what is relevant and important for well-being. . . . When information is appraised as having significance for our well-being, it becomes what we have called "hot information," or information that is laden with emotion. Subsequent processing takes place with this hot information, which means that the stuff of processing is no longer cold, meaningless bits . . . We are saying that it is not only possible, but in the context of most stressful events highly probable that emotion and information (and therefore cognition) are conjoined for large portions of the evaluative appraisal process. (pp. 276–277)

I have already alluded to emotions as barometers of change, but I would go further in describing them as barometers of meaning. Not only are theorists like Lazarus and Folkman pointing us in that direction, but support for emotion as an important part of our "knowing" comes from the work of Robert Kegan and his colleagues, who are positing new theories of the parallel developments of affect and cognition, and from Michael Mahoney, who forcefully addresses questions of meaning, emotion and the unconscious.

Going further with our definitions, the word "meaning" can be conceptually enlarged to join the elements of the noun and the verb. On the one hand *meaning*; on the other *mean-ing*. These complementary aspects dance in a dialectic of life, giving momentum to progressive states of personal knowing. As I have already suggested, "meaning" as a noun contains the elements of constructs, word systems, cognitive schemata, matrices of belief, orienting mechanisms, patterns of significance—in other words, the descriptors of that which creates meaning of life.

In the predicate qualities of "meaning" are process, movement, growth, personal intending, the evolution of personal synergies—the "from-to" growth and development which takes us both from what we don't know to what we know and from what we know to what we don't know, in various combinations of subject-object transitions and of subsidiary to focal knowing.*

"Meaning," then, is both *meaning and mean-ing; intention and in-tending; being and be-ing*. This "both-and," this noun and verb quality in our lives, is inherent in the words *adult development*—and is reflected in the metaphorical models of the lifecycle, as well as in the research wonderings of theorists in the field. Within the context of these perspectives, I interpret *meaning-making* as the forming and reforming of intention and significance; of what one has in mind and *how* one has in mind; and of the succession of synergies or gestalten of personal knowledge and meaning. And, if living *is* meaning-making—as Angyal, Kegan, and Fowler suggest—then, the vital focus for therapy is also meaning-making.

Meaninglessness is the negative contrast to a state of meaning when we are:

---

*In naming these sequences I have used terms from the theories of Robert Kegan and Michael Polanyi who are among those who address our passages of *knowing*.

- without a recognizable purpose or function
- without intention
- without significance
- without a design for living
- without an ordering, organizing system for making choices
- without a sense of direction in life.

Pulling this together, a sense of meaninglessness occurs when we have nothing to live for: nothing which provides a sense of purpose, dignity and self-respect; nothing which orders the myriad variables of everyday experience into a meaningful whole. A time of meaninglessness comes when we are unable to answer the larger questions of life: "Who am I? What am I created for? What is it I can contribute to life?" Inability to answer such questions is what contributes to the exquisite pain of meaninglessness.

In my work in career development I am continually impressed with the grief which floods people who have lost jobs or a career dream. Often this results from their failure to name themselves in unique definitions of who and what they are.

For example, Ron went through graduate school, graduated, and successfully passed the bar exam. Then he tried to kill himself. Why? Because his master plan broke down. At the end of all the effort he discovered that he really didn't want to be a lawyer, that he was disillusioned by what he was seeing in the profession. Thus he felt that everything he had done was a total waste. All the new skills, all the hard work, all the preparation and financial investment were left floating in limbo without a place to go. After a difficult year fighting depression and struggling to survive, Ron was able to see himself more clearly: He had a new philosophy of life which included understanding of his values and his purposes. As his therapist, I found it significant that he was able to return to law because he had recreated it in his own image.

Or, remember John whom I desribed in Chapter 1. He came for guidance because he couldn't find an academic position. He felt like a total failure because he hadn't become a professor—a goal, by the way, instilled from early childhood by his overly ambitious father. Very depressed, my client was ready to commit suicide. Little by little he put his thinking together in a new way as he recognized what a remarkable amount he was already accomplishing: teaching part-time at the university, successfully publishing works in political science, doing important research into governmental patterns and process. What was amazing to me was that he had totally overlooked these accomplishments. He gave them no credence because they did not fit his groundplan. In creating a new epistemology—a new way of knowing, thinking, and deciding about himself—he was finally free of his father's systems, able at last to shape his own goals and to fully appreciate himself.

In these cases, crisis occurred when the orderings of meaning were shaken. Out of the intense emotional pain of the crisis, energy was first mobilized for destruction, and then redirected into the hard work of the reorganization of personal epistemologies. Painful as it was, emotion gave energy for the difficult task of reshaping personal knowing.

The strong emotion of the crisis experience is evidence that meaning is a vital need for each one of us. Theorists describe this need in various ways. For Viktor Frankl it is the "will to meaning." Anton Antonovsky (1979) calls it a need for "personal coherence":

A sense of coherence is a global orientation that expresses the extent to which one has a pervasive enduring though dynamic feeling of confidence that one's internal and external environments are predictable and there is a high probability that things will work out as well as can reasonably be expected. (p. 123)

The strong pull to find form and predictability in one's perspective on self is demonstrated in the disaster studies of Irving Janis (1971) and his associates. These researchers discovered that survivors of disaster experience have had a self-shattering experience. Where they had felt invulnerable before they now felt vulnerable. Shaken by this new reality, these survivors moved into high cognitive gear to try to make sense of their disaster experience, to create a new image of its place in the events of their lives. Their awesome new sense of vulnerability had to be worked into a new, manageable image of themselves.

Kegan suggests that the most fundamental thing we do with what happens to us is to organize it. We literally *make* sense because our human being and becoming is the composing of meaning. Herbert Fingarette (1963) has proposed that the individual's presumed meaning-making may refer to a "scientific process of developing a logical, reliably interpretable and systematically predictive theory," or it may refer to an "existential process of generating a new vision which will serve as the context of the new commitment."

Whatever the description, we carry strong needs to create shape, form, and meaning in our sense of ourselves and of our lives. In his psychology of personal constructs, George Kelly (1955) has summarized these needs succinctly:

Man looks at his world through transparent patterns, or templates, which he creates and then attempts to fit over the realities of which the world is composed. The fit is not always very good, yet without such patterns, the world appears to be such an undifferentiated homogeneity, that man is unable to make any sense out of it. Even a poor fit is more helpful to him than nothing at all. (pp. 8–9)

Let us give the name *constructs* to these patterns that are tentatively tried on for size. They are ways of construing the world. They are what enables man, and lower animals too, to chart a course of behavior, explicitly formulated or implicitly acted out, verbally expressed or utterly inarticulate, consistent with other courses of behavior or inconsistent with them, intellectually reasoned or vegetatively sensed. (p. 9)

In general man seeks to improve his constructs by increasing his repertory, by altering them to provide better fits, and by subsuming them with superordinate constructs or systems. In seeking improvement he is repeatedly halted by the damage to the system that apparently will result from the alteration of a subordinate construct. Frequently his personal investment in the larger system, or his personal dependency upon it, is so great that he will forego the adoption of a more precise construct in the substructure. It may take a major act of psychotherapy or experience to get him to adjust his constructions system to the point where the new and more precise construct can be incorporated. (p. 9)

MEANING: A SYSTEMS PERSPECTIVE

I find myself convinced that elemental meanings unite and reunite in a shifting synergy of overall meaning. I also believe that some construct, some organizing principle—or overarching ideal—holds the elements of the systems together. And, finally, I believe that our meaning-making processes involve not only the *what* of meaning, but the *how* of our meaning—that we organize our meanings within principles and by means of principles in an ongoing epistemological process. In researching these premises I have found supporting theory within the literature of systems and within the systems concept of *synergy*.

Andras Angyal was one of the early psychologists who brought systems theory into his research, writing and therapy. Many ideas of significance were first developed in his 1941 book, *Foundations for a Science of Personality* and later elaborated and placed within the contexts of clinical experience and practice in his posthumously published book, *Neurosis and Treatment*. In a preface to that latter book he wrote:

The basic tenet of the holistic approach is that personality is an organized whole and not a mere aggregate of discrete parts. Its functioning does not derive from the functioning of its parts; rather the parts must be viewed in the light of the organizational principles governing the whole . . . any attempt to view the total human life as deriving from . . . fixed physiological features is bound to lead to a good many forced constructions. The approach "from above," from general patterns and trends, enables us to keep the perspective on the whole and offers a comprehensive framework for the understanding of the specific. (1965, p. xvi)

It is this concern for the whole which influenced the emergence of systems theory. In their book *Systems Thinking* (1977), two Dutch writers, Nicholas J.T.A. Kramer and Jacob de Smit, state their belief that the essence of general systems theory can be expressed as "the whole is greater than the sum of its parts" (pp. 33–34). This is the concept of *synergy*—a concept central, as I noted above, to my conceptualization of meaning.

The word "synergy" comes from the field of chemistry and medicine where it is used to describe the reality that certain combinations of chemicals or drugs create a reaction greater than the sum of the individual reactions. For example, when a person combines the intake of alcohol with Valium, the resulting impact on the physiological system is much greater than the reactions created by the independent action of each drug. Because of the power of this synergistic reaction taking the drugs in tandem can bring lethal result.

Synergy is a word whose inherent meanings have been adapted in various interpretive ways. The idea of synergy first caught my attention when I read an article by Maslow (1968a) entitled "Human Potentialities and the Healthy Society." In the article Maslow describes the efforts of anthropologist Ruth Benedict to arrive at a means of evaluating societies in terms of how well they served the welfare of the community. She needed a term that went beyond all available measures of behavior. In her struggle she finally arrived at the idea of classifying the *function* of behavior rather than the *overt* behavior. She needed descriptive, evaluative terms that avoided any projection of personal tastes and ideals. The concepts of "high synergy" and "low synergy" were the ones which she finally chose. "High synergy" referred to the positive reaction and interaction that occurred when people did things for themselves and at the same time did things for others. "Low synergy" societies were those where competitive, negative struggle resulted when people tried to enhance their own lives at cost to the lives of others.

Benedict's ideas were enlarged by Maslow, who felt the concept offered anthropology a chance to build a humanistic study of comparative culture and to escape from narrow scientism. Thus did a concept that started out in chemistry and medicine wander into the more humanistic fields of psychology and anthropology. Some of these further interpretations will be addressed in my discussion of therapy, but for our purposes here it is essential that we stay close to the original roots of the word. Some definitions from Buckminster Fuller's book *Operating Manual for Spaceship Earth* (1978) bring us back to these roots:

Synergy is the essence of chemistry. The tensile strength of chrome-nickel, steel, which is approximately 350,000 pounds per square inch, is 100,000 P.S.I. greater than the sum of the tensile strengths of each of all its alloyed, together, component, metallic elements.

Synergy is the only word in our language that means *behavior of whole systems unpredicted by the separately observed behaviors of any of the system's separate parts or any subassembly of the system's parts.* There is nothing in the chemistry of a toenail that predicts the existence of a human being. (p. 71)

When I conceptualize synergy I picture the holistic surge of energy which comes with an insight, with a new meaning, with a meaningful experience, an energy which cannot be explained in the dissection of parts. Two illustrations of this synergistic energy of meaning come from musical experience.

I always feel awe when I listen to an orchestra play, wandering down imaginative tracks as I picture each performer as a small child, practicing, learning to play, building the stepping stones of interrelated skills. I imagine all the parents hovering supportively in the background walking the delicate line between too much pressure and too little pressure. Then there are advanced trainings, the auditions, the practice, and finally, the remarkable moment when this vast diversity unites under the direction of the conductor. Talk about a whole that is greater than the sum of its parts!

Another synergy comes with the act of listening to music. I have found that I can listen in two ways: as a trained musical theorist who identifies modulations from key to key, the varying indications of tempo, and the kinds of instrumentation used by the composer; or as the naive participant who shuts off mental analysis and enters into simple enjoyment of the music. This experience is difficult to articulate because it is a synergy of many processes of thinking and feeling, but what I do know is that my whole being has been engaged. I can understand the parts of that music through the experience of that whole, but I cannot understand the whole through the experience of the parts.

Michael Polanyi has said something similar when he describes the loss of meaning when a poem or a metaphor is analyzed into its elements. Some essence of the experience of significance slips away. And yet, if we are to understand about poems and about particular metaphors we no doubt need the dissection. Again, what clarifies this for me is the recognition of the contrast between the whole and the parts as I study the parts through the eyes of the whole.

In contrasting the parts and the whole, Kramer and de Smit (1977) suggest we think of the letters, "M, a, e, t." In this juxtaposition the letters form a simple aggregate without meaning or system. If these same elements are rearranged into "team" there is a synergistic leap into system. The single elements, the letters, have come together into meaningful interrelationship. Carrying this further we can imagine the word "team" joining with other words in enlarging systems of a sentence, a paragraph, a book, and a system of knowledge. In this simple model is illustration of a series of *gestalten*. In like manner, we as human beings can take our elements — our words, our ideas, our knowledge — and arrange them into enlarging constellations of personal meaning.

Hierarchies are important in the consideration of systems. Without them systems research and theory can become loosely hung with neglect of some of the essential elements of the overarching systems. Economist Kenneth Boulding (1956, 1985) probes these hierarchies within his conceptions as he considers *The World as a Total System*. His definition of *system* is particularly helpful for a consideration of meaning-making in human development:

The broadest possible definition of a system is that it is "anything that is not chaos." We could turn the definition around and define a system as any structure that exhibits order and pattern. The orderly structures and patterns of which we are most immediately aware are those within our own minds, bodies, and behavior, but virtually all human beings have a strong conviction that corresponding to these patterns of mind and body are similar patterns in what might be called the "real world." We are also convinced that there are some pattern structures that we know and some, probably a great many, that we do not know. We have an enormous storehouse of images and structures within our minds to which we have access through consciousness and memory. These are undoubtedly coded in the structure of the brain and the nervous system, although exactly how this is done is still not really known. (1985, p. 9)

Boulding believes that one of the main tasks of general systems theory is to develop a certain "framework of coherence." One of his suggestions for accomplishing this is to arrange a hierarchy of systems according to "the organizational complexity of the various individuals of which these areas or systems consist." Following his own suggestion he offers an arrangement of systems from basic levels of the mechanical, the cybernetic, the "positive feedback," the creodic, and the reproductive, to the demographic, the ecological, the evolutionary, the human, and the social. To cap off this sequence of ever increasing complexity, he suggests the possiblity of what he calls the "transcendental systems" which "the religious experience of the human race especially has hinted at" (1985, p. 29).

It would certainly be presumptuous to suppose that systems complexity ended at the level of the human race. Just as an ant has very little conception of the human system that may be hovering over it, except perhaps a dim perception of something large and perhaps dangerous, or a dog perceives us as a benign deity and not as another dog, so we may stretch forth intimations of what is beyond us. Certainly our ideas about the transcendent have had a profound impact on human and social systems. (1985, p. 30)

What Boulding emphasizes in his classifications of systems is that each successively higher level embodies all the lower levels. Such a conceptualization of the organizations of life offers both an aid and a caution to the scientist by suggesting levels of entry for research. Indeed, Boulding suggests, the "methodology of empirial investigation should depend heavily on the nature of the system that is being investigated, and a lot of wasted effort — especially in the biological and social sciences — has been caused by attempts to apply a methodology that is quite appropriate, for instance, in celestial mechanics (a system where the basic parameters do not change) to systems that are highly stochastic, probabilistic, and where parameters do change." (p. 17) Thus, in studying the human being it can be very appropriate to study the atomistic processes; the problem occurs if this systems level is assumed to be all of what a human is.

Boulding's hierarchy gives suggestions for the difficult tasks of defining therapeutic objectives and of understanding approaches to a therapy of "systematic eclecticism." I can make choices about which level of the hierarchy I enter and I stay alert to which levels I might be ignoring. Translating this into my therapy with a depressed client, for example, I pay attention not only to the transcendent systems of personal meaning, but also to subsidiary systems of physiology and chemistry. I attend not only to questions of cognitive formulation but also to issues of personal health which may be addressed with suggestions for exercise, health care, and, if necessary, evaluation by a specialist in the chemistry of depression.

If we were to develop hierarchies of meaning-making systems we could go all the way from the semantic system of one word to the overarching ideologies which shape sets of values; from a single picture to the larger semiotic images which shape self-idealizations; from the behavior of running a word-processor to the writing of a book; from a simple job task to the overarching meaning of vocation. No one, as far as I know, has suggested a hierarchy of meaning-making, although I think many of the models of adult development offer conceptualizations of such hierarchies in moving from the more concrete processes of life to the levels of universal abstraction. By moving up and down *à la Boulding* in defining these levels of complexity of the human being, we gain new vistas into our clients' varying stages of meaning-making.

In considering hierarchies of systems and of meaning we are using an open systems concept. An open system interacts or is regarded as interacting with its environment. In the words of Kramer and de Smit (1977):

If a system is regarded as open, the state of the system and that of the environment influence each other: the system interacts with its environment. Hence there are relations between the system and the environment whereby at least one entity in the system influences the state of an entity in the environment or vice versa. (pp. 32–33)

If we adhere to a closed system with disregard for the relationships which exist between the system and its environment, we may lose the complexity of human meaning and interpretations which we have been affirming here. Again quoting Kramer and de Smit:

this approach often gives a reasonably quick insight into the system's internal functioning at an early stage of research but can also quickly lead to incorrect interpretations of the phenomena and to incorrect conclusions from these interpretations. (p. 33)

In using the systems approach I am describing here the therapist will pay attention to the interactions between systems and environments, and between systems and systems. I have felt concern that much of family systems theory has attended to one form of system, neglecting smaller systems and larger systems. The diagnosis often stops too soon. Or, in Kelly's words, "the range of convenience" is too limited, not allowing for meaning which is to be gained from attention to both the parts and the whole.

The Idealized Model

Another systems idea which is pertinent here comes from Gerald Nadler's book, *Work Systems Design: The Ideals Concept*.

I have suggested already that an ideal or overarching belief system shapes a system of meaning. This concept of the ideal as an organizing or modeling variable for the shaping of meaning is very close to what Nadler writes about in discussing the "idealized model" — a systems model used in business and industry. The idealized model is the ideal system which provides a measure of progress. It is the designer's ideal of what the finished product will be like; and it is the unifying concept in the system which has been set in motion. That model is kept central as a measure for the system — it is a way of making sense of the process and bringing the project to successful completion. It helps to organize and arrange the whole complex of resources required to achieve a purpose.

In like manner, organizing principles and models of our human systems help keep us on track in achieving goals or living meaningful lives. If these "idealized models" are big enough, we have lots of room to grow and to evolve. If, however, they are locked into limited systems or limited goals, they can stop us too soon or make us more vulnerable to failure.

John's story (p. 24) illustrates the enlargement of an idealized system of making sense of oneself and one's work. I find further illustration in the brainstorming of participants in one of my workshops on retirement planning.

The participants were psychologists who had found many of their life meanings in teaching, research, or therapy. These activities had brought order into many facets of their lives including lifestyle and interactions with family, friends, and colleagues. With their upcoming retirements they were facing major disruptions in this order, disruptions which could shake the very foundations of their meaning. In group brainstorming they played with new ideas of "what they wanted to be when they grew up." Considering career more in terms of vocation, one of the participants translated the teacher role into *being a catalyst* — a larger organizing principle than just being a teacher. In shaping this new model this man was able to conceptualize retirement activities as a writer, a volunteer, or a civic leader. For another participant who was a psychotherapist, *being a facilitator* was the shaping concept offering rich potential for service in leading workshops, teaching children on a part-time basis, and continuing to be available for students interested in research similar to her own. In the process of exploring their ideals these workshop participants opened their eyes to new ways of making sense of themselves and of their existence.

If meaning is the holding of some organizing model or ideal which shapes the system, then "meaninglessness" is the loss of such organizing principles. William Bridges' model of transitions acknowledges the power of this loss of meaning as he suggests three stages in personal transition: endings, a neutral zone, and then, new beginnings. Each stage has an importance of its own. As one grieves the old and faces the potential of a new form of life one walks through limbo, the time when things do not make sense. Bridges (1980) believes that the neutral zone, or the limbo time, is first of all a very difficult, frightening time; but, secondly, it is a very creative time. Because old elements of being are being resynthesized into "new beginnings" profound new opportunity is being given for new models, new ideals, and new ways of viewing the world. The reason the "neutral zone" is such a difficult stage is that old systems — old ways of making sense — have been lost, creating the time of walking the narrow pathway between two worlds. In Kegan's words, "All transitions involve leaving a consolidated self behind before any new self can take its place" (1982, p. 232). The challenge of this in-between time is to avoid retreating in fear, or building the limbo period into an extended moratorium.

In speculating further about the concept of the "idealized model" I look in on the darker side. The "idealized model" can be a negative model against which we measure ourselves; a model shaped out of negative early learning experiences and reinforced by the continuing repetitions which early reactions began. Much of this experience is unconscious, part of that which we know but which we do not know we know. Mahoney (1980) asserts, "it is reasonable . . . that many of the idiosyncratic acquired rules that direct a person's behavior are rarely 'accessible' to them" (p. 160).

Change begins with the understanding of the present. If we believe that the present includes many of the systems of the past, then we can accept this challenge to identify the preverbal, preconscious models and learnings which continue to shape us. I cite the experience of one of my clients to support this assertion.

Towards the end of our therapy together Maria offered a profound wisdom: "I can't forgive until I know what I am forgiving." She said this in the dramatic moment when suddenly she saw through into her own negative system, understood some of its sources, and was able to forgive and thus release her anger at her father who had abused her. This moment of resolution came after considerable struggle to bring into understanding the convoluted scenario of her family experience. Much of her personal model of self had been built on her role in the middle between father and mother. She was the bad person; she deserved punishment; she needed to keep on trying to resolve the old dilemma. Once this deeply internalized model of self was identified, challenged and released Maria became free to grow into new forms of who and what she was.

In *Self-Esteem and Meaning: A Life Historical Investigation* Michael Jackson suggests that our internalized images are constructed both of semantic systems and semiotic systems: out of our internalization of words and of images. These can be negative or positive and they can either facilitate or negate personal meaning and self-esteem. Whether helpful or not, these are the *meanings* of the individual client. And it is threatening to challenge these internalized models, even though to alter the models is to bring a more positive form of living. Mahoney believes that resistance by a client is really a form of survival struggle, because to give up one's inner images is to give up a shape of identity.

I think of Anna. When we talk about her self-image she says there is a void—an emptiness—a black nothingness. Exploring further we find an intricate network of negative self-statements: "I am unworthy, I am no good, I have no right to happiness. Why bother?" In our discussions there is a circularity as we keep following the premises around, constantly running into the rigid wall of her negative self-image. In the frustration of this experience, I have to remind myself that, negative as it is, this *is* her self-image. To release this, to change it, to leave that which shapes her very existence, is to face the terrifying world of the unknown. Joining, understanding, and respecting these inner images is my challenge as Anna struggles to redefine herself.

Wider perspectives on meaning open windows to a wide variety of approaches to our clients. In a supportive, caring manner we can seek to uncover the internalized, unconscious images, stories, beliefs, and semantic constructions which guide behavior; we can seek to enter into our client's world of knowing; we can seek to stand back and see the meaning in which the client lives; and we can seek to join in shaping new models of purpose and intention. One of our biggest tasks is not to trivialize the data or the process.

To emphasize this point and to prepare us for the next chapter I recount a story which Rollo May (1980) uses to introduce his book *Psychology and the Human Dilemma.* He whimsically tells the tale of the psychologist who is preparing himself psychologically for his entry through the pearly gates. He mentally rehearses all the questions he thinks St. Peter is going to ask at the moment of his entrance into heaven. But he is not prepared for the judgment which St. Peter puts on him. Here is St. Peter's pronouncement of the major sin: "You are charged with *nimis simplicando!*"

"You have spent your life making molehills out of mountains—that's what you're guilty of. When man was tragic, you made him trivial. When he was picaresque, you called him picayune. When he suffered passively, you described him as simpering; and when he drummed up enough courage to act, you called it stimulus and response. Man had passion; and when you were pompous and lecturing to your class you called it "the satisfaction of basic needs,' and 'release of tension.' You made man over into the image of your childhood Erector Set or Sunday School maxims—both equally horrendous."

I now present theories and models of adult development which make the effort to go beyond the sin of *nimis simplicando.*

As to individuality, there is no need to worry: we cannot dictate
deadly conformity to the life processes—they themselves will lead
to more diversity than we can comfortably manage with our
thoughts, our plans and our cures.

—Erik Erikson, 1961

We are all patchwork, and so shapeless and diverse in composition
that each bit, each moment, plays it own games.

—Montaigne, 1588, Book II, Ch. 1

Every discovery makes the living organism look less like a
predesigned object and more like an embodied drama of evolving
acts, intricately prepared by the past, yet all improvising their
moves to consummation.

—Suzanne Langer, 1967, p. 378

CHAPTER 3

Languages and Models
in Adult Development

DEVELOPMENTAL THERAPY is as much a language and an attitude as it is a
technique. To prepare us for therapy, therefore, I find it important to share
some of the words, forms and ideas which influence my thinking, questioning, and perceiving.

This chapter, then, is an excursion into theoretical material as I gather
ideas about adult development which are integrated into later discussions of
meaning-making, career development, creative aging, and marital meaning-
making. Out of the burgeoning material which we could discuss I am focusing on:

- the dialectical contrasts implicit in the words *adult development*;
- the metaphorical languages which shape developmental thinking;
- the power of models to influence cognition;
- shifting emphases in developmental paradigms;

- the featured languages and assumptions of Erik Erikson, Robert Kegan, and Michael Basseches—the three theorists who have strongly influenced this therapy.

THE LANGUAGE OF ADULT DEVELOPMENT

Consider the words *adult development*. In the coupling of those two words is a semantic dilemma. The word *adult* is the pluperfect of the Latin verb *adolescere*, "to grow up." Thus, an adult is someone who is "fully grown and mature." On the other hand, the word *develop* means "to unfold," and *development* is a sequence of unfoldings towards something. Here we have the contrast between a *fait accompli* and a process.

In these words are the dilemmas of adult development, both semantically and practically. The expectations of adulthood are the arrival at maturity; the realities of adulthood are the complex processes of adult development. We are frequently caught by the contradictions of that which we think we are and that which we are yet to be. On one side is the sense of *adult*, on the other side the sense of *adolescere* as the unfolding *process* and the stabilizing achievements and consistencies of *adulthood* create a dance of life and a dialectic between so-called opposites.

Writers, philosophers, and theorists have taken various positions along the human continuum from stability to change. If we listen to Montaigne, who wrote his essays in the 16th century, we hear a model of the unpredictability, complexity, and whimsical conglomeration of qualities called human. We hear inconsistency honored above consistency as he describes himself:

All contradictions may be found in me . . . bashful, insolent; chaste, lascivious; talkative, taciturn; tough, delicate; clever, stupid; surly, affable; lying, truthful; learned, ignorant; liberal, miserly and prodigal. (Frame, 1968)

Theorist Klaus Riegel would side with Montaigne, I believe, for he stated in 1978 that making a state of balance a goal is unhealthy since it "consigns growth and change to the status of necessary evils." Riegel also deemphasized attention to developmental plateaus where equilibrium or balance is achieved to give attention to development as continuous change.

At the other end of the stability/change continuum lie the trait theorists who emphasize empirical investigation of individual personality traits. These theorists would argue that "developmentalists have concentrated on the explanation for changes in the life course and have given less thought to factors which provide continuity. For the individual, however, continuity is as important as change, for it provides the basis for a sense of identity" (McCrae & Costa, 1982, p. 608). Therefore, "instead of asking how personality is changed by aging, we now can ask how the life course is shaped by enduring personality dispositions" (p. 611).

Speaking on behalf of a more encompassing position, social psychologist Thomas Blank writes that many dialecticians, including Klaus Riegel, have downgraded regularity and stability to the vanishing point, thus failing:

> to deal in a clear and unequivocal fashion with the equality of change and stability. They have failed to keep in mind that any model of social behavior and social cognition, any idea of development, that relegates stability and constancy to a subordinate position to change and imbalance and conflict is as misleading, as unreal, as those models and ideas that have subordinated conflict and change to the place allocated to equilibrium and regularity. (1982, p. 53)

We cannot choose sides here, because stability and change are simply two sides of a dynamic dialectic which creates the forward motions of human development. Without its necessary tensions human growth would either explode in frenetic instability or grind to a halt. Respect for this dialectic is evident in some of the more recent cognitive models as developmental theorists explore the "both/ands" of human experience with an increasing "willingness to transcend the polarity levels of analysis in favor of more comprehensive and complex models of human adaptation and development" (Mahoney & Freeman, 1985, p. ix).

But the themes and variations along the continuum from stability to change do illustrate the many points of view and emphasis as this exploratory discipline seeks its identity. In its emerging syntheses false illusions of "adulthood" do creep in, but many researchers are accepting the challenge of maintaining an attitude of respectful openness to diverse methods of research, and to the cross-fertilization of ideas from varying disciplines. Psychologists, sociologists, educators, gerontologists, philosophers, anthropologists, and systems theorists are among those joining in fostering and nurturing this discipline.

In working towards comprehensive theory we do well to listen to Harvard theorist Robert Kegan's (1983) playful aside when he recommends we just rent our theories for a while, rather than buying into them completely. The metaphor is apt because our theories are mental structures—the rooms that we rent—which give shape to the varying concepts with which we are working. And they represent our successive steps up the mountain.

METAPHORICAL LANGUAGE IN ADULT DEVELOPMENT

Metaphors shake and shape conceptual systems as they create new connections of thought and idea. They are like sparks which set off brush fires in the mind. More than this, George Lakoff and Mark Johnson (1980, p. 3) would argue that our ordinary *conceptual system* "in terms of which we both think and act, is fundamentally metaphorical in nature."

Metaphors are more than "mere language," therefore. Powerful means for structuring reality, they offer bridges between reason and imagination—

what Lakoff and Johnson call "imaginative rationality." From this perspective, metaphor is "one of our most important tools for trying to comprehend partially what cannot be comprehended totally: our feelings, aesthetic experiences, moral practices, and spiritual awareness" (p. 193).

These ideas lead me to consider a few of the central metaphors in adult development—metaphors which capture the organismic, proactive dynamic of the human journey and of human process.

What better place to begin than with *development*, a metaphor used so automatically that we don't often think of its metaphorical roots. The root meaning of *development* is "the seed which is gradually opened and uncovered." Through the years, the word has widened in its meaning to include the following definitions:

- to unwrap, to disentangle, to rid free;
- to open out of its enfolding cover;
- to unveil or lay bare to oneself; to discover, detect, find out;
- to cause to grow (what exists in the germ);
- to evolve;
- to grow into a fuller, higher, or more mature condition;
- to gradually unfold, to bring into a fuller view; a fuller disclosure, or a working out of the details of anything, as a plan, a scheme, the plot of a novel. (*The Oxford English Dictionary*)

Here then is the epigenetic, spiritual dimension which undergirds the developmental theory which I am featuring. Here are the organismic processes of self-discovery, personal growth, and the uncovering and living out of a human program for life. And here is the inherent assumption that "anything that grows has a ground plan, and that out of this ground plan the parts arise, each part having its time of special ascendency, until all the parts have arisen to form a functioning whole" (Erikson, 1968, p. 93).

Another metaphor in adult development pictures the journey of life as *the Way.* Religious tradition offers many illustrations of this usage:

Lao Tzu talked of the *Tao,* which in one translation has been translated as the Way. Buddhists speak of the *Maha-yana,* which is translated as the Great Way. Hindus refer to the *Deva-yana,* or the Way of the Gods. Christ said, "I am the Way." Moses showed the people of Israel the way out of bondage into the Promised Land. In Islam, the Prophet Mohammed led the Way to Mecca. There is the *sirat almusta-quim,* sometimes translated as the Straight Way, and there is the Sufic *tariqah,* or Way. The Straight Way is the theme in both the Psalms and the Gospels. The Sioux trod the Red Road and the Japanese sought the *Shodo,* or Holy Path. (Fowler & Keen, 1978, p. 4)

Confucious lived from 551-479 B.C., and his model of "the Way" is of interest because it is one of the earliest developmental models on record. In a review of developmental history, Colarusso and Nemiroff (1981, p. 4) write that Confucius succinctly described a personal yet representational journey, "indicating that at 15 he had set his heart on learning; at 30 planted his feet firmly upon the ground; at 40 no longer suffered from perplexities; at 50 knew the biddings of heaven; and at 60 could 'follow the dictates of his own heart, for what [he] desired no longer overstepped the boundaries of right'." In following the concept of *the Way* the adult works within a process of maturation with continuous effort toward self-realization. "A sense of inner direction must be endlessly discovered and put into action. The Way is inseparable from the person; it is experienced as an internal presence" (Fowler & Keen, 1978, p. 8).

Scholar Tu Wei-ming (1978) brings an important emphasis and interpretation to the model of Confucius. He says Confucianism is "not so much a state of attainment as a process of becoming." He calls the metaphor of *the Way* "a basic analogy" that "depends as much upon a sense of inner direction as upon a prior knowledge of the established social norms." Thus, Confucius' life was not meant to provide the one and only norm. As Wei-Ming explains, "the Master never instructed his students to follow him in order to find the Way. Instead, he inspired them to pursue the Way by realizing humanity — or adulthood, if you will — in themselves" (p. 125).

Closely entwined with the metaphor of "the Way" is the metaphor "life is a story" which Lakoff and Johnson believe is rooted deep in our culture. "It is assumed that everyone's life is structured like a story, and the entire biographical and autobiographical tradition is based on this story. What do you do? You construct a coherent narrative that starts early in your life and continues up to the present" (1980, p. 172). They name certain features which are present in a typical narrative: participants, parts, stages, linear sequence, causation, and purpose. When the life story is developed and told certain elements will be highlighted and others ignored because the narrator/participant is creating a coherent structure, a way of making sense of the story.

In this metaphorical understanding of life as a story are ideas for the meaning-making therapist to consider, for in the telling of the life story is opportunity for new features to be understood and highlighted, for new scenarios to be developed, for new possibilities and purposes to be considered. And the elements of the story which Lakoff and Johnson have suggested can become an effective outline for personal questioning. "Who are the people in your life who have been important? What are the experiences you remember? What do you think caused you to make that decision? What are your purposes, your goals, your plans for the development of your story?"

The theme of life as a story is also important from a theoretical perspective. Charlotte Buhler, whose biographical research gave important impetus to the evolution of developmental theory, emphasized this life story approach in the study of individual lives. Believing strongly in the "phenomenon of people wanting 'to live for something,' which becomes for them life's meaning . . .," she framed concepts of "self-determination" in lives directed towards the fulfillment of ultimate purpose. She also postulated the individual's lifelong simultaneous orientation to the present, the past, and the future. Because of her attention to this simultaneous orientation she believed that a biographical, narrative perspective must be maintained at all times (Buhler & Massirik, 1968, p. 21).

The narrative concept, or the narrative style of thinking, is important in my own approach to therapy. And recently I have found Jerome Bruner's *Actual Minds, Possible Worlds* (1986) a stimulating analysis of what he calls the "narrative mode": the side of the mind devoted to the "irrepressibly human acts of imagination that allow us to make experience meaningful. This is the side of the mind that leads to good stories, gripping drama, primitive myths and rituals, and plausible historical accounts" (from dust cover of the book). In such a narrative mode is a counterbalance for the more narrowly defined logical, analytical aspects of mental life.

Present in the stories of the Way, of the journey, of life as a story, are further metaphors of "phase and stage." These words are used rather interchangeably, but come from differing roots and thus provide differing cognitive structures for shaping understandings and expectations of life development.

Closely tied to a chronology of age, *phase theories* come from the metaphor of the passing of seasons and construe development as a continuing response to central life tasks. From this perspective, the life cycle involves a series of periods, correlated with biological age, during which a person must cope with a sequential unfolding of particular demanding situations. Thus, development entails the creation of ways of living, and means of understanding oneself, that effectively answer the changing requirements of living. The contribution of phase theory, therefore, is increased understanding of the nature of the inevitable demands of life.

Stage theories emerge from the biology of epigenesis and deemphasize some of the specifics defined by phase theories. In a summary of this Harry Lasker and James Moore (1980) write:

Contrastingly, stages of adult life identify levels of maturity that are relatively independent of the seasonal conditions in which they are found. Stage theories come from the insight that the same conditions are experienced in different ways, depending upon the psychological development of the persons involved. Thus, stage theories reveal that though the seasons of adult life present similar conditions for each person, response to these conditions will in part be determined by each person's level of development in various psychological domains. (p. 15)

Frequently, there is no neat and tidy dividing line between the theories of phase and stage, as will be evident in the theories of Erikson and Kegan described below. In fact, what often happens is that the earlier delineations of a developmental sequence are closely correlated with age, but become less so as the individual develops through adult life.

GRAPHIC MODELS

In considering the metaphorical frameworks for developmental theory, my mind leaps to the graphic models which are a natural outgrowth of the transformational cognition of metaphor. Indeed, this seems to be the way of our metaphors—they stimulate us to further orderings. It is a natural next step to come to the cognition of graphic, visual forms which help to make tangible that which is abstract. In these forms are images of comparison and contrast as well as measures of movement and progress.

Recently I gained new appreciation for the cognitive pull to visual form when I viewed a program on public television which suggested that the shapes of life give meaning to its elements. Four basic shapes were listed: the spiral, the hexagon, the helix, and the meander. These shapes are such an intrinsic part of nature around us that we often don't see them. But as the program so graphically illustrated, these forms are everywhere, bringing both an order and a program for growth.

As we proceed, then, take note of the varying shapes which theorists have used to tell developmental stories. Also, consider the cognitive systems and cognitive styles which are inherent in their structures. For example, how does a stepwise model contrast with that of a helix? Or a set of overlapping circles with that of linear progression?

To make this more specific, let us consider Erikson's model, which is traditionally offered in a linear, stepwise manner. However, this more formal model was transformed by his wife, Joan, who designed and wove a tapestry which incorporates in a graphic, picturesque way the interweaving sequences and developmental themes of life development. Her words describe this:

As you can see in the weaving, there is one color for each vital strength. In the fringe at the bottom—the warp—you can see them all: dark blue for trust; orange for autonomy and dark green for initiative; yellow for industry, and so on. From the start, there are gray threads to represent the dystonic elements (basic mistrust, shame, guilt, for example) over which the colors must maintain their dominance and brilliance, as well as their essential characteristics. When you study this weaving you no longer doubt that the warp must all exist from the start, otherwise the whole would not hang together. Also, you can clearly follow the threads as they continue up the years and add their character to the entire life pattern. In this way, everything is interwoven as, indeed, it is in life itself. (E. Erikson, 1981, p. 252)

The power of this model was revealed after a talk at Bennington, Vermont, where the Eriksons first shared this weaving. Joan Erikson reports that "many people came up to me and said how much help the weaving had been in explaining the epigenetic life cycle. They had, it seems, been hungry for something visual and sensual that brought it home." This illustrates my point that a differing model can shape and shake cognitive construction in the same way that a metaphorical leap can create a new translation.

SHIFTING EMPHASIS

As recently as 1966, Bernice Neugarten was commenting on the slow, uneven development of psychological attention to the broad landscapes of adult life:

The field of adult psychology and adult personality remains an underpopulated one among psychologists. The effect has been to speak metaphorically, that as psychologists seated under the same circus tent, some of us who are child psychologists remain seated too close to the entrance, and are missing much of the action that is going on in the main ring. Others of us who are gerontologists remain seated too close to the exits. Both groups are missing a view of the whole show. (Neugarten, 1977, p. 41)

In pondering this I can't help but note that ancient wisdom *did* pay attention to the "whole show." In fact, one of its theories came very close to some of the ideas which are being expounded today, as it placed its stages not only within the context of a whole life, but within the context of successive generations. This theory is the *ashrama* theory, codified in India some two and half thousand years ago by men like Manu and Gautama. In their wisdom they emphasized the connection between the person and his or her surroundings, and they described a generational sequence which has great similarity to the contemporary work of Erik Erikson. I cite this developmental scheme because it creates a link between the old and the new which illustrates certain basic themes in human development which have sometimes been downplayed within the contexts of contemporary theory — themes like hope, fidelity, love, care, and wisdom — themes which are now gaining renewed attention and importance, as I will demonstrate below.

These Hindu concepts unite within a stage-schema which includes specific tasks and virtues and which is correlated with successive age periods. Infancy is not explicitly considered but viewed as the individual's prehistory, a preparation for the first stage of "Apprenticeship (*brahmacharya*)" during the school years and adolescence during which competence and fidelity are learned; stage two is the "Householder (*garhasthya*)" during which the practice of love and care is developed; stage 3 is a period of "Withdrawal (*vanaprastha*)," a time of teaching "extended care" and involvement beyond the limits of the household; and finally the period of old age, "Renunciation (*samnyasa*)" which is the period of inner focus and the development of wisdom (Kakar, 1979, pp. 2–12).

A wisdom leaps the centuries, therefore, to join with contemporary theory as new streams of thought and research show growing complexity and sophistication, and as theorists move beyond discrete bodies of data or linear chartings, beyond a biased attention to the extremes of youth and age, to give increased appreciation to the many divergent paths which a human being's behavior, feelings, and thinking can take over the entire lifetime.

In these shifts in developmental thinking paradigms are being shaken.

Carol Gilligan has challenged models of adult development which feature and honor autonomy and self-development in contrast to nurture and other-development. She has correctly pointed out that "there seems to be a line of development missing from current depictions of adult development, a failure to describe the progression of relationships toward a maturity of interdependence" (1982, p. 155). She has also stated that:

Male and female voices typically speak of the importance of different truths, the former of the role of separation as it defines and empowers the self, the latter of the ongoing process of attachment that creates and sustains the human community.

Since this dialogue contains the dialectic that creates the tension of human development, the silence of women in the narrative of adult development distorts the conceptions of its stages and sequence. Thus, I want to restore in part the missing text of women's development . . . in focusing primarily on the differences between the accounts of women and men, my aim is to enlarge developmental understanding by including the perspective of both of the sexes.

And at the same time that Gilligan is asking theorists to consider the human dialectic of autonomy and care, of independence and nurture, progressive anthropologists and sociologists are reporting on current cultural trends showing that a narcissistic society is beginning to pay more attention to the human values of love and community. *Habits of the Heart* by Robert N. Bellah and his associates (1985), *Nine American Lifestyles* by Arnold Mitchell (1983), and *New Rules* by Yankelovich (1982) are among the current writings addressing these concerns. And there is a burgeoning of writing which develops Gilligan's themes of the feminine contribution to concepts of growth and development. For example, in *Caring: A Feminine Approach to Ethics and Moral Educations* Nell Noddings (1984) presents a well-reasoned discussion of the ethics of reason and justice vis-à-vis the ethics of care. And Mary Field Belenky and her colleagues (1986) are sorting the elements of feminine thinking in *Women's Ways of Knowing*.

Within the contexts of these shifts in developmental paradigm the theoretical streams which attend to cognitive form and epigenetic principle are growing and branching. The *genetic epistemology* of Jean Piaget provides a base for much of this emerging theory. Certainly it lies at the heart of the thinking of Robert Kegan and Michael Basseches; but other rich resources are provided by the work of George Herbert Mead, William Perry, Heinz Werner, Robert Selman, Lawrence Kohlberg, James Fowler, and Jane Loevinger. This is not to ignore the work of Sigmund Freud which penetrates many of these theoretical systems, but simply to acknowledge that he did not attend to the processes of adult development. Nor is this to ignore the developmental constructions of Daniel Levinson (1978), Roger Gould (1978), and George Vaillant (1977), but simply to acknowledge that their work does not feed the cognitive developmental streams in the same way as those cited above.

In sorting my cognitive constructive underpinnings, I name the strong influence of Erikson, Kegan, and Basseches, whose contribution is at the forward edge of exciting explorations of developmental theory. Even more, their theories complement the ideas of Carol Gilligan by giving strong attention to the dynamics of interdependence, of self and other, of love and care. In fact, Erikson (1974) has offered a helpful summary of the concepts of *care* as they are demonstrated in both individual life and culture. He also speaks of the tie between the ancient Hindu wisdom and the developmental wisdom which is pointing us towards community and interdependence:

From the point of view of development, I would say: In youth you find out what you *care to do* and who you *care to be* — even in changing roles. In young adulthood you learn whom you *care to be with* — at work and in private life, not only exchanging intimacies, but sharing intimacy. In adulthood, however, you learn to know what and whom you can *take care of.* I have said all this in basic American before; but I must add that as a principle it corresponds to what in Hinduism is called the maintenance of the world, that middle period of the life cycle when existence permits you and demands you to consider death as peripheral and to balance its certainty with the only happiness that is lasting: to increase, by whatever is yours to give, the good will and the higher order in your sector of the world. That, to me, can be the only adult meaning of that strange word *happiness* as a political principle. (p. 124)

In tune with such principles, Erikson, Kegan, and Basseches suggest the movements through forms of thinking which enhance people's capacity to pay attention to the viewpoints of others, to be open to new ideas, and to join and synthesize the wisdoms of the past with the wisdoms of the present. With varying degrees of emphasis and agreement, these three theorists also attend to the emotional, the ethical, and the spiritual. And although there is primary emphasis on constructive process, they cannot help but attend to *content* as they offer new languages and new ideas which spark leaps of insight and understanding in the field of adult development.

And now we plunge into theory as we focus on Erikson, Kegan and Basseches. Here can be found many of the ideas and wonderings which shape my therapeutic questionings and therapeutic emphases. Here, too, are vocabularies which are incorporated into the dialogues of meaning-making and into the constructive forms of developmental therapy.

Erik Erikson

In his delineation of eight stages of psychosocial development (see Table 1), Erik Erikson based his theory on Heinz Hartmann's idea of an average expectable environment of cradle, nursery, family, school, peer group, marriage, children, and maturity. The first five stages are elaborations of Freud's oral, anal, phallic, latent, and genital stages and the last three stages take the subject from adulthood to maturity. What he describes in this translation is the interaction of the individual with succeeding environments

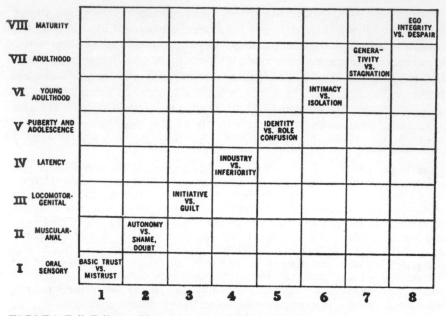

		1	2	3	4	5	6	7	8
VIII	MATURITY								EGO INTEGRITY VS. DESPAIR
VII	ADULTHOOD							GENERATIVITY VS. STAGNATION	
VI	YOUNG ADULTHOOD						INTIMACY VS. ISOLATION		
V	PUBERTY AND ADOLESCENCE					IDENTITY VS. ROLE CONFUSION			
IV	LATENCY				INDUSTRY VS. INFERIORITY				
III	LOCOMOTOR-GENITAL			INITIATIVE VS. GUILT					
II	MUSCULAR-ANAL		AUTONOMY VS. SHAME, DOUBT						
I	ORAL SENSORY	BASIC TRUST VS. MISTRUST							

TABLE 1 Erik Erikson: Eight Stages of Life Development
Adapted from *Childhood and Society*, Second Edition, by Erik H. Erikson, by permission of W. W. Norton & Co., Inc. Copyright 1950, © 1963 by W. W. Norton & Co., Inc. Copyright renewed 1978 by Erik H. Erikson.

which bring a sequence of learnings: Trust vs. Mistrust, Autonomy vs. Shame, Initiative vs. Guilt, Industry vs. Inferiority, Identity vs. Identity Confusion, Intimacy vs. Isolation, Generativity vs. Self-Absorption or Stagnation, and Integrity vs. Despair or Disgust (1978a, p. 26).

Erikson's placement of the word "versus" between the successive developmental polarities is carefully calculated, for it is in the contradictions of the two polarities — in the facing of one against the other — that the individual comes to terms with successive stages of psychosocial development. In Erikson's sequence, then, first one part of the ego identity and then another is tested in interaction with the environment as it either surmounts or fails to surmount its vulnerability. Each step is an altered perspective with a different capacity using a different opportunity. Each comes to its ascendence, meets its crisis, and finds its last solution towards the end of its stage. Thus, each new stage founds itself upon the previous stages, so the manner in which initial crises have been met must affect the chances of resolving later ones.

But Erikson cautions us against making this sequence too rigid or too neatly resolved. He writes in 1961 that the "idea of a *resolution of developmental crises* without any leftover of loose ends fits modern man's idea of a *perfect adjustment,* as if developmental crises were so many efficiency tests applied to an organism with accidental flaws in design and production."

Indeed, to think of Erikson's successive stages as so many neat little steps up the ladder of life is to miss the rich complexity of his conception. A commentary by Herant A. Katchadourian (in Erikson, 1978a) develops this point:

At each phase, components from each of the eight major tasks are present simultaneously as "precursors," "derivates," and as the decisive "crisis" itself. Thus, childhood does not end nor adulthood begin with adolescence. Rather, the adult is anticipated in the child and the child persists in the adult. This is the thread that gives continuity to Erikson's developmental scheme. (p. 51)

Charles Hampden-Turner (1981, p. 132) offers similar interpretation as he writes that at each of Erikson's stages "the seeds of the challenges have already been planted" and in "every individual both child and adult are present, and both meet in the other." He also makes the point that once a person is out of phase with the age-appropriate stage of reorganization and integration his or her needs are often seen as illegitimate and the odds against the deviant multiply. That is an important idea for the developmental therapist, for it is all too easy to stigmatize our clients with a label rather than to name and allow that necessary working-through of the developmental processes which have been interrupted.

Thus, there is no simple, perfect, resolution of each crisis. Each is involved in another. And, according to researcher Vivian Clayton (1975, p. 123), "Most people never progress through all of *Erikson's* life cycle stages to the point where the resolution of the last crisis becomes relevant to them. They become fixated at earlier stages of development and therefore never resolve earlier crises which would make possible the emergence of the highest of all human virtues, wisdom." Refusal to change or to face the crises can occur through either the process of foreclosure or a prolonged moratorium. In the former case, the individual denies the crises that occur at each development stage. As a result,the individual does not reorganize or integrate his accumulated experiences to his advantage. "This is the individual who, at 50, handles problems in the same manner as he did when 25 years of age" (Clayton, 1975, p. 123).

In the case of the prolonged moratorium, the individual faces a life crisis and is unable to resolve it. His commitments will be vague until he decides which direction he will follow . . . delaying a resolution only delays commitment. . . . Both the processes of foreclosure and prolonged moratorium, therefore, contribute to fixation and shield the individual from change and growth. Therefore, many people simply do not complete the life cycle. They die uncommitted, unresolved and frustrated, never having arrived at the stage where they could fully integrate and utilize accumulated years of experience and knowledge. (Clayton, 1975, p. 123)

What is sometimes ignored in the analysis of Erikson's sequence of psychosocial tasks is the parallel development of the *virtues* of *hope, will, competence, fidelity, love, care, and wisdom*—those qualities "with which human beings steer themselves and others along the path of life," and which provide an overall vision for healthy human beings and society. "In all their seeming discontinuity, these virtues depend on each other: will cannot be trained until hope is secure, nor love become reciprocal until fidelity has proven reliable. Also, each virtue and its place in the schedule of all virtues is vitally interrelated to other segments of human development . . . " (Erikson, 1966, pp. 204–205).

In naming these abstract achievements "virtues" Erikson pondered his language:

. . . one is at first tempted to make up new words out of Latin roots. Latin always suggests expertness and explicitness, while everyday words have countless connotations: to optimists they make virtues sound like gay and easy accomplishments, and to pessimists, like idealistic pretences. Yet when we approach phenomena closer to the ego, the everyday words of living languages, ripened in the usage of generations, will serve best as a means of discourse. (Erikson, 1966, p. 204)

Erikson named *hope, will, purpose, and skill,* as the rudiments of virtue developed in childhood; *fidelity* as the adolescent virtue, and *love, care, and wisdom* as the central virtues of adulthood.

In discussing *fidelity* as the developmental challenge of adolescence, Erikson describes the adolescent as a "contradictory combination of shifting devotion and general perversity"—the emerging human being who is sometimes "devotedly perverse" and at other times "perversely devoted." These contradictory elements, however, are a part of the search for identity, for an inner coherence, and a durable set of values. And the struggle is for a sexual maturity which prepares the young person for next stages of mating and parenting. Certainly the working-through and learning of fidelity lead to the *love, care, and wisdom* of evolving maturity.

What contributes to the successful development of the virtue of fidelity, Erikson believes, is society's rituals, rites of passage, ideologies, and demands. This is thought-provoking and disturbing as one ponders a society which lacks such social supports and confirmations, and as one observes the inability of many people to form lasting commitments to a partner or to the deeper principles of love, care and wisdom. Indeed, what seems to be happening is a preponderance of *disconfirmation* that is interrupting the sequential development of human qualities which contribute to meaningful interdependence in human relationship.

Once the capacity for fidelity has been worked through and internalized, the groundwork is laid for the reciprocal experiences of love. *Love* is defined by Erikson as a shared identity, a mutual verification, a finding of oneself as one loses oneself in another. Love involves a mature and responsible genitality, and a later ability in life to replace certain forms of sexuality with the shared tenderness and companionship of old age.

Care involves both generativity and the need to be needed—what Erikson calls a "generative responsibility." "Care (in all the various meanings of *caritas*) is a quality essential for psychosocial evolution; for we are a teaching species." Erikson sees this virtue building on the concept that "adult man is so constituted as to need to be needed lest he suffer the mental deformation of self-absorption, in which he becomes his own infant and pet." Further, in addressing psychosexual needs and responsibility, Erikson writes, "It is essential . . . that the control of procreation be guided not only by an acknowledgement of man's psychosexual needs, but also by a universal sense of generative responsibility toward all those brought more planfully into the world. Such care includes the guarantee to each child of a chance for such development as we are outlining here." In summary, "As adult man needs to be needed, so—for the strength of his ego and for that of his community—he requires the challenge emanating from what he has generated and from what now must be 'brought up,' guarded, preserved—and eventually transcended" (Erikson, 1966).

Wisdom. This is the virtue which comes as a climax of life—the out-growing, culminating, integrating achievement of all the virtues. This is the virtue which represents the successful resolution of the final psychosocial crisis of "integrity versus despair," as the individual puts his or her life into perspective within the losses as well as the achievements of later life. In wisdom can come the ability to maintain the "wholeness of experience," even as the body capabilities decline. And, if we follow Kegan's model it is the time of the transcendence of embeddedness and differentiation, of subject and object. It is also the time when other high points in adult development take on extra meaning—the high points of faith (Fowler, 1981; Fowler & Keen, 1978), of spiritual development (Jung, 1957), of enlightened, flexible, open forms of cognitive process (Basseches, 1984; Loevinger, 1982; Perry, 1970; Sclman, 1969) and of the dialectical unions of caring and justice (Gilligan, 1982; Kohlberg, 1984).

But what does all this say for a developmental therapy? What can we take from Erikson into the therapy room?

First of all, a language which can shape our questioning as we analyze our clients' capacities for trust and autonomy, for example, or the intertwining growths of identity, intimacy, generativity, and the integrations of age. We can use these conceptual forms for analyzing client development as we design therapeutic programs according to individual need: A client who has never established a sense of trust will be supported and encouraged in the fulfillment of dependency needs; a client whose psychosocial deficiency is in the realms of autonomy will be offered the creative contradictions which can thrust him or her into greater self-effort and differentiation.

Secondly, by using the terminology of *virtue* we can begin entering human domains often neglected by traditional psychotherapy. Certainly, the terminology of the virtues smacks of the metaphysical and the "touchy/feely" but it also smacks of humanness, of interdependence, and of the nurture and love which is all too often ignored in our psychological languages. Furthermore, these successive virtues are representations of increasingly complex cognitive constructions as earlier orientations become reformed within the new. Thus do I consider Erikson's framework of "virtues" a successive, incorporating set of cognitive systems which frame and direct life through particular attitudinal and cognitive lenses. Indeed, to maintain hope is to hold an attitude which keeps one open to experience; to incorporate love is to view one's partner and one's society with appreciation and sensitivity; to achieve wisdom is to move through a ladder of cognitive form to the achievement of a perspective on life from a place on the side of the mountain.

And, finally, in using Erikson's theories we honor the complexities of particular life problems which take on a new hue according to the psychosocial contexts of successive stages of aging. Thus, the intimacy questions of a 20-year-old are different from those of a man who has just retired; the trust issues of a high school student are different from the trust issues of an old woman who has just entered a retirement home; and the integrity challenges of the older person are not faced until one has lived through the previous periods of life.

ROBERT KEGAN

To his theoretical development Kegan brings the experience and perspective of an active teacher, clinician and researcher as he works to fill gaps in the interrelated constructive-developmental theories. These he describes as not yet mature, and still far from full potential stature as paradigm:

With very few exceptions, the work of the Piagetians ("neo" or otherwise) must still be characterized as about *cognition,* to the neglect of *emotion;* the *individual,* to the neglect of the *social*; the *epistemological*, to the neglect of the *ontological* (or *concept*, to the neglect of *being*); *stages* of meaning-constitution, to the neglect of meaning-constitutive *process*; and (forgive the awkward ex pression of this last) what is *new and changed* about a person, to the neglect of *the person who persists through time.* (1980, p. 406)

He summarizes these "multiple neglects" as a "truncation" in the paradigm which has somehow ignored the creative motion of life which includes the "social, the ontological, the process, the person who is doing the developing." In this Kegan sees evolving human beings as much more than their stages of development—they are "persons who are a motion, a creative motion, the motion of life itself" (1977, p. 8). Thus, for him, theory building is not "about the doing which a human does; it is about the doing that a human is." For Kegan, then, human beings are "constitutive meaning-makers" who are continually working to make sense of their worlds by actively constructing their reality systems. And he describes this process of meaning-making as a "simultaneously epistemological and ontological activity; it is about knowing *and* being, about theory-making *and* investments and commitments of the self" (1982, pp. 44–45).

In postulating a developmental sequence of meaning-makings, Kegan hangs his conceptual framework upon the model of the helix because it shows graphically the "way we revisit old issues but at a whole new level of complexity," and because it gives a picture of evolutionary balances which are "slightly *im*balanced" (1982) (see Figure 1). Upon this helix he has hung a number of evolving, interactive patterns: the affective and the cognitive; the dependent, the independent, and the interdependent; the institutional and transcendent; that which has found its balance in an "evolutionary truce" and that which is in the disruptive throes of transition. All this is a complex mix of shifting patterns which are moving through shifting meaning-makings towards the human capacity to hold a dialectic of embeddedness and differentiation in a transcendent interdependence. These move-

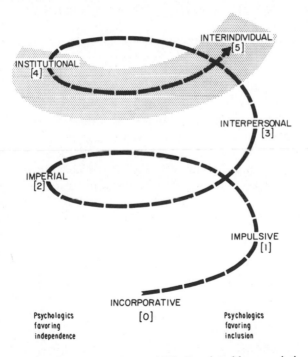

FIGURE 1 The Helix Model from Kegan, 1982. Reprinted by permission.

ments of growth complement and affirm many of Erikson's ideas as he points us towards a wisdom of love and care.

I have looked for ways to describe Kegan's work without reducing his rich vision to simplistic summary. For this reason I find myself approaching his helix from differing angles and differing perspectives as I read and incorporate his work. One way is to track his stages through their evolving definitions as we consider growth from the undifferentiated stage of the infant who is "all self" through intermediary movements of assimilation and accommodation towards the transcendence of the "Stage 5" individual who has achieved the "transforming dynamic of interdependence" where "now there is a self to share" (Kegan, Noam, & Rogers, 1982). These formulations (see Figure 1 and Table 2) are of help in examining and describing the dynamics of client problems to determine therapeutic emphasis and approach—to contrast the self-orientations of a Stage 2 person with the other-orientations of the Stage 3 individual; to see how autonomy and self-centeredness on the one hand may be leading into the emerging reciprocity of intimate relationship. To contrast these two orientations with the later self-definitions of a Stage 4 and the mature interdependence of Stage 5 is also to appreciate the shifting dynamics of self and other and to respect the increasing complexities of human cognitive construction and meaning-making. Particularly helpful, also, are the descriptions of transition which enable us to view our client's disturbances in developmental terms rather than in those of medical pathology.

The further I go in tracking the schemata, however, the more I draw back in accepting stage definitions which are too tightly defined. Particularly I wonder how the so-called "feminine" and "masculine" elements of human development (nurture and care on the one hand, autonomy and agency on the other) can be removed from particular stage assignments (notably Stages 3 and 4) and placed within the contexts of a dialectic of human development. Perhaps we need another model—of the braid, or of overlapping helixes, for example—to show how culture has shaped men and women in differing ways—a model which will portray the tensions of differentiation and embeddedness as they are lived out within differing forms, differing contexts, and differing definitions of dependence and independence. It certainly seems that we need models which free love and care from the connotations of the loss of self and identity.

Whatever these concerns about the specifics of stage progression, I value Kegan's model because it points us towards new understandings of our evolving meaning-makings and towards the interdependence of mature love. In this valuing and evaluation I incorporate his metaphorical language, which couches developmental questions in imaginative new ways: *holding environment, cultures of embeddedness,* the *evolutionary truce,* which incorporates Piaget's conceptualizations of *equilibration, assimilation and accommodations.*

Holding Environment. In using this terminology Kegan cites Winnicott (1965) who writes of "the envelope of care—the holding environment" which provides three very significant functions: (1) *Confirmation*—a supportive (not restrictive) "holding on" of the person as the individual is given acknowledgment and recognition. For, as Kegan says, we each need to be able to excite someone—"to turn the lights on in their eyes." (2) *Contradiction*—a "letting go" as the individual is encouraged within the framework of the holding environment to reach out beyond the current embeddedness to new steps in personal differentiation. And with the knowledge that the holding environment remains as a supportive backdrop for new experience the person is enabled to grow and change. (3) *Continuity*—a kind of "sticking around" as the individual keeps a sense of ongoing support and personal consistency within new forays into life. (In my own terminology I see each successive holding environment as *a dependency fulfilled which becomes a dependency resolved.* Thus does therapy become a powerful milieu for offering the supportive but freeing relationship of continuity, contradiction, and continuity.)

Holding environments or *cultures of embeddedness* are found within successive contexts as the child moves from the mothering culture and the parenting culture to the role-recognizing cultures, which can include both school and family as institutions of authority and role differentiation, and the peer gang with its requirements for a certain kind of role-taking. These cultures are replaced by the culture of identity or self-authorship, which can be achieved within contexts of love and/or work. And finally, if the individual has worked through developmental stages of embeddedness and differentiation, she or he arrives at the transcendent culture of interdependent intimacy which, for Kegan, means a "genuinely adult love relationship." Each of the successive cultures would ideally provide the supportive elements of confirmation, contradiction, and continuity—the essential qualities of holding environments.

In describing these successive holding environments Kegan uses another term important in his vocabulary—the term *evolutionary truce* which he develops from Piaget's concept of equilibration and its language of assimilation and accommodation:

Central to Piaget's framework—and often ignored even by those who count themselves as Piagetian—is this activity equilibration. Whether in the study of the mollusk or the human child, Piaget's principal loyalty was to the ongoing conversation between the individuating organism and the world, a process of adaptation shaped by the tension between the assimilation of new experience to the old "grammar" and the accommodation of the old grammar to new experience. This eternal conversation is panorganic; it is central to the nature of all living things. Piaget's work has demonstrated—and the work of many modern biologists in other areas confirms—that this conversation is not one of continuous augmentation, but is marked by periods of dynamic stability or balance followed by periods of instability and qualitatively new balance. These periods of dynamic balance amount to a kind of evolutionary truce: further assimilation and accommodation will go on in the context of

TABLE 2 Forms and functions of embeddedness cultures. From Kegan, 1982, pp. 118–120

Evolutionary balance and psychological embeddedness	Culture of embeddedness	Function 1: Confirmation (holding on)	Function 2: Contradiction (letting go)	Function 3: Continuity (staying put for reintegration)	Some common natural transitional "subject-objects" (bridges)[a]
(0) INCORPORATIVE Embedded in: reflexes, sensing, and moving.	Mothering one(s) or primary caretaker(s). *Mothering culture.*	Literal holding: close physical presense, comfort and protecting. Eye contact. Recognizing the infant. Dependence upon and merger with oneself.	Recognizes and promotes toddler's emergence from embeddedness. Does not meet child's every need, stops nursing, reduces carrying, acknowledges displays of independence and willful refusal.	Permits self to become part of bigger culture, i.e., the family. High risk: prolonged separation from infant during transition period (6 mos.–2 yrs.).	Medium of 0–1 transition: *blankie, teddy,* etc. A soft, comforting, nurturant representative of undifferentiated subjectivity, at once evoking that state and "objectifying" it.
(1) IMPULSIVE Embedded in: impulse and perception.	Typically, the family triangle. *Parenting culture.*	Acknowledges and cultures exercises of fantasy, intense attachments, and rivalries.	Recognizes and promotes child's emergence from egocentric embeddedness in fantasy and impulse. Holds child responsible for his or her feelings, excludes from	Couple permits itself to become part of bigger culture, including school and peer relations. High risk: dissolution of marriage or family unit during transition period (roughly 5–7 yrs.).	Medium of 1–2 transition: *imaginary friend.* A repository for impulses which before *were* me, and which eventually will be part *of* me, but here a little of each. E.g., only I can see it, but it is not me.

(2) IMPERIAL Embedded in: enduring disposition, needs, interests, wishes.	Role recognizing culture. School and family as institutions of authority and role differentiation. Peer gang which requires role-taking.	Acknowledges and cultures displays of self-sufficiency, competence, and role differentiation.	marriage, from parents' bed, from home during school day, recognizes child's self-sufficiency and asserts own "other sufficiency."	Recognizes and promotes preadoles-cent's (or adoles-cent's) emergence from embeddedness in self-sufficiency. Denies the validity of only taking one's own interests into account, demands mutuality, that the person hold up his/her end of relation-ship. Expects trustworthiness.	Family and school permit themselves to become secondary to relationships of shared internal experiences. High risk: family relocation during transition period (roughly early adolescence, 12–16).	Medium of 2–3 transition: *chum.* Another who is identical to me and real but whose needs and self-system are exactly like needs which before *were* me, eventually a part *of* me, but now something between.

(continued)

TABLE 2 Continued

Evolutionary balance and psychological embeddedness	Culture of embeddedness	Function 1: Confirmation (holding on)	Function 2: Contradiction (letting go)	Function 3: Continuity (staying put for reintegration)	Some common natural transitional "subject-objects" (bridges)[a]
(3) INTERPERSONAL Embedded in: mutuality, interpersonal concordance.	Mutually reciprocal one-to-one relationships. *Culture of mutuality.*	Acknowledges and cultures capacity for collaborative self-sacrifice in mutually attuned interpersonal relationships. Orients to internal state, shared subjective experience, "feelings," mood.	Recognizes and promotes late adolescent's or adult's emergence from embeddedness in interpersonalism. Person or context that will not be fused with but still seeks, and is interested in, association. Demands the person assume responsibility for own initiatives and preferences. Asserts the other's independence.	Interpersonal partners permit relationship to be relativized or placed in bigger context of ideology and psychological self-definition. High risk: interpersonal partners leave at very time one is emerging from embeddedness. (No easily supplied age norms.)	Medium for 3–4 transition: *going away to college, a temporary job, the military.* Opportunities for provisional identity which both leave the interpersonalist context behind and preserve it, intact, for return; a time-limited participation in institutional life (e.g. 4 years of college, a service hitch).

(4) INSTITUTIONAL Embedded in: personal autonomy, self-system identity.	*Culture of identity or self-authorship* (in love or work). Typically: group involvement in career, admission to public arena.	Acknowledges and cultures capacity for independence; self-definition; assumption of authority; exercise of personal enhancement, ambition or achievement; "career" rather than "job," "life partner" rather than "helpmate," etc.	Recognizes and promotes adult's emergence from embeddedness in independent self-definition. Will not accept mediated, nonintimate, form-subordinated relationship.	Ideological forms permit themselves to be relativized on behalf of the play between forms. High risk: ideological supports vanish (e.g., job loss) at very time one is separating from this embeddedness. (No easily supplied age norms.)	Medium of 4-5 transition: *ideological self-surrender (religious or political); love affairs protected by unavailability of the partner.* At once a surrender of the identification with the form while preserving the form.
(5) INTERINDIVI-DUAL Embedded in: interpenetration of systems.	*Culture of intimacy* (in domain of love and work). Typically: genuinely adult love relationship.	Acknowledges and cultures capacity for interdependence, for self-surrender and intimacy, for interdependent self-definition.			

a. In the construction of this column Kegan acknowledges indebtedness to the thinking of Mauricia Alvarez.

the established relationship struck between the organism and the world. (1982, pp. 43–44)

Each of these successive "cultures" and "truces" contribute to the development of more progressively encompassing systems of thinking, emotion, and relationship. He calls these evolving systems "stages" or "given knowing systems" with each stage "distinguished by a kind of active balance between what is taken for 'self' and what is taken for other." Kegan cautions that the "stages, even at their very best, are only indicators of development. To orient around the indicators of development is to risk losing the *person developing,* a risk at no time more unacceptable than when we are accompanying persons in transition, persons who may themselves feel they are losing the person developing" (1982, p. 277). These successive balances involve not only shifts and balances in the individual's internal equilibrium but a larger equilibrium which is created by the "progressively individuated self and the bigger life field, an interaction sculpted by both and constitutive of reality itself" (1982, p. 43).

But how do I take Kegan into the therapy room?

If I believe that people's constructions of the world can frame their interactions with others then I will want to know about these constructions. If I believe that development implies a direction along a path of increasing complexity of thought and relationship, then I will seek to facilitate that development. If I believe that mature love is the result of learning to be fully oneself at the same time one is able to fully relate to another, then I will be facilitating personal growth and development in the service of this goal. If I believe that transitions are painful because a way of making sense of the world is falling apart, I will join my client in experiencing that transition fully — facing the pain, accepting it, understanding it, using it, rather than avoiding it, sedating it, or denying it. If I believe that principles of growth and the values which they contain are valid goals for therapy, then I will join with people like Kegan in teaching and modeling *norms for growth* (1982, p. 293). Indeed, that is the purpose which I have maintained and will maintain throughout this book.

MICHAEL BASSECHES

Building on the theories of Piaget, which he considers "the most elaborate example of work" within the tradition which he is espousing, Michael Basseches goes beyond Piaget's more formalistic description of mature thought to a level of cognitive development which opens windows on cognitive possibility in adulthood. In doing this he breaks the hold which both the psychoanalytic and the stage-by-stage developmental theories have maintained on the study of adult life. His dialectical thinking offers a way to conceptualize adult development in entirely new ways — ways which show the rich potential for the individual to think in open, flexible, evolving kinds of movements through cognitive forms. Building on the roots of Piaget's "genetic epistemology," then, he points us towards concepts of adult cognitive development which honor universal programs for life at the same time they suggest the uniquely individual.

Basseches argues against popularized perspectives of adult development as the confrontation of predictable crises, speaking for the alternative viewpoint that adult development is the "achievement of more epistemologically adequate forms of cognitive organization." Though he accepts the concepts of predictable, normative "life-courses" which include tasks and crises specific to a particular culture, and though he would not negate the importance of working through these issues, he points to *development* as the progressive achievement of more effective, encompassing forms of thinking. In his words, "Simply confronting a new task or crisis is not, in my mind, development" (Basseches, 1984, pp. 311–312).

A central theme in dialectical thinking is contradiction. Basseches quotes Hegel: "Contradiction is the source of all motion and vitality; only in so far as something contains contradiction does it move, has it drive and activity" (1969, p. 545). From the contradiction of a basic thesis, a paradigm, a way of thinking, and the resulting disequilibrium comes the movement into a *"more inclusive* form."

Out of his belief that a detailed conception of the processes of dialectical thinking can be of value for cognitive psychologists in their study of adult thinking, Basseches has broken dialectical thinking into 24 component *schemata* — "specific types of moves-in-thought which dialectical thinkers tend to make." And he sees these schemata operating either as individual strategies of thinking or as an "organized whole" which represents a new form of equilibrium. In this he argues that individual schemata "may be employed in thought prior to, during, or after the formal operations stage," but the use of these dialectical schemata as an organized whole is a cognitive stage beyond Piaget's formal operations stage.

Thus, although a person can learn each of the cognitive moves, one-by-one, what constitutes a genuine stage beyond formal reasoning is *"the organization of the discrete tactics into a coherent whole,"* when the mind makes a cognitive shift into new, dialectical forms of organizing principles.

Basseches has named four categories of cognitive schemata which are further subdivided into a total of 24 schemata: (1) motion-oriented schemata, (2) form-oriented schemata, (3) relationship-oriented schemata, and (4) meta-formal (or transformation-oriented) schemata (see Table 3).

Motion-oriented schemata "describe moves in thought which function either to preserve fluidity in thought, to draw the attention of the thinker to processes of change, or to describe such processes" (1984, p. 73). Thus, when we describe the thesis-antithesis-synthesis movement in thought we are

TABLE 3 Michael Basseches: The dialectical schemata framework. From Basseches, 1984, p. 74

A. Motion-oriented schemata

1. Thesis-antithesis-synthesis movement in thought
2. Affirmation of the primacy of motion
3. Recognition and description of thesis-antithesis-synthesis movement
4. Recognition of correlativity of a thing and its other
5. Recognition of ongoing interaction as a source of movement
6. Affirmation of the practical or active character of knowledge
7. Avoidance or exposure of objectification, hypostatization, and reification
8. Understanding events or situations as moment (of development) of a process.

B. Form-oriented schemata

9. Location of an element or phenomenon within the whole(s) of which it is a part.
10. Description of a whole (system, form) in structural, functional, or equilibrational terms
11. Assumption of contextual relativism

C. Relationship-oriented schemata

12. Assertion of the existence of relations, the limits of separation or the value of relatedness
13. Criticism of multiplicity, subjectivism, and pluralism
14. Description of two-way reciprocal relationship
15. Assertion of internal relations

D. Meta-formal schemata

16. Location (or description of the process of emergence) of contradictions or sources of disequilibrium within a system (form) or between a system (form) and external forces or elements which are antithetical to the system's (form's) structure
17. Understanding of the resolution or disequilibrium or contradiction in terms of a notion of transformation in developmental direction
18. Relating value to (a) movement in developmental direction and/or (b) stability through developmental movement
19. Evaluative comparison of forms (systems)
20. Attention to problems of coordinating systems (forms) in relation
21. Description of open self-transforming systems
22. Description of qualitative change as a result of quantitative change within a form
23. Criticism of formalism based on the interdependence of form and content
24. Multiplication of perspectives as a concreteness-preserving approach to inclusiveness.

using dialectical thinking of this type. Or if we show understanding of events or situations as movements of development or of a process, we are also illustrating these forms of dialectical thinking.

A second category is *form-oriented schemata*, which shows thinking that acknowledges the idea of transformation or motion through forms. Boulding's hierarchy of systems could be a form-oriented schemata, or Bateson's attention to the interconnectedness of systems — of patterns within patterns. In fact, this question-and-answer sequence with Bateson from Goleman (1978) is a nice example of what dialectical, form-oriented thinking is about:

GOLEMAN Does this mean that whenever we propose a theory of behavior, with specific entities in particular relation to each other, we freeze the dance and so miss the larger patterns which connect? That, for example, the Freudian's id-ego-superego or the behaviorist's stimulus-response can never be more than a small part of a much larger story?

BATESON Exactly!

So, in this set of schemata an element or phenomenon is seen within the context of the whole, and it is assumed that this contextual relativism influences how we view that element within that whole.

A third category is *relationship-oriented schemata*, which "serve to direct the thinker's attention to relationships and to enable the thinker to conceptualize relationships in ways which emphasize their constitutive and interactive nature and thereby permit them to be related to the idea of dialectic" (1984, p. 75). This can include an understanding of the interactional dynamics which occur in relationships of differing types. This can include criticism of those cognitive moves which try to keep things separate.

The fourth category of schemata that Basseches has articulated is what he calls *meta-formal schemata.* In this category he has included nine different cognitive moves which play the role of "*integrating* the categories of relationship and motion with the category of form. They enable the thinker to describe (a) limits of stability of forms; (b) relationships among forms; (c) movements from one form to another (transformation); and (d) relationships of forms to the process of form-construction or organization" (1984, p. 76). In this kind of thinking can be a search for contradiction, and an acceptance of contradiction — what Basseches calls two characteristics of dialectical thinking. "Not only is contradiction viewed as positive within the context of the dialectical perspective, it also is viewed as necessary" (1984, p. 123).

How, then, do I take Basseches into the therapy room?

To fully appreciate the complexity and depth of Basseches' thought one must take time to study these schemata and to think oneself into the process. Here I have only given the flavor of a powerful set of ideas which influence my thinking and my therapy. But I direct you to these schemata as excellent resources for constructive questioning, which further becomes the active teaching of new ways to think. As therapists, then, we can ask:

- In what ways do you think you are changing?
- What would it be like to get rid of your success/failure ideas by thinking in some new ways?
- How does it feel to know that these tasks of growing and changing are never finished? That you are in process for the rest of your life?
- Let's compare and contrast how you are now with the way you were when you first came to therapy.
- What would it be like for you to take a different perspective on this?

What else do I take from Basseches into the therapy room? Perhaps most important for me is a loosening of fixed schemes which might lock me into cognitive sets. It is a freeing and releasing of labels as I turn to my clients' movements through cognitive form. This becomes a model for enrichment rather than for cure as I attempt to open my clients to new experience of thought, affect, and behavior; and as I become increasingly alert to my own structurings of thought which may or may not facilitate client development.

I also reflect on Basseches' values position as I work with clients. Concerned about the strong egoistic orientation of much developmental psychology—about the big push to self-actualization, success, and personal autonomy and narcissistic preoccupation—he raises important and thought-provoking questions about positivistic empiricist traditions which keep value judgments and science strictly apart. In contrast, he embraces a developmental tradition which "has the potential to directly counteract, rather than to play into, the egoistic, subjectivistic tendency in American popular psychology." He says this tradition, rather than equating human development with self-enhancement or getting as much out of life as possible, gets beyond the "narrow boundaries of the egoistic self." Most importantly, he states that the tradition which he espouses honors and incorporates the "pursuit of a truth and a collective good which transcend the individual" (1984, p. 8).

These values statements are in harmony with the values statements of Erikson and Kegan, for each has pointed to the need and the challenge of evolving human relationship, of the meaning-making of self and other, and of the development of the virtues which lead to the wisdom of later life. These values also carry some of the flavor of the writings and teachings of Confucius and the Hindu, as they point to the ultimate giving and caring which can arise from individual development. Certainly these values are in harmony with what Carol Gilligan is saying as she challenges the independence-dominated, self-oriented theories which have been named as programs for life. And, as I have already mentioned, these values are reflective guides to some of the hidden developmental changes which are taking place in American life as people reach from their places of aloneness to a greater sense of community.

SECTION II

A Bridge to Therapy

Debasing assumptions debase human beings; generous assumptions exalt them.

—Gordon Allport 1968, p. 16

In part, it is a professional helper's persistent recognition that her own meaning for a set of circumstances might not be the same as the client's that leads us to call her a sensitive listener; her understanding of what goes into the way her client makes meaning and what is at stake for him in defending it that leads us to call her a psychologist; and her understanding of what to *do* with her understanding that leads us to call her a therapist.

—Robert Kegan 1982, p. 3

Let's not try jamming facts into a theory. I've known a lot of good men who've messed themselves up doing that. The trick is to fit the theory to the facts.

—Detective Stilton, Sanders, 1983, p. 232

CHAPTER 4

Ties Between Theory and Therapy

IN PREVIOUS CHAPTERS I have described contributions of thought to conceptions of meaning and adult development. Now it is time to show how these varying streams unite under an umbrella of similarity and intent in a conceptual system which shapes the processes of developmental therapy. I also hope to demonstrate that a wide variety of theories and a broad base of knowledge contribute to the creative process called therapy. In fact, I am helped here by the image of the "creative know-it-all" described by Roger von Oech:

The creative person wants to be a know-it-all . . . Because he [or she] never knows when these ideas might come together to form a new idea. It may happen six minutes later or six months or six years down the road. But he has faith that it will happen. . . . Knowledge is the stuff from which new ideas are made . . . the real key to being creative lies in what you do with your knowledge. Creative thinking requires an attitude or outlook which allows you to search for ideas and manipulate your knowledge and experience . . . by adopting a creative outlook you open yourself up to both new possibilities and to change. (1983, p. 6)

This creative outlook is a world view which I seek to foster not only in myself but also in my clients as we make meaning together. It is an outlook which shines through the developmental beliefs, attitudes and processes which I describe below.

In translating theory into psychotherapy practice, I emphasize again the significance of our theories. They form screening devices, filters and explanations. They call us to attention and suggest methods and logics for categorizing, organizing, and creating a meaning. For us, as therapists, they influence perspectives on the client as person, what goals we project, and which questions we ask. They are the cognitive shaping mechanisms for choosing the interventions of psychotherapy and for defining and measuring change.

Because theories influence our therapeutic choices in all aspects of therapeutic practice they can not only open new vistas for exploration but also limit us. Indeed, ignoring Detective Stilton's warning, we may try to jam the facts into preconceived theories, forgetting that the "trick is to fit the theory to the facts." A central therapeutic task, therefore, is to name our theories, our assumptions, our boundaries and limits, while maintaining an openness and responsiveness to the serendipity which occurs with our client.

Our clients come with *their* sets of theories and assumptions, many of them unnamed. They, too, bring tendencies to jam facts into predetermined theories or to use mental templates which limit the realities of their worlds. Indeed, the initial impetus to therapy is usually found in theories gone awry: theories which no longer function in enabling the client to make sense of his or her world, or theories which have locked cognitive, affective, and behavioral movements into a circularity which blocks the reordering of personal experience. In the moment of crisis, the emotions which provide motivation for therapy also signal that the cognitive structural system is no longer assimilating and accommodating in a rhythm which keeps life on an even keel. Because the theoretical systems may be breaking, much of the challenge of the initial therapeutic dialogue comes in the naming and facing of the theories which no longer make meaning for the client.

Acknowledging the vital role of theory, then, the purpose of this chapter is to move from the theoretical to the practical. It is *not* my purpose to say "this is it" in terms of a specific technique or a specific approach. Although I will be illustrating and offering specific approaches to therapy, I also believe that therapeutic specifics spring from the unique dynamic between individual client and individual therapist. What I *am* describing is a paradigm, a body of metaphor, a conceptual window, through which I view my client and from which I develop my questionings.

A central premise in all this is that the therapist joins the client in a dialogue which seeks to make sense of life. A secondary premise is that crisis and therapeutic resolution can provide impetus to movement from less sophisticated, more rigid and closed systems of thinking to more encompassing, flexible conceptualizations in terms of both intrapsychic process and one's dialectic of contexts and relationships. The movement of therapy proceeds in a back and forth motion between thoughts, feelings, and behaviors of past and present in sorting the overlapping, intertwining systems which can give a springboard of meaning for the future.

Some might argue that I have widened the lens too far, that a body of theory gathered in the spirit of the "creative know-it-all" becomes fuzzy, messy, and nonscientific. As we progress, what I propose to show is that this multidimensional, interdisciplinary point of view gains meaning under a larger umbrella which *does* bring system and order to therapeutic process. In doing this I presume to take the title of "systematic eclecticism" which Gordon Allport (1968, pp. 3–27) suggested as a goal for therapy and thinking. Whether this goal is fully achieved remains to be seen, but at the least it provides a sense of meaning, purpose, and direction for this book.

Goals for psychotherapy provide the springboard for our discussion and form our first category for discussion. These lead naturally to a set of *assumptions about the person* who is our client. The third category summarizes *assumptions about developmental process* as a cognitive system for conceptualizing both therapy and the client. This discussion closes this chapter and prepares us for Chapter 5, which is a bridge to therapy.

GOALS FOR PSYCHOTHERAPY

Goals form a tacit dimension for therapy. Another way to say this is that goals are the internalized values which the therapist finds important for therapy. These goals or values can range from the reduction of symptoms to the structuring of behavioral programs to the imaging of plans for the future. Goals also give measuring points for change.

Goals are sometimes painted in concrete, discrete terms. But if goals are too simple or too definite they reduce planning and purposes to black/white terms without much flexibility of choice and error. To avoid this, I start by couching these therapeutic goals in a language of concepts, large ideals, large reference points for meaning. As we progress, however, these abstract goals become increasingly translated into the specifics of the *doing* of therapy.

This list of goals is not closed or complete. I like to think of it as an open system which has the potential for receiving feedback and for being "recognized" as the complexity of each individual client's dilemma presents itself. What is being offered here, therefore, is a speculative starting point for further consideration and application.

An initial goal is *to join each client where he or she is*. This means attending to the feelings, the thoughts, and the wonderings which have brought the person into the vulnerable position of exposing the most private elements of self. Respecting our client's vulnerability *and* natural wisdom, we can offer an "indwelling" with the client in a therapeutic meeting place where the client can feel accepted and honored where he or she is. The establishment of this environment of meeting and disclosure, then, is an initial goal in therapy.

Goals unite with theory at this point in shaping my approaches to the person. In my case, I was trained as a Rogerian therapist where reflection was the rule and questioning was somehow not acceptable (at least with my own supervisor), and where the ideal for the interaction with each client was "unconditional regard." Through experience I have broken with this strictly reflective style. Increasingly I have paid attention to the kinds of questions which are raised, teaching and nurturing a kind of Socratic method of question and answer. Though I use paraphrasing techniques constantly and consider them exceedingly valuable at times when the client needs to feel heard, I also value the posture which I call "constructive contradiction."

But in the early stages of therapy it *is* essential to create a caring, supportive environment which builds the relationship between client and therapist and provides a resilient springboard for later interventions — what family therapist Carl Broderick calls an investment in the client's "emotional bank," as ongoing, sensitive attention is given to client pain and client need. But the process can't stop there. As the client is gradually brought to the edge of safety the therapist alternately leads and steps back, reinforces and contradicts, in a kind of contradiction of what *is* in the service of what *is to be*. It is a dynamic interaction in which dependencies need to be fulfilled in order for dependencies to be resolved.

A similar model is offered by Kegan when he describes the "holding environment" in family life and marriage (see Chapter 3). He suggests that a good family provides confirmation, continuity, and contradiction as three key ingredients in rearing the child. When these are provided, the child grows up with a sense of trust in the world around him or her and begins to move out of the home as parents not only support but also contradict in leading the child to personal initiative and autonomy. Therapy is like this. As a holding environment it can offer these functions: first of all in the establishment of trust born of confirmation and continuity, and then in the creative contradiction which can lead the client to name his own choices and directions.

Therapeutic ploys which manipulate, demean, or reject the client do not fit in here, which means that "a treatment that is essentially manipulative, for example 'paradoxical intention' is eschewed if its rationale is not clear to the patient, or if it cannot be applied with the informed consent of the patient" (Bedrosian & Beck, 1980, p. 129). In contrast, what is adopted is *creation of a genuine therapeutic dialogue*. Martin Buber's model of the dialogue of "I-Thou," for example, is rich and suggestive of its elements.

The dialogue is like a game of chess. The whole charm of chess is that I do not know and cannot know what my partner will do. I am surprised by what he does and on this surprise the whole play is based. (1965, p. 178)

But more than that:

The chief presupposition for the rise of genuine dialogue is that each should regard his partner as the very one he is. . . . To be aware of a man . . . means in particular to perceive his wholeness as a person determined by the spirit; it means to perceive the dynamic center which stamps his every utterance, action, and attitude with the recognizable sign of uniqueness. (Buber, 1965, p. 79)

In genuine, fully receptive meeting the therapist offers his or her presence in the creation of a unique dynamic for recovery, reconciliation, and renewal. Indeed, what unites many disparate therapies is the relationship of client and therapist, a relationship which provides a "healing through meeting . . . a kind of confirmation that does something to repair the disconfirmation that causes 'mental illness'" (Friedman, 1985a, p. xii).*

The therapeutic dialogue is unique because it is necessarily one-sided with the client and therapist assuming differing roles. Indeed, they cannot be equal. The therapist is the listener and the helper, not the one who is being helped or listened to. And with a kind of detached presence the therapist offers the contradictory elements which bring the client to moments of awakening and surprise. The therapist is the person who wrestles *"with* the patient, *for* the patient, and *against* the patient" (Friedman, 1985b, p. 14). It is not just a passive acceptance or a simplistic reinforcement of what is; it is a challenge to the individual client to recreate self by facing oneself, by naming oneself, and by daring oneself.

Another therapeutic goal is to *fully explore the feelings within the crisis experience* and to *face and use crisis experience as the energy for constructive change.* This means helping the client touch the emotions of the crisis experience in an acceptance and reshaping of those emotions. In this approach I encourage the cognitive understanding of feelings at the same time they are expressed, believing that these emotions lose their controlling power as they are addressed and named. This is a process of encouraging clients to "walk into their fears—to stare them down" as they defuse them by dealing with them. From being ruled and haunted by their emotional ghosts, clients move towards new appreciation of these very feelings, learning to know them and to use them.

An accompanying goal is *helping the individual face basic "existential fears" without building neurotic defenses.* By "existential fears" I mean those which seem to be built into the fabric of human existence—fears which are common to us all and which are a part of being human. This is an idea from Paul Tillich's *Courage to Be*—an idea which I have found helpful

---

*To study Buber and Friedman is to discover rich resource for greater understanding of the meaning and power of dialogue.

for myself as well as for my clients. This means, again, acknowledging, facing, accepting, and using fears in the service of growth. It means that what Tillich calls "basic existential anxieties"—the anxiety of fate and death, the anxiety of emptiness and meaninglessness, and the anxiety of guilt and condemnation—are taken as part of the givens of life. Yes, they are painful, but no, they cannot and must not be avoided if one is to live life in a creative, courageous fashion (Tillich, 1952).

In writing about therapy and emotional expression I cite Michael Mahoney, who criticizes those cognitive therapists who ignore the emotional expressions of the individual. Mahoney believes that we as therapists must pay attention to previously interrupted sequences of emotional life experience. He does not endorse the idea of diffusely stored feelings that accumulate and spill over into symptomatic expressions. "More tenable is the notion that 'catharsis' is not the discharge of amorphous energy but rather the expression of previously inhibited affect associated with a given belief or memory . . . it is possible that such expressions may actually facilitate belief change, if they reduce the arousal and its CNS [central nervous system] interference" (Mahoney, 1980, p. 165).

Belief change is central to the shifts in world view which we are describing in a meaning-making therapy. It is a cracking of old systems of thinking which militate against creative process and reinforce negative emotions and negative thought. The therapist struggles against "belief-keeping" in order to encourage constructive processes of "belief-making." This does not necessarily challenge particular beliefs; rather, it challenges a *way of thinking* which interferes with new approaches to and new understandings of the realities of one's world.

This cognitive approach has a spirit and flavor different from that of cognitive psychologist Albert Ellis. I do not tell a client that her beliefs are "irrational" or inappropriate; to me that smacks of a form of arrogance that presumes the therapist knows best what is true. Rather, I seek to lead clients to their own insights about belief in a process which respects the integrity and logic of that belief. And, believing that the past has created belief patterns, I direct attention to exploring how the past is still exerting its power in the present. "What were the 'thou shalts' and the 'thou shalt nots' of your family? What did your father believe? Did he believe that he was right? How do you think your fear affects you right now? Is that fear from the past?" On and on, as together we examine the edicts of authoritarian figures or the inherited ideologies of families; as we examine opinions based on black/white, opinionated interpretations; as we verbally joust around ideas, comparing and contrasting beliefs of every sort. In such dialogue is the challenge to name the contents of belief, and to examine the ways of *making* belief. In the process I model and share my own beliefs, but I would hate to see my client leave my office with beliefs imposed from without rather than born from within.

In the therapeutic dialogue, I join others like Arthur Koestler, Roger von Oech, James Adams, and Silvano Arieti in respecting and defining creative thinking, and actively teaching techniques of "conceptual blockbusting" (Adams, 1974) in order to shake apart rigid pathways of cognitive process. I find myself as therapist examining thinking style in a search for the giveaway phrases which reveal dualistic, limited cognitive process. This can be the "never," the "always," the "absolutely," the "I can't," the "there's only one right way"—all of which illustrate a world view built upon right/wrong, black/white perspectives, upon broad generalizations and frantic avoidance of anything that smacks of "failure" or of the less-than-perfect (Lazarus, 1971).

A therapeutic goal, then, is *to teach, facilitate, and reinforce creative thinking processes*. Using the definitions of Arieti, this means teaching abilities to think freely, to be somewhat gullible in entertaining varying possibilities, and to keep oneself open to the creative gestations of mystery and wonder (Arieti, 1976, pp. 372–379). It means teaching personal attitudes of trust and openness, which help the individual live with ambiguity without a heavy burden of threat and anxiety. It also means teaching the guidelines of discipline and focus which help to translate the abstract into pathways of action. In the process of teaching such attitudes, the therapist delves deeper into the realms of individual meaning-making, cognitive structures, and constellations of belief and attitude to help the client reorder that which is blocking the creative process.

A parallel goal is the stimulation and encouragement of *dialectical thinking patterns*. With the schemata of Michael Basseches as a measure and a model (see Chapter 3), the therapist can question in a manner which opens thinking. Questioning can inject elements of novelty and surprise; of wondering; of a paradoxical perspective on an idea or a behavior. Questioning can lead the client to new levels of abstraction, and to new ways of comparing and contrasting, of seeing both sides of an issue, of considering another point of view. And the question and answer process can both feed forward and feed back to therapist and client, leading them to larger and larger versions of the same questions.

EXAMPLE OF QUESTIONING

The creative, dialectical forms of thinking which I have been describing are born of, and facilitate, the achievement of another therapeutic goal, which Kegan has described as the *subject/object transition*. Einstein's words at the beginning of this book are a metaphorical statement of this transition. I quote them once again to illustrate my point:

. . . a new theory is like destroying an old barn and erecting a skyscraper in its place. It is rather like climbing a mountain, gaining new and wider views, discovering unexpected connections between our starting point and its rich environment. But the point from which we started out still exists and can be seen, although it appears smaller and forms a tiny part of our broad view gained by the mastery of the obstacles on our adventurous way up.

As we step outside our systems of thinking and feeling we become more able to look into our problems from new vantage points. It is the shaking of old systems in the creation of the new. It is the experience of no longer *being* the problem, but *having* the problem. My client, Jana, described the subject-object transition in herself in this follow-up letter a few months after the close of her first therapeutic sequence:

You have helped me to that one step further in my thinking so that I can get out of whichever circle I'm caught in. Of course, after so many years of "circling," I still need a lot of practice on actually using the exits.

In this therapy the therapist is a teacher of both knowledge content and cognitive structure. The two feed off from each other. One new idea can spin through the cognitive system. Or a model or a metaphor may bring novelty into comparison and contrast. The teaching method can be semantic free-association which alerts the client to the powerful systems of meaning entwined around each word. Content can include varying life skills, understanding of a developmental sequence, stress management, behavioral control and discipline, crisis use and resolution, models for personal growth and development, assertiveness training, or tools for conceptual blockbusting. One day in therapy with Nick I was delighted by his whimsical statement, "I have just completed Learning 101 and am now ready to move on to Learning 202." And in this statement I found affirmation of my belief that a client can walk away from therapy with *content* as well as process — new knowledge of coping mechanisms, larger conceptual pictures of personal growth and development, and increased understanding of what thinking is about.

The facilitation of creative aging is another goal for a meaning-making therapy, as we help clients build an active preparation for the tasks of old age. An essential part of this process is helping individuals look ahead to the end points of life by asking in constructive ways, "What helps me to age well and to live as effectively as possible until the day I die?" Most people never ask that question, unfortunately, so another therapeutic challenge is to teach a long view of life which incorporates such questions into the decision-making of adult life. For the therapist it means asking: "How do we help our clients handle the despair which is a part of old age? And how do we help them build the integrity which is the counterbalance for that despair?"

Many of the theories of adult development do offer some sort of a model for creative aging. Whether they tell us this is *the way or the goal*, they do suggest by the very sequential nature of the model that these are significant passages and stages of life. For Erikson, again, it is working one's way through the psychosocial tasks of life. For Kegan, it is the evolution towards a blending of self and other, of embeddedness and differentiation, of dependence and independence. For me, it is the flexible designing and redesigning of successive systems of meaning in an effective, synergistic enlarging of one's interaction with life. A therapy of meaning-making, therefore, becomes a therapy of creative aging, a theme which I will be developing fully in Chapter 13.

The uniting goal in all of this is the *fostering of "meaning-making."* I have already discussed many aspects of this in the goals described thus far, but think the focus can be narrowed helpfully by considering the following as tangible steps to this goal:

- Establish a climate of trust and acceptance, joining the client in his or her meanings and presenting problems and pain.
- In partnership with the client identify and name the wide range of facts, assumptions, and speculations which are part and parcel of the complexity of his or her meanings.
- Keep the mind open to this wide range, not judging prematurely or narrowing the range of convenience too soon. This means giving attention to contexts of meaning, to differing personal systems, while considering both history and the present, the concrete and the abstract, the sensory and the cognitive/affective, in evaluating all aspects of the presenting problem and the presenting person.
- Begin the creative patterning of this wide collection of data and theory being just a bit "wild" in the process. This means incorporating the "free thinking" and the "gullibility" which Arieti describes as significant aspects of creative thinking.
- Help clients to think about thinking so that they begin to understand their own epistemologies, their own ways of ordering their world, their own structurings of meaning and meaning-making.
- Incorporate within the process the experiences of confirmation, continuity, and constructive contradiction which both respect the integrity of the client and honor his or her need for a supportive holding environment while engaged in the awesome task of moving from one way of being in the world to a new way of being.

The central figure in the therapeutic drama is, of course, the person who is our client. An overarching goal in everything we do, therefore, is the facilitation of this person. How we honor and name this person is the focus of this next set of assumptions. As a bridge to that discussion I quote a brief commentary by Erik Erikson as he pondered the meaning of identity—a commentary which provides another goal for helping the person: *to facilitate a sense of sameness, continuity, and the "real me" in creating a life of meaning:*

As a *subjective sense* of an *invigorating sameness* and *continuity,* what I would call a sense of identity seems to me best described by William James in a letter to his wife:

> A man's character is discernible in the mental or moral attitude in which, when it came upon him, he felt himself most deeply and intensely active and alive. At such moments there is a voice inside which speaks and says: "This is the real me." (Erikson, 1968, p. 19)

ASSUMPTIONS ABOUT THE PERSON

What *are* the filters and lenses we use in viewing our clients? If we depend only on normative data or statements of universals, we may miss the person. If we depend only on the intuitions of the moment, we may lose the historical/cultural, psychological, physiological understandings of what a person is all about. If we focus only on techniques, strategies, and diagnostic evaluation, we may miss the essence of individual meaning, putting our clients at the mercy of our manipulations, imposition, and interventions. And if we label our clients with a discrete category from *DSM-III* we may be hooked into stereotype.

These negative possibilities are concerns for the therapist. As I ponder this I pull into my consciousness some very powerful warnings from two researchers in creativity and semantics: James Adams' words that a label once applied makes us less likely to notice the actual qualities or attributes of that which is labeled (1974, p. 80), and Gordon Allport's warning that "Labels of primary potency act like shrieking sirens, deafening us to all the finer discriminations that we might otherwise perceive" (1954, p. 179).

But we cannot give up our models and our structures. To find answers to the dilemma requires the dialectical ability to look two ways and to recognize which view is dominant in our thinking at a particular therapeutic moment. In his seminal wisdom, Carl Jung stated the challenge:

> If I want to understand an individual human being, I must lay aside all scientific knowledge of the average man and discard all theories in order to adopt a completely new and unprejudiced attitude. I can only approach the task of *understanding* with a free and open mind, whereas *knowledge of man, or insight into human character, presupposes all sorts of knowledge about mankind in general.* (1957, p. 18)

> If the psychologist happens to be a doctor who wants not only to classify his patient scientifically but also to understand him as a human being, he is threatened with a conflict of duties between the two diametrically opposed and mutually exclusive attitudes of knowledge, on the one hand, and understanding, on the other. This conflict cannot be solved by an either-or but only by a kind of two-way thinking: doing one thing while not losing sight of the other. (p. 19)

Jung's challenge translates into a caveat that we keep respect for the universals of *persons* at the same time we approach the uniqueness of the individual.

Each person is both a reactive and a proactive being. In fact, following a model articulated by Gordon Allport (1962), I can view my client through three lenses: as reactive being, as reactive-being-in-depth, and as a "being-in-the-process-of-becoming"—the positivistic, the psychoanalytical, and the humanistic perspectives on the human being. I approach my client with respect for all three. Acknowledging that conditionings and reinforcements have shaped me as well as my client, I seek to sort these influences with my client and name them. This is also true of looking for the unconscious, tacit dimensions of thinking, affect, and memory. But when I reach the conceptualization of the person as a "being-in-the-process-of-becoming," then I may not only hold a body of knowledge about stimulus and response and about unconscious functioning, but also move toward something that is much more active.

This perspective puts the person solidly in charge of personal meaning-making. As active meaning-maker the person can build new awarenesses, new thoughts and planned purposes into the pauses between the stimulus and the response. This is an idea from Rollo May, who feels therapy gives opportunity for building such pauses by helping the client to use creative thought in breaking automatic reaction to trigger experiences. Building these pauses the individual is more able not only to act differently, but also to gain a new perspective on personal choice. Further, according to Allen Wheelis' message in *How People Change*, the more we know we are determined, the less we are determined. Which is to say, once we understand the sources and power of our learnings and conditionings, we can rise above them.

Thus, *new personal awareness can bring change*. I often say to my clients, "Once you are aware you are already different." Those few words are usually reassuring because they offer a window into change. Often, with those ideas in their thinking, clients begin to see the continuum of growth and development, and to gain recognition of how new understandings, new beliefs, new meanings can "shake up the works" in making them different. They come to recognize how previous learnings have produced emotional "triggers" which represent unique vulnerabilities. These triggers often continue through life, but by standing outside their learnings with new understanding clients seem better able to name the patterning, recognize the reactions, and build in moments of thought and choice in the ongoing dynamics of stimulus and response.

Naming the person as a "being-in-the-process-of-becoming" brings the past into the present in moving towards the future. Thus, another assumption is that *each person is a mixture of the past, present and future*. This constitutes a "time-binding quality" which enables the person to include the systems of the past and the present in an orientation towards a future. It is what Michael Mahoney describes as the "I was, I am, and I will be" of human process. It is the attention to how the past is shaping the present and the future which is a basic part of meaning-making process.

But our futures also shape our present. In the words of Vicky, "How am I to know who I am unless I know who I am to be?" That profound question acknowledges the power of goals, purposes and meanings — all a part of a future which has been conceptualized — in leading us to important decisions and choices in the present. And, certainly, what shapes this future are the meanings, ideals, perspectives, memories which we bring to it. This future-oriented perspective about the person influences therapy in creating an approach with a multidimensional perspective and a multidimensional approach.

As a "time-binding" being, then, *each person comes to therapy with designs and purposes which contain the meanings, models, and ideals which form a tacit dimension for personal meaning-making.* In a client's natural wisdom is a theory of life, a personal construct of meaning or meaninglessness. Sometimes this wisdom is hard to find because it is a part of unarticulated experience — that which is variously called endoceptual, primitive, or unconscious. This wisdom is sometimes the child's wisdom, shaped in response to emotional and psychological needs, met and unmet, early in life. Though this wisdom may not fit adult life, it was built as a needed response to early experience. It was the child's way of surviving in the real, sometimes brutal, world of the family.

Because the task of the therapist is to enter into a client's meaning systems, it also becomes the task of the therapist to help the client name these systems of family, relationship, work or self. By understanding the sequences and patternings of this past he or she is more fully able to understand the present. Although the knowledge of the moment does not predict the future, its knowledge guides questions and goal-setting towards the future in a qualitative analysis of what has worked and what has not worked in the past. In the naming and ordering of this experiential knowledge, the client can make new meaning in new orderings and reorderings of experience.

Acknowledging that old systems are operating in the present, family systems therapy has pointed the way in looking at the influences of "family of origin" — of the learnings, modelings, behaviors and beliefs of the family system. And the influence of family ideology as it passes through the generations is being researched in a number of different ways. Paul C. Nagel's book, *Descent From Glory* (1983), a study of four generations of the John Adams family, is a remarkable commentary on the powerful influence of family meaning systems, as it demonstrates how the Adams family's sets of ideals brought a kind of either/or swing in lives of the descendents — either leading the individual to success in the public arena or to personal tragedy when unable to live up to the family ideal. When a family member incorporated a belief system out of synchrony with personal style or personal needs, tension and tragedy often resulted. As Charles Francis Adams, John's grandson, poignantly revealed, his family history was "one of great triumphs in the world but of deep groans within, one of extraordinary brilliancy and deep corroding mortification" (cover page).*

In this theory and therapy *the person is viewed as an organic being rather than a mechanistic machine.* Chronological ascent and decline in a movement towards a built-in obsolescence becomes replaced as a model for human life. Human beings are seen as capable of mental and spiritual growth even though their bodies show physical decline. Acknowledgment is given to the *possibilities for new growth in the mature brain, stimulated in part by mental activity.* "Neural modifiability in the mature brain appears to be multi-determined. The presence of multiple mechanisms for the reorganization of neural structures requires the abandoning of any conception of the brain as a static, slowly decaying brain" (Colarusso & Nemiroff, 1981, p. 74).

My friend Helen, now in her eighties, has modeled processes of organic growth which include continuing enlargement of perspectives on life, and evolving philosophies of her place in the order of things. She says that as her body loses some of its functioning she has needed to give increased attention to the opportunities for growth in her mind and her spirit. It is not easy, she says, to refocus attention from physical fitness to mental, emotional and spiritual fitness, but she feels that is what aging is all about. Carl Jung has offered that same thesis in his statement that the therapeutic questions of the middle and later years of life are spiritual ones.

With the framing of some of therapy's questions as spiritual ones the therapist moves into a domain not often populated by helping professionals trained in a traditional mode. In the spiritual domain are large *meaning* questions which reflect the cycling and recycling of the meaning questions of life. What is interesting to me is that therapeutic process often leads naturally to these larger, more abstract issues, so that I often find clients asking questions which can be framed as "spiritual." Indeed, I consider Erikson's sequence of "virtues" a sequencing of those human characteristics which lead the enlarging, universal interconnections and perspectives of spiritual meaning and capacity. (Some of these "spiritual" qualities will be raised in Chapter 13 as we consider the role of the therapist in facilitating creative aging.)

The person has the ability to stand outside of self and look in. We have already talked about this in discussing the subject/object transition, but I cite it here as a remarkable capability of the human being. This capability is demonstrated in the ability to ask "Who am I?" and to order life with systems of meaning. The capability is certainly found in humor, where the person steps outside of self in order to laugh at self. Genuine humor seems to contain the elements of detached perspective. Because of this I feel much

---

*McGoldrick & Gerson (1985) offer a detailed genogram of the Adams family which highlights these patterns of success and tragedy.

growth has been achieved when my client and I can laugh together. This is a moment of novelty, of surprise, of a creative flash, when we frame the therapeutic dilemmas in new ways.

In therapy, therefore, the therapist can tap human capacities to look in on self as object, using any and all techniques which facilitate the process: the creation of personal stories, the imaging of a future, the use of models, the introduction of metaphor, the reframing of language, the painting of pictures. All these techniques shake thinking, drawing in the power of imagination and novelty. I will be detailing and illustrating many of these techniques in Chapter 7.

These assumptions about the person are not complete, but I have offered this selection as an introduction to the "person-in-the-process-of-becoming" and as a stimulus for what is to come. Now it is time to consider some of the underlying assumptions about developmental process.

ASSUMPTIONS ABOUT DEVELOPMENTAL PROCESS

Many of the assumptions about the person as "being-in-the-process-of-becoming," about the meshing, time-binding qualities of past, present, and future, about the spiritual qualities of the person, lead us into another discussion of the developmental assumptions which influence a meaning-making therapy.*

With a long view of life, the developmental theorist and therapist see *development as an ongoing dynamic process* which starts at birth and continues to the end of life. With this perspective less attention is given to equating behavior and development with biological chronology and more is given to the potential for personal growth and change throughout all of life. In that attention is appreciation for the complexity of overlapping systems within the human being: the physical, the social, the emotional, the cultural, the communal, the cognitive. The dynamic complexity of evolving, overlapping, and integrating systems also makes us appreciate the vast potential of the individual (icluding us as therapists) to widen capacities to name and integrate the meanings of the systems. As William James (1902, p. 428) asserted, "There never can be a state of facts to which new meaning may not truthfully be added, provided the mind ascend to a more enveloping point of view."

Again, *a developmental perspective honors the fact that even though a person's body is wearing out, human awareness, understanding, and wisdom can continue to evolve until the end of life.* This assumption feeds back to the one we have already addressed in honoring the organic quality of the

---

*I want to give special acknowledgment to Colarusso and Nemiroff, whose pioneering work *Adult Development* (1981) offers sets of assumptions which feed into my own. In my synthesis here I mesh their ideas with those of Allport, Mahoney, Bedrosian, Kegan, Rogers, Angyal, Buhler, and the many others whose thinking influences my own.

human being, and in respecting the spiritual developments which can occur as the person grows older. With such belief the therapist will be more open to work with the elderly, not labeling them rigid and incapable of change.

In the words of Colarusso and Nemiroff, *"The fundamental developmental issues of childhood continue as central aspects of adult life but in altered form"* (1981, p. 67). Accepting certain aspects of trait theory, the developmentalist sees the traits taking on new color, new flavor, new constructions as the person moves into new contexts and relationships, as well as into the cognitive restructuring of perspectives on self and others. The adult story develops through solution and resolution of old problems seen in the light of the new.

Take the problem of shyness, for instance. Jerome Kagan suggests that this quality of temperament may be one of the characteristics of a child which appear at a very early age:

Of all the temperamental qualities that have been studied — activity, irritability, and fearfulness are the most popular — an initial display of inhibition to the unfamiliar (what parents call "shyness," "caution," or "timidity") and its opposite (what they call "sociability," "boldness," or "fearlessness") are two qualities that seem to persist from the first birthday to late childhood . . . . unlike most behavior, the conditions for inhibited or uninhibited behavior toward others are present continually. Many moments of every day are punctuated by interactions with other people that require a decision to withdraw or to participate. Each time one chooses either course, the relevant habit is strengthened, making this disposition an intimate part of each person's character. (1984, p. 65)

One of Kagan's theses which is important here is that such predisposition towards shyness does not *determine* how one will be. Certainly, shyness will show differing manifestations throughout life depending on how the characteristic is addressed. If it is honored as a personal quality less attention will be given to altering the quality. And with the lowering of concern about the quality it may actually diminish as a quality! (Sam Keen once whimsically wrote, "Deliver Us from Shyness Clinics.") A developmental perspective once again honors the belief that we each have the capacity to alter how we view a characteristic, how we use it, and how we order our lives around such a characteristic.

In this developmental perspective, psychosocial tasks are not believed settled once and for all; they can recycle in new forms within varying contexts and at differing stages of adult development. I image this as cycles within cycles within cycles, or systems within systems within systems. Professor Henry Maier of the University of Washington reports that every time he enters a new city or establishes himself in a new domain he cycles through Erikson's eight stages of psychosocial development in miniature as he faces renewed problems of everything from trust to generativity. I have certainly found this cycling and recycling present with each adventure into a new job. And we need only think of the aging person to realize that the search for meaning in old age brings into sharp focus unresolved questions of generativity, intimacy, and trust in personal integrity. What was resolved once is not resolved once and for all.

"The developmental processes in adulthood are influenced by the adult past as well as the childhood past" (Colarusso & Nemiroff, 1981, p. 69). When we build on a Freudian perspective, or on any of the other theoretical systems which make current problems a reliving of the past, we may forget the trauma of six months or a year ago which has left an imprint upon the human personality. To reinforce this assumption in my thinking, I often recall the research of Irving Janis into the powerful impact of disaster on people's cognitive systems. Disaster shakes trust levels as it reveals a vulnerability previously unknown, and it thrusts people into intensive modes of problem-solving in order to place the experience within an overarching perspective on life (Janis, 1971). This could be called meaning-making in high gear, as the individual seeks to make sense of what does not make sense, and to grieve the loss of a form of innocence which shaped life before. (In this regard, one only needs to study the research into concentration camp survivors to see the powerful effect of an adult event upon the shaping of personal reality.)

In another sharpening of sensitivity and awareness a *developmental perspective respects the influence of physical change on the cognitive and the affective*, an influence which can shape the processing of progressive challenges of adult development. Here again is the place where the therapist must maintain the ability to move through hierarchies of systems in considering the problems of the client. Taking time to research the influences of the biological in current life transitions and personal crisis may well be as significant as seeking for the cognitive developmental structures.

It is the adult who has the capacity to study the adult. And, I would add here, the interest. If one looks into the literature of adult development one finds cases of how a particular developmental experience leads a researcher to study a particular aspect of adult development. Daniel Levinson is an example of this:

In embarking upon this work I seemed to be entering a lonely and uncharted territory. The study reflected in part my intellectual interest in the possibility of adult development. The choice of topic also reflected a personal concern: at 46, I wanted to study the transition into middle age in order to understand what I had been going through myself. Over the previous ten years my life had changed in crucial ways; I had "developed" in a sense I could not articulate. The study would cast light on my own experience and, I hoped, contribute to an understanding of adult development in general. Later it became evident that this decision reflected more than my personal feelings. There is a growing desire in our society to see adulthood as something more than a long featureless stretch of years with childhood at one end and senility at the other. (1978, p. x)

It *is* the adult who studies adulthood and it *is* the adult who reflects biases, personal dilemmas, and private developmental challenges when studying the adult. This realization and this assumption lead me to consider how my own developmental levels influence what I see, hear and model for my client; and how my own "adult" perspectives may either facilitate or hinder client process. For me, this particular assumption is both a caution and a challenge to keep sensitive to the interaction between one's own developmental processes and those of the client.

The developmental viewpoint reduces the danger of simplistic stereotyping of people which reduces them to normative portraits. The point is that we respect the vast permutations of adult life. Bernice Neugarten is among those who say we are less alike at 65 than we were at 18 because of the increasing dividing and subdividing of personal variables in interaction with life experience. One need only look around to realize how ludicrous it is to lump people "over 65" into one class of citizen, as though to enter this age group is to become homogenous with everyone else of the same age. When we respect the vast permutations of adult life, we will be more likely to honor the complexity of individuals and the dialectic between stability and change, between the universal and the unique, and between the internal experience of the person and that of shifting relationship.

Colarusso and Nemiroff have suggested that the *personal meaning of an event determines its emotional response.* This assumption fits well with all that I have said thus far about using emotions as barometers of meaning and change. Within this perspective emotions are honored as signals and guides to stages of meaning-making — a means to understanding the particular cognitive structures which are shaping the client's world. These concepts are at the core of the cognitive model of emotions and emotional disorders.

By looking at depression or anxiety as signs that a person's world is in upheaval we can speak to the *dangerous opportunities of crisis as the challenge of constructive change.* This is a theme which I have already addressed in a number of ways, but I mention it again as one of the developmental assumptions which underlies my therapy — an assumption which shifts the emphasis from treatment and symptom reduction to the harnessing of the energy of the crisis experience. With this developmental perspective on emotions and confusion, I am less likely to lock my clients into a diagnostic label, and more likely to imagine them in terms of emerging health.

With a developmental perspective I can use differing models of adult development as lenses for viewing clients and for adopting alternative approaches to therapy. Each theory and therapy can move forward in a dance of figure-ground. This dance creates its choreography in response to a particular client, a particular problem, a particular moment in movements through time. Such a dance honors the fluid, shifting, multidimensional qualities of a meaning-making therapy which is built on verb forms rather than on fixed, discrete definitions or labels.

For example, I can look at Vicky, whose story is told in Chapter 5, as struggling with the foundation questions of trust which have never been resolved — a foundation which must be developed if she is to enjoy the warmth and love of human relationship. I can look at her as caught at a "Stage 2" in Kegan's model of the helix. Or I can see her as developing cognitive structures which take her from formal thinking into dialectical constructions. Each of these perspectives is in the back of my thinking, and each can take its turn in helping Vicky become a more trusting, evolving, aware, and effectively intimate kind of person.

The developmental therapist *internalizes a caution to meet the person rather than the stage, and to aim for the person rather than a level of development*. Robert Kegan states this caution clearly:

The greatest limit to the present model of developmental intervention is that it ends up being an address to a *stage* rather than a person, an address to made meanings rather than meaning-making. . . . The existing model of developmental intervention too easily translates into the goal of "getting people to advance stages," an extraordinarily reduced (not to mention presumptuous) relationship to the evolution of meaningmaking. The stages, even at their best, are only indicators of development. To orient around the indicators of development is to risk losing the *person developing*, a risk at no time more unacceptable than when we are accompanying persons in transition, persons who may themselves feel they are losing the person developing. (1982, p. 277)

To reinforce and illustrate all that has been written thus far I introduce you now to Vicky, whose astute commentary on her own developmental process takes us far beyond form and formula into the intangible and the wonderful in human meaning-making.

. . . we must all gather up the important pieces of our experience, make a synthesis of them and ask significant others in our lives, "Will you accept this configuration of what I am?" Upon such questions and the answers sanity itself depends.

—Charles Hampden-Turner, 1982, p. 132

The psychotherapist is thus enjoined to learn to know the patient and to recognize him in his partnership to the world. But—and this must be added at once—an objective knowledge by itself is not enough. In order to "discover" this patient as a whole person, the psychotherapist himself must enter into the partnership with him. This means: I do not truly recognize this other person *as a partner* so long as I make him an "objective" object of my own cognition but only when I experience him as a partner *in my own meeting with him*.

—Hans Trüb, 1952, p. 19

CHAPTER 5

A Bridge to Therapy

IT IS TIME TO CATCH our breaths a bit and prepare for the next stage of this book. We have had a fairly heavy dose of theory in examining concepts of meaning and adult development, and assumptions about the client as person, about developmental theory as a cognitive window for therapy, and about goals for therapy which grow out of these sets of assumptions. It is time now to move into the practice of therapy, but there are a few points I want to make before moving directly into that discussion:

- Therapy is a negotation process around change.
- To determine what makes a difference is difficult.
- Feeling questions are important in pacing change.
- "How do you believe you are changing?" is an important question I frequently ask my clients.
- Questions asked *after* therapy help give meaning to the therapeutic experience.

To highlight and illustrate these points I am using my former client, Vicky, as a research source in considering change and in alerting us to one of the most significant contributions the therapist can make to therapeutic process.

As I move into this section on therapy I join the story of therapeutic process in an active way. At first I thought of detaching myself, retreating to the stance of the third person, but somehow that would defeat the meaning of the therapeutic dialogue. In the manner of that dialogue, therefore, I will play several roles as I share this material with you: Yes, sometimes quite detached and theoretical — other times right in the middle of the fury. Perhaps at times I will seem arrogant as I report "this is what worked" or "this is how I understood that moment," but those reactions are the ones which reveal my emotion, my excitement, my involvement. And as far as I'm concerned, that is what the role of therapist involves — the role of active participant in process. Certainly, it was often in the moments of strong emotional connection that the movements of therapy began.

Therapy is a negotiation process around change and to ferret out just what makes a difference or just what *is* different is sometimes difficult. Acknowledging that verbal reporting and behavioral cues are simply not enough to keep a synchrony with my client's experience, I also frequently ask, "How are you feeling *right now?*" In fact, I frequently use this question to close a therapy session, to see if I have missed something, or if I have negated my client's feelings or meanings in any way. Often I am amazed at how unaware I am of what my client is thinking or feeling, frequently shocked at how off base I have been in the therapeutic directions which I have chosen. These are moments of awakening, bringing renewed appreciation for the amount of learning that can come from my client if I will only listen in an open, naive fashion

I pace therapeutic experience with another question which helps me check my perceptions of process against those of my client. I often ask, "How do you believe you are changing?" This question requires a certain naming and defining of the client's version of change separate from my own. Sometimes clients are at a loss for words, not yet able to stand outside themselves and look in. At other times, still dependent on my versions of "the truth," they tend to parrot my words and phrases, not coming to their own definitions at all. In other instances, however, clients verbalize with great insight the progress they are making, demonstrating with remarkable clarity newfound abilities to think about their own thinking, to see their problems, and to understand that, indeed, life is not a completed project, but a project in process.

Not only is it helpful to ask these questions while in the processes of therapy, but it is also helpful to be able to look back *after* therapy to articulate the changes and assimilations which have taken place. Therefore, I often ask clients for a summary of therapy after it is completed. This usually takes place at the time of the final session. Not all therapies go through the more extended periods of time required to bring about in-depth cognitive developmental change, but when clients do name the steps of change there is a level of understanding and articulation of personal meaning-making which bodes well for future growth and development. Vicky was one of those who was willing and able to do this.

Vicky first came to me when she was 21 and stayed in therapy for about two years before closing her initial sequence. Then she reappeared at significant turning points during the next five years. Each re-entry was precipitated by some new developmental problem in her search for meaning — in relationships, in her art, and in her self-understandings. Recently she moved out of the state, but she has taken time to write a response to my final questions to her: "How do you believe you have changed? How are you different today than when you first came for therapy?" Here is her letter:

Hi . . .

I suppose I understand more about who and why I am now than I did then. I think that has to do with a strengthening in acceptance/responsibility for myself. Instead of so readily taking others' judgment and reading of who I am to be "truth," I tend to accept [that truth] as "their truth." The important part being that I can also accept that I often know the more precise/honest "truth" about myself since I am able to see it from the inside. And there's a crux . . . sometimes "from the inside" lacks a certain objectivity.

So, while I have more insight/knowledge about the "me" they are judging, sometimes they have more insight through their "clear vision." But this is to be balanced . . . Sometimes I am clear because of my insight, sometimes less clear. Sometimes they are objective because of the distance, sometimes ignorant. Which brings up the "labeling" we often talked about. I catch myself labeling and see the ridiculousness it can be. You used to have to point it out to me — now I see it myself. It is so automatic? A very hard family trend to break. I sound so very opinionated and rigid at times when my natural self is far from that place. The less I know the more fixed I sound. I don't agree that ignorance is bliss . . . it's just easier.

I don't think that I'm as hard on people as I used to be. I don't demand as much, because I'm less self-centered, I'm more forgiving because I'm more self-understanding, and I'm more attentive because I'm more accepting. While there are still people with whom I have tremendous difficulty relating, I am less hard on myself about it being my stupidity and inabilities at fault. But, at the same time, I have passed thru the phase of assuming it to be their problem . . . it feels more like "our challenge." And while ignorance/comfort still irritates me, I have become more allowing of others' rights to stay or move in the direction they want to. (The more generalized the more frustrated I become. Specifics I can deal with . . . balance again . . . in certain cases I'd rather have vagueness . . .) I'm more accepting of my wisdom and more understanding of my ignorances.

My interactions with others, specifically, have changed to a small degree . . . maybe not so small . . . I don't hate mother like I used to. I don't resent the people I once did, which eases the game-playing. My interactions with others, generally, have changed to more guarded and protective of myself. I don't work so hard at acceptance.

You know . . . I think the largest change is that *I can see* that what I want in life is very different from what most people think I should want and think they want.

When they hear me, they say, "Yes, of course, wouldn't that be idyllic . . . But it's not realistic." I honestly don't believe the second statement. It is possible. I do it. Perhaps one of the most awesome/fascinating/curious perplexities of human nature (whatever that is!), to me, is the way the majority sleeps through life. The questions like "Where do you get your ideas?" I wonder . . . what do they think about all day? Anything? . . . the difference now, in making the last few statements, is a lacking of assumption of right or wrong. I'm not better—neither are they—just different. The "why" is still very important, though. It is what keeps me exploring.

I don't think I expect perfection nearly as much as I used to, though there are still so many areas in which it is still being strived for.

I am definitely more vocal than I was before, yet not as vocal as, perhaps, a time since then. I am also better at listening—in reference to the one who is speaking instead of in application to self.

Along with all this . . . my image has changed from an unsure one—therefore grasping at others' images and beliefs—to a more solid, though still wavering, one that sees my art as me. I don't see the separation. I used to attempt to see some line, some boundaries, where the art was and where it wasn't. I've finally realized that it's everything I do. It's me. I think that is perhaps the gap that exists between the artists and the "workers." It seems that those people don't know what it is to have a constantly burning passion—one that consumes if it isn't released. I still believe that every human has it—but I see more easily that it happens in different intensities. It is still my challenge to find the materials needed to ease this difference. I have, to this point, sought to build bridges between them and me . . . perhaps it is more important to focus energy on reflecting their own passion with mine by just being me. Hmmm . . .

I have quoted this letter in its entirety because it illustrates so many aspects of dialectical change as well as movement to a more independent, and yet concerned, level of development. Vicky is able to compare and contrast her present with the past. She has new perspectives on herself, new measuring points for personal choice and interpretation. She seems better able to examine her own positions, coming to new understandings of her relationships and opinions vis-à-vis others. Her personal boundaries and lines of identity are better defined and she can protest with less generalization and labeling, with less of the judging and reactive response which used to characterize her dynamic with others. In the past, if someone objected to her interpretation of herself, of an event, or of an attitude or belief, she became either very outspoken and angry or very depressed and withdrawn. There seemed little choice between the two extremes. What is delightful in her new stance is that she *does* have an in-between in a dialectic between her position and that of another person. As she says, "It is *our* challenge."

What brought about Vicky's change?

Just as it is difficult for researchers in psychotherapy process and outcome to arrive at agreement on the significant variables in effective therapy,* so it is hard here to name a specific set of change processes which

---

*For an indepth discussion of some of the latest research in therapeutic change see *The American Psychologist*, Vol. 41, #2, 120–130 (February 1986). Particularly note Hans Strupp "Psychotherapy: Research, Practice and Public Policy (How to Avoid Dead Ends)" in this issue.

brought Vicky to her outcome. In fact, I find it presumptuous to do so. Although Vicky came for therapy one or two times a week for a considerable length of time, between every therapeutic session she was living life, hard at work, seeking to resolve the dilemmas of interaction and reaction which interfered with her intimacy and with her identity as a person. In a cybernetic process she returned each week to report on her experience, bringing new thoughts, new insights, new questions, new behaviors, new emotions, *and* new relationships. Sometimes it was a cyclic process: three steps forward, two steps back. At other times it was a leap, a new gestalt, a dramatic new way of knowing the world — processes which could never be neatly charted or graphed from a linear perspective.

In thinking about this I have likened Vicky's therapeutic loops and leaps to the negotiation process described by social phenomenologists Jaber Gubrium and David Buckholdt (1977):

A world is being negotiated. It is being generated around the occurrence and is being elaborated. Its conceptual apparatus is being developed and its logical conclusions are being drawn. Contrary to the popular maxim against "jumping to conclusions," which suggests that such jumps may somehow be prevented so as to promote reason in daily living, "jumping to conclusions" is at the very heart of living a meaningful existence. People cannot help doing so in order to *get on* with the reasonable business of daily living . . . Once an occurrence has been redefined as typically something other than previously believed, again, in a flash, another whole world is generated. (p. 65)

But, in honoring all the significant work that Vicky did outside the therapy office I don't negate the processes of therapy. Certainly, Vicky *did* commit to therapy and she did continue to come week after week after week. She did find the therapeutic environment safe and receiving, a place for personal expression and questioning, and a place for the dynamics of emotion and protest. Those elements were significant. But what else was significant? What was it that *worked* in therapy? Which technique was the salient one? Which question the expanding one? Which interpretation the most revealing one?

Vicky had her answer. At the close of one sequence of therapy I asked her, "What was it I did that made a difference?" Her answer was so simple and so direct that it rather took my breath away. In fact, I did a double take, somehow disappointed that she didn't cite some very important moment in therapy. Her answer also constituted a kind of constructive contradiction to some of my pet theories of what had been happening between us.

"You believed in me." Belief? What did I believe in?

After thinking about this I came to some answers. For one thing, I believed in Vicky's passion for art and joined her in that passion. In fact, there was no way I could know her meaning and her meaning-making without joining that passion. When I joined her there and when I believed in her I did not label her swings of intensity "manic-depressive." Rather, I honored her style and her creative temperament. At the same time, however, I could and did challenge Vicky to anchor her passion within the necessities of economic survival, of the balance of self and other, and of the disciplines of her art. I could and did teach her abilities to soften the extremes of emotion which might carry her into emotional disorganization—abilities which offered a dialectic of passion and control. These were not concerns imposed upon her by a therapist who thought she knew better (and, yes, sometimes I thought I did); they were the concerns which Vicky kept bringing to our therapy sessions; they were *her* concerns.

Other belief? I believed in Vicky as a person, a person who was an artist, a daughter, a sister, a wife, a friend; a person who was struggling on a very private level with large questions of meaning and purpose. "How am I to know who I am unless I know who I am to be?"

I believed in Vicky's health when many outside the office wanted to label her unhealthy. I believed in her change when others labeled it nonexistent. I believed in her style, in a certain "kookiness," a certain wonderful capacity to look at the world with fresh eyes. And underneath all my particular "believings" in her were my basic beliefs in human growth and development, and in the powerful opportunitites for cognitive, affective shift—for new windows on the world—at moments of crisis and emotional distress. My beliefs sustained *me* when I might have doubted. Vicky knew this, and, apparently, it was this belief that sustained her.

Again, I cannot write about Vicky without writing about her artistic passion, because that was what emerged as her base of meaning and meaning-making. It was her art in dialogue with her relationships, her personality style, and her shifting cognitive perspectives which shaped much of her personal identity. If I were to chart the processes of her therapy in order to satisfy the requirements of an insurance company or of a policy-making committee, I would have a very difficult time. Or, if I were to label Vicky with a discrete DSM-III definition I'm not sure where this artistic passion would fit in. In dealing with art I have moved away from those observable, measurable domains to those which require different rules for understanding.

The value and importance of art, philosophy, and religion are not—as in science— that they reach generally agreed-upon conclusions, but that they continue to expand and deepen the possibilities of our being, to make us more human rather than more machinelike. The goals of these domains do not aim toward agreement and conformity but toward diversity, communication, and choice; toward individuality and uniqueness; toward modes of feeling, thought, and behavior that can be tested individually only. (LeShan & Margenau, 1983, pp. 191–192)

I have quoted Lawrence LeShan and Henry Margenau because they call attention to differing domains of personal reality and suggest that we must interpret these domains through lenses and methodologies appropriate to the domain in question. If I were to be truly "scientific" I would have to deal with what LeShan and Margenau call the sensory, "touch-feel" domains of reality. I could measure traits and I could chart behavioral patterns. I could develop genograms of family history and I could plot patterns of pathology within the statistical guidelines of the MMPI. And I could chart Vicky's passages of life development through the eyes of varying theories of adult development (and, yes, I touch on that later), but—and this is a big *but*—I must remember what domains I am dealing with and not lose one for the other. In such loss would be the loss of Vicky as artist and person.

I return again to the both-ands, to the dialectical thinking which somehow sustains me in the middle of all these dilemmas. I am both subject and object with a Vicky—bringing in my techniques and my knowledge, and joining her in deeply personal connections of passion and artistic intention. I cannot just passively reflect her; there are times when I must actively engage her. I can't impose my goals upon her; and yet, I cannot *not* bring my own goals and values to therapy.

Hopefully, this brings us to a certain humility about the *art* and the *science* of therapy. And, hopefully, it brings us to a certain humility about our work with our clients. We can learn from Vicky and others like her who have walked through personal doorways to look at themselves and their relationships in transformed ways. But let's not lose them in the process.

With these caveats I plunge into the objective sides of therapy while maintaining attention to the subjective. Rollo May is helpful to me here:

> we are not simply describing two alternate ways of behaving. Nor is it quite accurate to speak of our being subject and object *simultaneously*. The important point is that our consciousness is a process of oscillation between the two. Indeed, is not this dialectical relationship between experiencing myself as subject and as object just what consciousness consists of? The process of oscillation gives me potentiality—I can choose between them, can throw my weight on one side or the other. However we may alternate in dealing with someone else—say, a patient in therapy—when we are dealing with ourselves, it is the gap between the two ways of responding that is important. My freedom, in any genuine sense, lies not in my capacity to live as "pure subject," but rather in my capacity to experience *both* modes, to live in the dialectical relationship. (May, 1980, p. 9)

In Section III I will be focusing increasingly on techniques, exercises, and cognitive processes in therapy, making them figures upon the ground of theory and assumption which has already been established. This figure/ground dynamic continues to shift, ebb, and flow, however, because therapy is not a fixed "something." And our clients are not fixed "somethings." Therapy is a moving and a proceeding in a dialectic of the tangible and the intangible, the explainable and the unexplainable. Thus, although at this point in the development of this book it is timely to allow theories and assumptions to retreat into the background, the tacit influences of belief and believing must be neither ignored nor forgotten. As Vicky has so poignantly suggested, they may be among the most significant influences on change.

SECTION III

A Meaning-Making Therapy

The therapeutic moment cannot be truncated from the past; but if it is genuinely therapeutic, the meaning in which the past appears must be one that never before existed. When past meanings are merely resurrected, there is no therapy, only stereotype, ritual and compulsion. . . . The problem of life is to make sense—*make*, not find.

—Huston Smith, 1965, p. 44

. . . events that are apparently unconnected from one view become interconnected when a broader viewpoint is taken. . . . Theories within theories—none of them telling the final truth at all.

—Jeremy Hayward, 1984, p. 152

Nothing that strikes our eyes or ears conveys its message directly to us. We always *select* and *interpret* our impressions of the surrounding world. Some message is brought to us by the "light without" but the meaning and significance we give to it are largely added by the "light within" . . . What I sense, what I perceive, and what I think become blended into one single act of cognition.

—Gordon Allport, 1979, p. 165

CHAPTER 6

Steps to Meaning-Making

THERAPY IS A DOING rather than a fixed package of theory and technique. That contrast is important, for to treat therapy as a noun—as a static body of doctrine and methodology—is to risk a mindset which treats therapy as some magical entity which is to provide pat solutions to all types of problems. In contrast, a process therapy such as "meaning-making" takes its energy and form from imaginative exploration and sensitive adaptation in the service of clients, believing that it is in its cyclings and recyclings, in its endings leading into new beginnings, that each therapeutic sequence gains a life and a narrative uniquely its own.

Thus, when I name a series of therapeutic steps for therapy I do so with attention to the cycling, recycling, intertwining processes which take place under the umbrella of what I have called "steps to meaning-making." This framework gives us a way of categorizing our efforts, but is not meant to be rigidly or universally defined and applied. In saying this I also acknowledge that it is the rare client who moves neatly through all these stages, but I affirm that the effort to do so leads towards effective therapy—a therapy which brings increasing capacity to make meaning of self within the contexts of personal history and relationship, and to continue personal meaning-making as an active process of life which transforms the static event of "identity crisis" into the fluid patterns of "identity process."

As an outline for this overview, therefore, I use the following "steps to meaning-making." Each of these will be enlarged and enriched within the discussion below.

- The *establishment* of a holding environment which includes the supportive qualities of confirmation, continuity and creative, constructive contradiction.
- The *gathering of data* in the joining with client meaning. This can include many therapeutic techniques and many ways of looking at the data.
- A search for *patterns and process* in the understanding of old meanings in the creation of the new. This includes the naming of personal philosophies and cognitive structurings, as well as patterns of history, of emotion, of image and ideal, of behavior, of stimulus and response.
- Reinforcement of new abilities to think about one's own thinking — to stand outside and look in. This is the time to integrate and reconcile new insights with past history, understandings, and experience. This is the time of *therapeutic closure*.

Establishment

The ingredients of the establishment stage are simple, quite obvious, and yet, profound and far-reaching — essential, in fact. They include: the shaping of an atmosphere of receptivity and trust; a joining with the meaning-making of the client; and the mutuality of introduction which takes place between client and therapist. The time of therapeutic beginning is thus a remarkable time of learning and sharing, of trying out limits, of arriving at a shared language, of creating understandings — in other words, a time of getting acquainted and initiating the dialogue of therapy.

How we greet our clients and how we introduce them to the therapeutic process sets the tone of therapy. Many elements of simple human courtesy are a part of this: explaining the arrangements of furniture, sharing a few simple moments of personal introduction before the business of therapy is begun. In these beginnings are the practical aspects of fee, insurance claims, understandings about confidentiality, and the arrangement for appointments. And in these early moments can be brief explanation of what therapy is about.

Because I take notes I usually ask my client whether this is threatening or not. If it is I put my pad away and make notes at the end of the hour. What I do explain, however, is that by gathering words, phrases and pieces of philosophy, by noting significant points of history, by indicating moments of emotional peak and valley, I am able to brainstorm on paper, developing and connecting ideas as we go along. (In fact, I have increasingly come to realize that note-taking is a way to translate divergent thinking into a *convergence* which identifies important themes for each session and brings clarity and focus to the therapeutic dialogue.) What I don't always explain is that I scan language constantly for the fine semantic meanings which reveal the mind sets of my clients. But I make my point that note-taking is a definite part of my therapeutic technique, a springboard to further questioning, and a guide to the patterning of experience which develops through our sessions together.

Clients obviously have every right to ask about these notes, and I share them if it seems helpful to the therapy. In fact, with both Nick and Vicky, written transcripts of particular therapeutic sequences have facilitated much new personal understanding and insight. Clients also can do their own note-taking, and quite a few of my people copy my technique, bringing their pencils and pads to therapy as they, too, synthesize and take note of bits and pieces of new thinking, possibility, and insight.

The primary modality of this early stage is a receptive, reflective style in the manner of Carl Rogers' "client-centered" listening. This style enables me to be supportive and focused at the same time that I listen to several levels of functioning: to the conscious statements of the crisis experience or the presenting dilemma; to the nonverbal signals of body movement and personal rhythm; to the fluctuations of emotions as revealed in facial color, in eye movements, in laughter and tears; and to the kinds of words which are chosen and the phrases which seem to form a leit motif in the client's story. While I listen to these more obvious manifestations of personal functioning, I am also gathering the data which will guide me to "ways into" my client's unnamed, unconscious processes.

The Rogerian "client-centered" approach does color much of what I do, but I share some concerns with Kegan that this approach has been one of the most misunderstood of techniques:

Though it would be hard to tell from the way many therapists and counselors make use of it, the client-centered response is something quite different than "saying back to the client what the client said to you," "pulling for affect," or "offering support." Like any technique, it can only stop being a technique when it is embodied by a person with a specific set of ideas and hopes which he is himself trying to bring to life through the medium of the "technique." (Kegan, 1982, pp. 277–278)

But Kegan does more than critique the Rogerian approach, he redeems it by placing it in context: "where language is the central medium of communication I do not know a more effective way of establishing that context than by the client-centered response. Properly understood, it is an extremely powerful instrument" (1982, p. 278).

In the context of language and dialogue, therefore, the Rogerian modality is very helpful. Certainly it is a powerful tool for the establishment stage when confirmation is begun. And throughout therapy the Rogerian technique can bring therapy back to center, back to a focus on the client. Indeed, "reflective listening" *is* a discipline for the therapist in terms of attention, language, mental process, and attitude.

In these early hours of therapy, it may sometimes be very important to give the client "permission" to maintain feelings, to maintain a troublesome relationship, to perpetuate so-called "symptoms." For example, a client may have had much advice from friends and family that she *should* give up the friend who is abusive. But what she may not have received is an understanding and appreciation of the deep grief she is experiencing as she leaves that friend. Or of the good parts of that friend which drew her to the relationship in the first place. Often she is feeling an intense shock or disbelief that this person she loved so much is not the person she thought he was. And in that she feels shame or anger towards herself. During these times of intense emotion and self-blame we may need to cool the process a bit, to allow the client to *feel* rather than to think, to "indwell" in the experience.

What unites these early experiences of therapy is the concept of joint meaning-making. If client and therapist are to make meaning together, they have to come to know each other, trust each other, and work with each other. In these initial steps the therapist is already offering steps to healing and growth, gently introducing questions born of dialectical thinking while offering caring, acknowledgment, and confirmation as early antidotes to feelings of rejection, confusion, and alienation. Whatever is done in these early hours of therapy can either make or break the therapeutic partnership, can either facilitate or hinder the steps to emerging meaning. And in these early movements towards more complex meanings are also steps to openness, curiosity, flexibility; to the making sense of oneself and one's purposes; to the meanings that will facilitate a kind of synergistic interdependence in which one can have a sense of self while caring for and working in harmony with others.

In the experience of emerging dialogue the therapist starts coming across as a unique personality in his or her own right. Here is where the therapist's style begins to reveal itself. In my case therapeutic style moves across polarities of approach and reaction from passive to active, reflective to directive, tangible/concrete to abstract/intuitive, cognitive to behavioral, analytical to poetic. There's nothing particularly unusual and significant about this stylistic description except to emphasize that in the kind of therapy I am describing therapeutic style can and must be flexible as it adopts differing stylistic responses according to the personality and needs of the client. I've been helped in this by continually realizing that this meaning-making dialogue is a human dialogue, which can incorporate the ups and downs of every kind of interpersonal communication. Although knowledge and technique inform and lead the process, they don't have to form an imposition *upon* the process.

As clients begin to identify and react to differing facets of the therapist's approach there may be new dynamics of relationship to work with. Indeed, the client may find elements of the therapist's personality which are disturbing, or a style which intrudes on his or her own. Certainly, the therapist is more than a passive, reflective figure; he or she is a wondering, concerned, involved figure with whom the client will not always connect.

In my own experience, the issue of cognitive style is the one that sometimes rears its ugly head. My approaches and my questionings reflect a brainstorming, intuitive approach to problem-solving. I like to start with the wide picture, the broad schemes, the diverse facts, as the statements of my client trigger new avenues for exploration. Occasionally this style puzzles a client, or even overwhelms him, particularly if he wants or needs a therapy of discrete, inductive steps—a therapy which has a shape and form in advance rather than a shape and form which evolves as therapeutic process develops. Or particularly if he wants a therapist who gives him all the answers in a few simple sessions and sends him on his way. Several times clients have faced me with this. What has been valuable about our confrontations is that we generally become more genuine in our communication, more sensitive and aware, and more open to other ways of thinking about ourselves and our thinking processes. Most clients who confront these stylistic differences stay with me, but those few who cannot find resolution are referred to another therapist more in tune with their style.

As such differences are resolved, and as an environment of trust is created, therapy begins to gain a life of its own. Out of early questions about the presenting problem and the life situation of the client, as well as many other questions which are triggered by the question and answer, statement-reflection process, come the explorations which begin to reveal the underlying cognitive/affective constructions which have shaped the life of the client.

DATA GATHERING

At the same time that the therapist is establishing an environment of support, the data gathering process begins. This will continue throughout therapy and will intertwine with the other cycling and recycling steps of therapy. But there will be an increasing intensity and sophistication in the data gathering process as each individual therapy shapes its uniqueness, as the perceptions and vocabularies, the thinking styles, the kinds of questionings of both client and therapist arrive at common meeting grounds.

This is the time when the language of the *dialectic* takes on new meaning within the mental dialogue of comparing and contrasting, of the collision of ideas, of the playing off of one idea against another as one position is juxtaposed with another, as one point of view faces off against its oppositions. In this exchange comes the "fruitful collision of ideas from which a higher truth may be reached." This is a communication and a collaboration as well as a technique—what Windy Dryden (1984) calls a *collaborative empiricism* which can translate into an exploratory search for personal variables, both conscious and unconscious, which continue to construct and guide personal life.

The meaning-making therapist engaged in this "collaborative empiricism" believes that a better way to think and a better way to find personal equilibrium comes from a "way of thinking which recognizes all theories— all answers to life—as provisional, awaiting new data, new experiences, new relationships with other people, to be reconstructed in ways that incorporate more" (Basseches, 1984, p. 337). Basseches further says that the "opportunity to pursue goals of synthesizing systems through critical reflection in an atmosphere of personal support is hypothesized to stimulate the development of dialectical thinking" (1984).

As therapy develops its own momentum, then, the therapist works with the client in a kind of critical reflection within an atmosphere of support and emotional acknowledgment which has been developed in the first hours of therapy. This is the momentum which builds as the therapist helps the client to:

- experience and understand aspects of self previously repressed;
- develop better integration and more effective functioning;
- become more similar to the person he or she wishes to be;
- become more self-directing and self-confident;
- become "more of a person, more unique and more self expressive";
- become more adequate and comfortable in coping with the problems of life. (paraphrasing of the words of Carl Rogers, 1961, p. 479)

In this time of emerging data search the therapist's creative questioning must be sensitive to client need, not putting clients on the spot, not coming across as an inquisitor, not neglecting the feelings and intents of the client. Rather, using the client's tentative statements of the problem, or the expressions of unique metaphors, behaviors, and emotion, the therapist can build and expand the networks of verbal exploration. At the same time, the therapist can be modeling and actively teaching a kind of questioning approach— a cognitive style, a cognitive activity—which compares and contrasts the elements of one's being and one's life. Certainly, in the dynamics of creative questioning is an initial training ground for the capacity to think dialectically as we compare and contrast bits of personal history, feeling, and attitude; one person's approach with another; one stage of personal history with the present; one opinion with a contrasting point of view. For example:

- I am wondering if you would look at this from another angle?
- Let's compare your feelings as a child with the anger you feel right now. How does that feel to you?
- What do you think is your reason for reacting that way?
- What about that other person's opinion? How does it fit with your own?
- How is your current friend like the friend you had in high school?
- Would you say your mother has changed in the last few years?

In a search for the categories of questions which will open cognitive doors for both myself and my client, I turn to a wide variety of theories, particularly those which suggest the tasks and challenges of developmental process. In their schemata are stimuli for comparison and contrast and for the emerging "catching of similarity" (see Chapter 7 for further discussion of Silvano Arieti's wonderfully apt words), which is essential in the construction and reconstruction of meaning.

The theories of *Erik Erikson*, for example, contain rich material for questioning as I contemplate the psychosocial development of my client. Is this a trust issue, never resolved? Or a case of too much trust without the counterbalance of mistrust? Is this a person wrestling with personal intimacy in a transition from adolescent identity search to the intimacy questions of young adulthood? Or is this a person facing the generativity concerns of middle age and aging as the threat of personal stagnation moves in? What about hope? And faith? And wisdom? What about relationship, work, purpose, integrity, the chronology of age, of spiritual concern? Erikson's theory provides windows for looking at these developmental issues which are framed and reframed through successive life periods, as old questions gain new richness in the contexts of new experience and new relationship.

The theories of *Andras Angyal* also suggest new ways to form our questions. Although he did not cast his ideas within the framework of stages, his is definitely a developmental model with his systems perspective of a gestalt of past, present and future.* His theory is also a point of departure for considering early life patterns to see how they were established and how they have been reinforced and maintained. Frequently clients are very relieved to see current response shaped by the early survival experiences of the child, and they often find insight into ways they can change, or ways that they can accept and handle the learned responses of an early age. This is the time in therapy when I report Angyal's idea that we all have "neurotic trends" and "health trends"—that we are not simply "neurotic" or "healthy"—that the challenge is to reinforce a healthy response and to diminish negative blocks to effective living. This cognitive framing removes clients from stereotype

---

*The limits of this book have prevented me from detailing Angyal's theory, but his book *Neurosis And Treatment: A Holistic Theory* has created a powerful impact on my work, and offers complementary material for both theory and therapy.

and gives them a new approach to themselves. Typical questions which build
on Angyal's theory include, "How did your family handle anger? How did
you respond to your father's outbursts? How do you think you became the
rebel in your family? And how is that continuing now?"

Robert Kegan's theory is also rich with suggestion for both questioning
and teaching. Frequently I draw his helix model on the blackboard, demonstrating the alternating stages of "differentiation" and "embeddedness"
which move towards the transcendent stage when alternating currents of
human interaction are brought to new synthesis and balance. This is a
wonderful model for marital therapy, as clients name some of the stuggles
and dynamics of togetherness and separateness, of self and other. With the
model we can question the stage they are in — whether they are struggling
with attachment and intimacy, or whether the struggle is with self-definition
and self-articulation in relationship to others. Through Kegan's theoretical
eyes I can further attend to questions of cognitive complexity, of life development, of passages of "knowing," and of possible constellations of depression. I might also use his "Subject-object Interview" to tease out the structure of my client. This simple exploratory tool can raise questions as well as
provide a relatively quick history of important experiences, current emotion-
al/psychological dilemmas, and levels of cognitive construction.

Most recently, my questioning has drawn on the ideas and proposed
dialectical schemata of *Michael Basseches*. The way I frame my questions
can introduce dialectical forms of comparison and contrast, of movements
through time, of the elements of one's being within the context of the whole,
and create windows on the kinds of thinking which are taking place, whether they be "black or white," generalizations, or a self-absorbed unawareness
of another's position. Certainly, these schemata are mirrors for reflecting
and analyzing the thinking and verbal style of the client, and for stimulating
new cognitive approaches to comparison and contrast.

In my questioning I am searching not only for cognitive constructions of
thinking and feeling, but also for reference points for meaning. Here, once
again, I can draw on the ideas of Erikson and Kegan, or I can turn to ideas
like those of Daniel Levinson, who suggests more concrete contexts for
ordering life experience. He calls his "theory of life structure" a way of
conceptualizing answers to the question, "What is my life like now?" To
answer that question, he says, we begin to identify those "aspects of the
external world that have the greatest significance to us." What gives significance, he believes, includes relationships to "significant others" such as
friends, lovers, spouses, parents, bosses, teachers, and mentors.

A significant other might be a person from the past . . . or a symbolic or imagined
figure from religion, myth, fiction, or private fantasy. The other might not be an
individual but might be a collective entity such as a group, institution, or social
movement; nature as a whole, or a part of nature such as the ocean, mountains,

wildlife, whales in general, or Moby Dick in particular; or an object or place such as a farm, a city or country, "a room of one's own," or a book or a painting. (1986).

He further writes, "These relationships are the stuff our lives are made of. They give shape and substance to the life course. They are the vehicle by which we live out — or bury — various aspects of our selves and by which we participate, for better or worse, in the world around us."

I like these ideas of Levinson and find them an interesting check list for questioning. But I would also go further than the external sources of meaning to those internal sources which include the central images, central conceptions, central goals, central values which a meaning-making therapist must consider. Certainly the shift from making "significant others" the source of meaning to internalized sources of meaning is one of the major shifts identified in developmental sequence — the shift when dependencies fulfilled become dependencies resolved. In the answers to questions about sources of meaning — whether external or internal — comes new questioning and new insight for the therapeutic process.

The questioning, searching process involves considerable redundancy as the therapist and client approach the central concerns from differing angles. This process is like walking around the elephant, or examining the facets of the prism, or drawing the little bits and pieces of the portrait. I explain this redundancy to my clients because some are bothered by it — particularly those who want quick results, and who need a sense of precision and direction about what they are doing.

In using varying theories as sources of questioning, the therapist's mind no doubt moves back and forth from one to another, in a kind of cognitive dance of figure/ground where theories move forward and back according to the particular needs of each client. In this it can be valuable to go back to professional notes, to current research and reporting, to books on speculative theory, to keep fresh and open to new ideas in an avoidance of cognitive ruts. Frequently one new idea will stimulate life, novelty, excitement, and cognitive reframing as therapy takes off in a contrasting direction.

Questioning brings a growing body of information about the client, but it also serves as stimulus for thinking as the client is challenged to process the "facts" of personal knowledge with new insight and understanding. Let me quote Gregory Bateson and Robert Glaser once again (see Chapter 1) as they give names to these processes. First of all, Bateson sees these steps as the weaving of "three levels of abstraction:"

the first, a concrete level of ethnographic data; the second, more abstract level, the arrangement of data to create "various pictures of the culture"; and the third, most abstract level, a self-conscious discussion of the procedures by which the pieces of the jigsaw are put together. (1958, p. 281)

And this is what is happening as data-gathering begins to move into the "patterning and processing" stage described below. Progress is made as the client comes to better ways to "express, recognize, and use diverse and particular forms of knowledge" and as client and therapist tease apart "the levels inherent in one's attempt to understand a phenomenon" (Glaser, 1984).

IN PROCESS

In process: those words are absolutely key in this whole business of change—a willingness to *not* have everything neatly defined and settled once and for all. Indeed, to acknowledge *process* is to acknowledge the three steps forward, the two steps back, the expansions and contractions, the frustrations and "failures" as the very human dialogue of therapy continues.

This is the time of observing and expressing feelings, and of using whatever means possible to help the client translate feelings into emotional expression and verbal articulation: imaging, role playing, playing with tools of Gestalt psychology, free associating, meditating, writing—whatever will work to complete old emotional sequences and to understand and enhance the new.

This is the time of taking the big and little bits of personal history, habits, and attitudes to see how they form constructions of the world. This is the time of comparing and contrasting, of naming and ordering, of speculating and wondering, of challenging and questioning. This is the time when the therapist gently leads and confronts at the same time she reflects and allows. It is the time of dialogue, of the dialectic, which encourages imagination and the leaps of creative wondering. It is the time, hopefully, when old systems of thought, feeling and behavior release their hold to be transcended by the new.

This is also the time of accelerating partnership between therapist and client as the therapist, building on whatever trust has been established and developed, leads the client to be *what he can be.* Here is where Martin Buber's description of *confirmation* takes on particular meaning within the spirit and behavior of the constructive contradictions of active dialogue:

Confirming means first of all, accepting the whole potentiality of the other and making even a decisive difference in his potentiality, and of course we can be mistaken again and again in this, but it's just chance between human beings . . . And now I not only accept the other as he is, but I confirm him, in myself, and then in him, in relation to this potentiality that is meant by him and it can now be developed, it can evolve, it can answer the reality of life. (1965, p. 182)

Within the spirit and form of this confirmation the therapist also wrestles "*with* the patient, *for* the patient, and *against* the patient" (words from Friedman, 1985b, p. 14). I don't think we as therapists have always been taught these contradictive forms of the therapeutic process, particularly in the Rogerian approach. We have been taught to interpret, to reflect, to advise, to intervene, but have frequently neglected the stimulating novelty and surprise of verbal jousting, of playing ideas off against each other, of disagreeing as one human with another. One of the reasons for this, I believe, is that our culture has often created a semantic equation (and all too often, a physical equation) that conflict equals violence. Or that disagreement is unkind (May, 1953). Or that argument is bad or negative. These beliefs and attitudes cause people to be afraid of protest or of argument or of disagreement, losing their genuineness as they negate spontaneous thought and feeling. *This is not to speak on behalf of angry outburst or destructive putdown.* Rather, this is to speak on behalf of thoughtful, constructive expressions of points of disagreement or differing perception. Through such exploratory dialogue can come new recognitions, new constructions, new understandings of one's personal patternings of reality. Through such dialogue can also come new abilities to assert oneself, to know oneself, and to understand oneself.

Richard Walton believes in the power which lies inherent in creative, constructive conflict:

First, it [conflict] may allow new motivation and energy to be discovered by the conflicting parties. Second, the innovation of individuals may be heightened due to a perceived necessity to deal with the conflict. Third, each individual in the conflict situation can develop an increased understanding of his own perceptions by having to articulate his views in a conflicting and argumentative situation. Fourth, each person often develops a firmer sense of identity; conflict allows values and belief systems to emerge into fuller view. (1969, p. 50)

But we have to be cautious here: In order to honor the integrity of our client — potential, meaning, emotions, sensitivities, style, whatever — we must continue to respect, respond, and prize that which is different in that person. So even though there are forms of contradiction or of conflict, we are not talking about negating or discounting our clients, or imposing pronouncements that what they say is "irrational" or "inappropriate." Rather, by questioning, by reframing, by using reflective language, by teaching, we interrupt cognitive/affective/semantic sequences through creative exploration and collaborative engagement.

Contrasts between cognitive, affective systems become more apparent as this therapy continues. It is exciting when a client begins to see these contrasts, comments on them, and acts upon them. Awakening awarenesses do not always bring alterations in personal functioning, however, but the insights and "ahas" are preparatory work for fresh cognitive synthesis and behavioral change.

What do I mean by the contrasts between systems? I image it this way: The client carries a body of memories, conditionings, learnings, all of which create "evidence" of the old image, the old belief, the old way. Somehow, conceptualizing this as the holographic image (Pribram, 1976) through which everything is processed and ordered makes sense to me, particularly when one is aware of the tenacious hold that these central images have on life choice. In these images is the "evidence," the "proof" that the individual is a certain way and that they really can't change. But, little by little, through the change process glimmers of new memories, conditionings and learnings begin to accumulate — the sudden flash of awareness, the feeling that has not been there before, an understanding which opens up a world of thought never contemplated before. Here is the emerging creation of a new system, of an "evidence" that a new way is possible. And it is here that the client may sometimes be caught between two lenses on the world.

I had one client with whom I diagrammed these contrasts and she could see them and acknowledge her dilemma. In one system of thinking was her sense of void, her emptiness, her firm belief that she was worthless, her firm belief that it was useless to make new friends because ultimately they would reject her. In her words:

- I am different and don't belong.
- Whatever I do will lead to failure or rejection.
- Other people won't recognize any change in me so why bother?
- My values don't fit this world.
- I cause trouble.
- I should have been able to prevent myself from being like this.
- I don't want to be like my father, but I am and I hate it.
- I have always been alone because there's something wrong with me.

And as we challenged this system of thought and feeling we continually collided with what I called her "cognitive equation" — her inner "therefores" which reinforced the cognitive process and the defining of her personal reality. This is the descriptive, circular statement we created after one powerful session: "I'm different, therefore I'm junk, therefore I should be thrown in the junk heap, that brings feelings of pain, then I withdraw, which makes me different, which makes me believe that I really am different." And so the wheel of thought and affect turned and turned back upon itself. This was what we were trying to interrupt; simplistic counterstatements were simply not going to do the job. But her emerging ability to stand outside herself and see the equation was a dramatic sign that she *was* beginning to change.

In her emerging ability to see herself in new ways came windows into a new system of thinking — a system congruent with personal qualities long blocked or negated: her qualities as a mischievous, fun-loving, playful kind of person, who just might have the possibilities of friendship and meaning in her life. But even though she could see her contrasting systems intellectually, her feelings and deeply internalized memory systems held tightly to the old way. Also, in many ways, her logic system was just not ready to accept the new evidence. She still could not risk letting go of the one image she had of herself that really made sense, the one image which was able to order her world in fairly predictable ways. (And I still ponder one profound question which she threw out during this particular discussion: "Is it *real* enough if only I believe it?" In other words, is the new "evidence" strong enough to counteract all the old "evidence" that she had collected throughout her life that somehow she was not okay?)

The therapeutic work that remains is the continuing supportive work which can both challenge and affirm her as I honor a more positive self-construction, as I care for her and provide the real, live experience of new relationship. That work continues. There is no way that she or I can predict the final stages of release, transition, and reconciliation.

In the words of another client, Laura, "If I am not real nice and real good, the world will come crashing down . . . the world should be nice and good . . . I find it hard to take praise seriously and insulate myself against disappointment. I will be found out. I am afraid of people's expectations. Fearful of disappointing someone—having them not like me—finding out I'm a fake. I have very high expectations of myself."

Laura was caught by expectations which kept her cycling through the struggles to be nice, to protect herself against the world crashing down. In so doing she rejected praise and protected herself not only against the expectations and rejections of others but also against the discovery of herself.

With hard work Laura made progress in reframing perspectives on herself as she opened her feelings and thought not only to herself and to me but to people outside the therapy room. Well into that therapy she asked a question which pointed to shifts in her thinking: "How do I let someone else into the continuity of myself? Now that I have something to give, how can I let someone else in?" The very fact that she could ask such questions showed that her protective barriers were tumbling and the willingness to risk herself was growing.

Sonny was wrestling with the pain of divorce. He discovered that leaving his wife was like the nonresponse of a brother whom he idolized. We spent considerable time trying to understand why the two relationships triggered similar emotions of anger, bitterness, hurt, and resentment. Finally Sonny was able to name the common variables in the two relationships: "These are people on pedestals, they are charismatic and self-centered, vital, alive, sharp, successful, *but* they do not give back the love that is given them. They are very important in my life because they provide a 'constant,' a sense of being there, of something to relate to."

In the losing of these very important people Sonny lost a sense of the ideal—of the models which he was seeking to emulate. In this loss of the ideal was anguish as he began to see their negatives. "The loss makes me question my own behavior because it doesn't fit the model of 'Good people are rewarded; bad people are punished.'" In his disillusionment Sonny began to express his bitterness: "These are people who shouldn't get God's gifts." And, further, "I lost the ability to see the real world and now I have to redefine the framework." He then went on to express his rage, to grieve the loss of the ideal, and to wrestle with his feelings that two people could "get away with these things," and that other people in his culture "trivialize" the seriousness of the problem. In this stage of therapy, therefore, Sonny identified his philosophy, his models, his dreams and ideals at the same time he saw these crack. Indeed, his system of living and dreaming did fall apart, making it necessary for him to shape a new cognitive system with a transformed set of meanings and ideals.

Jennifer, a young woman wrestling with fears about intimacy and connection with people, moved rather quickly through her therapy, using writing and models to articulate what was going on. In her efforts she discovered a self-defeating pattern of human relationship which had guided her behavior since adolescence — a pattern which she articulates below:

- I want to please, I want approval from those I care about.
- Pleasing others is accomplished and approval is gained through achievement . . .
- Achievement requires concentration on self.
- Concentration on self prevents recognition of other people's needs . . .
- Then, other people feel uncared-for and neglected.
- Connections are broken or prevented.
- [I feel] left alone, lonely and unconnected.
- Protect self by extreme independence which requires concentration on self . . .

In diagramming this sequence Jennifer saw the pattern which kept cycling back upon itself in a self-defeating way. Out of her astute observations and interpretations she began to change and reshape the achievement cycle into a new sequence of choice and behavior that more nearly reflected her own wishes and desires and freed her to enjoy others while she was more able to enjoy herself.

As systems of feeling and conception begin to break in times of crisis, in times of therapeutic collaboration, in times of reflective discovery, then client and therapist alike can begin to see what was not seen before. As one client said, "I have examined the foundations and see the cracks that are there." When a client is able to say this, therapist and client have moved over a barrier from being in the problem to having the problem — and thus, are moving towards the final stages of therapy when the transformational, integrative work is brought to some sort of creative resolution.

THERAPEUTIC CLOSURES

When I use the term "closures" I think of them in a cyclic, renewing way — as endings which are active and going somewhere, not creating a *period*. I also think of closures as recycling into new beginnings which in turn lead to new endings. This reflects Freud's suggestion in *Analysis terminable and interminable* that the door to the therapy room remain open with a termination which is flexible and open-ended.

Which raises a point: Coming from traditional psychotherapy, we have been trained to think of "successful or unsuccessful terminations." Indeed, much of our research into psychotherapy is couched in those terms. I was certainly trained to construct therapy in this way and can't help but remember when during my therapeutic internship a client returned after a year's absence. My supervisor commented that somehow we had failed in our efforts to help this woman because she still had some of the same problems that we worked with before. And I agreed. But now I have come to believe that that was an arrogance on our part, a supposition that we were supposed to be the wise, all-knowing fixers. To look at the same case within the perspectives of developmental process is to see this young woman at emerging stages of readiness. Work that needed to be done had to have a kind of life preparation for new therapeutic work to be successful.

I think of therapy, then, in the cyclic, circling terms of the "revolving door." I also think of it under an umbrella of lifelong learning. This is neither to encourage client dependency nor to prolong therapy, but simply to paradoxically encourage independent decision-making by allowing clients free movement both in and out of the therapy door. In viewing therapy in this manner we do not ignore our "failures," our inappropriate approaches to clients, our insensitivities. What we *do honor* is the integrity of developmental readiness and the personal learning experience which may bring a client back to therapeutic process.

In the final hours of therapy the chilling moments of recognition and awareness give clues to the coming closure. Other signs are there as the intensity of feelings is lessened, as the person usually becomes more spontaneous and willing to share thoughts and feelings, and as the problems which are brought to the therapy room begin to wane. There is a shift in energy as confusions are sorted, named, and resolved. This is a good time as clients are more able to step outside their problems with new understanding and direction. And many seem to realize how very important it was for them to understand the roots of the negative patterns in order for change to come about. As Lorraine stated, "I have to know what I am forgiving in order to forgive." And Lucille: "I can untie the knots when I know how they were formed and which knots I am loosening." And once the patterns have been identified and placed within a perspective of personal history, therapy often moves rapidly to the time of closure.

The time of closure is a time of interpretation and reintegration, therefore, as the past becomes meaningful within the contexts of the present, and as the present takes on new hues through the naming of the past. Together therapist and client have moved from the initial stages of conflict and confusion into the times of search — what Loder calls an "interlude for scanning" which includes looking for "possible solutions, taking apart errors, keeping parts, and discarding others." From this searching process comes insight, intuition, or a new act of imagination which, Loder (1981, pp. 31–36) writes, "appears on the border between the conscious and unconscious" and offers a resolution of some sort "in a form readily available to consciousness." This is the moment of turning point when the individual attains a new perception, perspective, or world view. The original conflict is freed as the person gains a new energy which comes with the new awareness, the new knowing. In this final stage, therefore, the client interprets and integrates the new with the old in a restructuring of the past. This is the time of genuine developmental movement as the person moves from former cognitive/affective construction to a new narrative of self. And it generally seems that the new system of knowing is larger, more encompassing, as it incorporates increased self-knowledge and self-undertanding. Indeed, the categories of self will never again be the same.

To bring successful closure, therefore, it is essential that the client name and shape new understandings to bring about new orderings in a making sense of things. To ignore this vital step is to lose the power of cognitive meaning-making.

To facilitate these namings and integrations I ask my client to name their changes and to describe what the time of closure means to them: "What are you feeling? How do you think you are different? Is there any sense of unfinished business? Are there problems which may arise in the future?" We question, we discuss, we compare and contrast, reinforcing and anchoring the emotional and cognitive learnings of therapy. We also examine shifts in habits, in behaviors, in outlooks, in the active, practical experiences of love, play and work. We share ideas about newly-named identities and perspectives on self.

Natalie's words in our final session together demonstrate these processes of closure:

THERAPIST So you were saying that this period is exciting for you, too?

NATALIE Yes. I'm interested in it in an intellectual sort of way — because I am able to step back outside of this and then look in again. And I can take everything that I was emotionally involved in previously, and look at them all sort of in separate packages, and see how it has affected my behavior up to this point. And, also see how it's still affecting it. But, being able to look at it that way, now, almost makes it as though I can take it and rearrange things a little bit, which is intriguing to me.

THERAPIST And this feeling of being able to rearrange, what does that do for you?

NATALIE Well, it gives me some hope. . . . After a while that makes me feel like, "Hey! I'm in charge here . . . I'm in charge here and I really can reorder things, reorder my decisions, or my behavior, or whatever." Uhhm . . . well, I feel good. It's not easier, necessarily, but it's . . . I think it's easier to know what to do.

THERAPIST How do you know what to do? How does that help you to know what to do?

NATALIE Well, I think what it is . . . . Maybe it's because it identifies it. And the definition of the identification. . . . But I can use an analogy . . . is that okay? It'll be easier for me then.

THERAPIST All right.

NATALIE Uh, it's like if you're—if you have a class, for instance, and you don't get a syllabus, and there's no guideline and you just know you're supposed to learn biology. Okay. So you know you're supposed to learn biology, but if you don't have any assigned chapters to read, specific topics to write about, or know what you're going to be tested on . . . it's like you're sort of putting your energies in all these different areas and it's hard to make sense out of anything. But if you're given guidelines, and you know that you're going to study biology, or the physiology of the brain . . . or if you know what you have to write about . . . well, when you know these things you know how to use the class . . . I don't know if that's really that clear, but . . .

THERAPIST I like what you're saying . . .

NATALIE I guess, it seemed like before, you know, that all the emotions stayed attached to my father, or my friend, or my mother—all those things. Well, it truly affected my behavior. And, I knew that, but I didn't know why or how or what to do with it. I'm not sure, but it looks like now that it's all compartmentalized.

THERAPIST And, again, what does that do for you?

NATALIE Uhmmm . . . (pause) . . . it makes me feel separate from it all, somehow. It makes me feel like I was usurped by it all before, and, uh, caught in a web that I couldn't get out of. But now I feel separate from it all. So it's like feeling them, and the emotions are still there, connected with all those people and circumstances, and it's still affecting my behavior (laugh) . . . but . . . but now I can see it. I can see it so clearly.

THERAPIST Now what does that do for you?

NATALIE I don't know. Somehow it . . . it gives me some freedom. That I feel like I am enjoying the freedom of being outside of the emotional web, even though I still have the emotions. (Pause) I feel like I make choices differently now, too. I mean, not that I have or am . . . but it's just this sort of intellectual . . . intellectualizing that I'm doing about it now . . . there is an immense amount of freedom that I'm feeling associated with . . . with some choices. *Oh, I don't feel like I'm making any sense!*

THERAPIST Oh, I think you're making a lot of sense. You're terrific! Just sort of go with it, because I think as you grow to express it it will probably make more sense.

NATALIE Yeah, 'cause, uh, I was thinking lately how I have this sort of window on my growth, and I was trying to explain to somebody today, as a matter of fact, where I was in my own personal growth and what issues I was working with—love, compassion—because I saw that through realizing all of my emotional relationships with the past that I had all these separate egos operating in me . . . (sigh) . . . and they are very interesting to me because in trying to integrate . . . I don't know if all those will ever get integrated, but I can see how one particular sort of ego is operating off of all of those emotional webs from the past, but if I allowed that one ego image to continue to operate I'm not going to be very happy . . .

Natalie's closure illustrates several important points about a meaning-making therapy. First of all, these words are a beautiful illustration of the subject/object transition—of moving from being within the problem to standing outside the problem, from the position at the foot of the mountain to the place on the side of the mountain where she can look down and see where she has been. Secondly, she illustrates the reality that therapy is not necessarily "finished" at the close of the final session. Indeed, Natalie had to quit because of her financial concerns as well as a new job. We had not done everything that could be done, but she had come a long distance in naming herself, in stepping outside of herself and her emotions. She thus was better prepared to work through many of her concerns on her own. And, finally, she also illustrates the "revolving door" because she returned two years later at a time of crisis which also proved to be a new stage of developmental readiness as she began to deal more intensively with her fears about intimate relationships.

In the final hours of an effective therapeutic sequence client and therapist become more known to each other. From the heavy involvements of the therapeutic experience client and therapist begin to emotionally move apart as the therapeutic connections lose their power. Certainly this is the resolution of the transference experiences, but more than that, it is the movement of the client to a position of greater equality with the therapist. This is subtle and not always achieved, but when it happens I find myself much more able to share myself as person as we finally walk out together through the therapeutic door. In this emerging sharing as we say "goodbye" we can also acknowledge that no learning experience, no therapeutic process, is going to solve all problems; that is a spirit which leaves room for future contacts and future learnings.

And, just as there can be many differing therapies under the umbrella of a given therapy—short-term, long-term, career, marital, grief, stress management, for example—there can be many types of closures and many types of movements through the revolving door: abrupt endings, the nicely resolved endings, referrals to someone else, or the vague, ill-defined endings which spread out over weeks but never really come to conclusion. What I have been describing is an ideal which serves as a guide and a hope for therapy.

Lasting improvement seldom follows any approach in which
patients are coerced into abandoning their deviant responses by
methods decided in advance by the therapist.

—Arnold Lazarus, 1971, p. xi

. . . the more eager we are to make a diagnosis and a plan of
action, the *less* helpful do we become. The more eager we are to
cure, the longer it takes. . . . In this and in many other situations,
to give in is to overcome, to be humble is to succeed.

—Abraham Maslow, 1961

Using words to name objects, feelings, or events is not a harmless
form of contemplation, a "gentle breeze" on the surface of things
that leaves them unchanged or a mirror of preestablished
qualities, relations or dimensions. Rather, words represent a
decision as to what aspect of the world to disclose. Our understanding of reality is constituted by the language we use to express
it. Consequently, the possibilities for multiple true descriptions of
our lives are virtually inexhaustible.

—Stuart Charme, 1984, p. 15

CHAPTER 7

Techniques of Therapy

THE TERM "TECHNIQUE" troubles me just a bit, for it seems too pat, too
definite, for the more fluid, global processes which I am describing here.
And it is all too easy to focus on technique to the neglect of the person. But
we need technique—that "mechanical or formal part of an art"—in order to
join discipline and practical detail to the more intuitive processes of therapy.
Therefore, as I describe "techniques" below I approach them with a respect
for the dialectic of technical repertoire and intuitive process. Therapy does
arise from technical specifics, but like an artist's creation it must leap beyond its colors, its brush strokes, its carefully plotted subject matter, to a
synergy of the whole. But without the specifics of technical expertise the
translation would never take place.

Much of what I was describing in the previous chapter can be called
"technique": establishing a therapeutic relationship, questioning, engaging
in dialogue, stimulating dialectical thinking, reflecting client affect and cognitive statement, comparing and contrasting pieces of personal history and
information, teaching new ideas, contradicting, sorting theories for new

insight and question, and patterning personal bits and pieces into a new whole. These more global approaches to client meaning-making suggest contexts and opportunities for the more specific techniques which I will be naming below. What is to be remembered is that all of these unite under the cognitive umbrella of *constructive, developmental meaning-making* — an umbrella that gives a shape, a cognitive form, and an organizing principle to therapy as it postulates and orders goals and methods, and suggests a framework for accessing and joining client reality and client process. (And I can't help but think of the data gathering, patterning processes of therapy as addressing the client as a kind of "walking eclecticism" who needs some overarching meaning to organize the diversity of self. So much of this book is about just that!)

Within an effort at "systematic eclecticism," then, this therapy bridges areas of psychological neglect as it encourages the therapist to move up and down abstraction ladders of theory and practice; as it respects and facilitates the person's capacity to assimilate and accommodate new forms for shaping personal reality; as it considers the broad range of human thought, behavior, and emotion from reductionist elements to synergistic whole; and as it draws on a broad range of technical approach and expertise. All this is done in the spirit of Allport's meaning "that by striving for system *in an eclectic manner*, we may actually achieve a comprehensive metatheory. When such a time comes eclecticism merges into system" (1968, p. 24).

CREATIVITY AS TECHNIQUE

There is another language which incorporates its own technique as it opens thinking and feeling to transformed constructions of personal reality. This is the language of *creativity*. Because much of what I think and do in therapy can be subsumed within this category, I take time to summarize and define what Arieti calls its "attitudes and conditions." This may seem a side journey into theory, but I don't consider it so. What I have to describe is tangible, specific, and central to the further techniques elaborated below.

Among those who have researched creativity, Arthur Koestler, Silvano Arieti, and Howard Gruber offer ideas which can be fruitfully translated into therapeutic techniques and teaching. But one approach which has been particularly useful to me has been Arieti's description of ten "simple attitudes and conditions for fostering creativity." I also like his whimsical description of himself as a therapist who doesn't "resort to toxic procedures, the setting of strange milieus, or the performance of difficult tasks" (Arieti, 1976, discussion on pp. 372–383).

Arieti names *aloneness* as a first condition for creativity. But this should not be "confused with protracted or painful loneliness imposed by others, or by one's psychological difficulties. Nor should it be confused with withdrawal from others, persistent shyness, or constant solitude." Rather, aloneness means the ability to remain alone for short periods of time in order to listen to the inner self and to come in contact with personal emotions, thoughts, and resources. I think of therapy as a time of creative aloneness. Although two people are present, it is a time to back away from the world, to be quiet, and to listen to oneself with both head and heart. Perhaps one of the spinoffs from therapy is a quieting of the spirit, and an achievement of comfort with oneself which enables such creative aloneness.

Second and third conditions for creativity include *inactivity* and *daydreaming* to allow creativity to proceed at its own pace. Unfortunately, our culture is oriented to activity and accomplishment and can be quite critical of a person who daydreams or appears to be inactive. But, as Arieti says, we are not advocating withdrawal, excessive loafing, or extremes of fantasy life, but a constructive approach to the *allowing* of personal creative process. I find this important in considering therapy, because both client and therapist can be impatient, unwilling to allow answers to develop in their own way. To foster a creative, allowing attitude, and to provide receptive conditions for inactivity and daydreaming honors Maslow's challenge for therapy: " . . . to give in is to overcome, to be humble is to succeed."

Not only are there conditions which are helpful to creative discovery process, there are two kinds of mental sets or attitudes which are essential— *free thinking* and *gullibility*.

What Arieti calls "free thinking" is not free association but a "state of abandon," of "freedom from inhibition." He believes that if the mind is open and nonjudging in its processing of information, awareness of similarities (that is, analogies) between perceptions, apperceptions, concepts, and even systems and abstractions will tend to occur repeatedly as the mind creates new patterns and connections. I see this as an essential attitude and condition if the therapy is to progress from simple data gathering to the patterning and ordering present in the middle and later stages of therapy. A willingness "to catch similarities" also adopts a dialectical willingness to remain open to opposing positions as one seeks creative synthesis, or a willingness to either allow the tension between "opposites" or to transcend them.

The sixth condition of *gullibility* is complementary. Arieti means by this a "willingness to explore everything: to be open, innocent, and naive before rejecting anything. It means accepting (at least temporarily or until proved wrong) that there are certain underlying orderly arrangements in everything beyond and within us. More than the inventing of new things, creativity often implies the discovery of these underlying orderly arrangements." In this, however, there is a selective quality in which the person engages in a kind of cognitive dialogue of trust and mistrust, receiving, sorting and sifting without some sort of discrimination, but to the extent that insights are not discarded "a priori as nonsense."

The seventh creative element is the *remembrance and inner replaying of past traumatic conflict.* From Arieti's viewpoint this means remembering, acknowledging, and integrating former psychological conflicts of the effects of trauma. It also means using these former conflicts with both a sense of familiarity and a sense of distance in the service of new growth. This is a dialectical capacity which sees the present in the light of the past, in a comparing and contrasting of the varying periods of one's life and of the progressive evolutions and growths which have taken place. This is also a manifestation of the kinds of reconciliation which take place in the later stages of therapy.

Finally, Arieti lists the ninth and tenth conditions necessary for creativity as *alertness* and *discipline*. "Many would-be creative persons, especially in the artistic fields, like to believe that only such qualities as imagination, inspiration, intuition, and talent are important. They are reluctant to submit themselves to the rigor of learning techniques and practicing discipline and logical thinking, on the pretext that all these things would stultify their creativity." In terms of therapy, I liken this to the wish of some clients to truncate the developmental process because they are unwilling or unable to face the pain of personal transition, or to current tendencies in our society for quick success or the instant high. The message from this for our clients is that change does take time, it does take effort, and it does take practice. But, in the words of M. Scott Peck, "Once we truly know that life is difficult — once we truly understand and accept it — then life is no longer difficult. Because once it is accepted, the fact that life is difficult no longer matters" (Peck, 1978, p. 15). Or, the idea from Rollo May (1981) that our freedom is born of limits — of the disciplines, the learnings, the heritage, the focusings which bring the creative movements from the moments of insight to the active translations into the world.

In Arieti's descriptions, then, are the dialectical contrasts of creative process — free thinking and gullibility on one side, and the discipline, acuity, control, checking and discussion, on the other hand — which provide a foil and a mirror for each other. In these descriptions are also didactic resource material for teaching clients new habits and for stimulating new behaviors. Furthermore, shaped and guided by these creative attitudes and conditions this therapy continues to encourage exploratory dialogue, dialectical thinking, and emotional expression with techniques that stimulate the evaluative comparison and contrasting which shake the old into the creation of the new.

TESTS AS TOOLS FOR SELF-DISCOVERY

In the spirit of creative cognitive adventure and "collaborative empiricism" (Windy Dryden's term) the therapist and client search, name, and hypothesize together. And it is in this spirit that exploratory tools are chosen.

But, you may ask, "What purposes do tests serve within the contexts of developmental meaning-making? And what principles guide the therapist's choice of evaluative tools?" To answer these questions is to return again to the purposes of this therapy:

- To join the client in his or her meaning-making.
- To use whatever means possible to discover the internalized, unconscious images, stories, beliefs, and semantic constructions which guide or influence behaviors, emotional expressions, and cognitive formulations of reality.
- To continually seek to identify systems of meaning and the referents and contexts for those meanings.
- To identify and name the cognitive processes and forms which guide one's choices.
- To pull all these discoveries about oneself into a coherent form which makes sense of personal reality.

For most clients tests are rather fun if they are administered in a spirit of creative self-discovery. This means all results are shared so that the client has every opportunity to join the therapist in the interpretative process, and to fully understand the rationale for giving the tests and for the results which are achieved. By following these guidelines the therapist maintains a more effective dialogue which provides the confirming, supporting energy for developmental growth (see again my discussion of dialogue on p. 67).

One tool particularly valuable for the cognitive therapist is Alfred Adler's *"early recollections"* technique. Adler (1958, 1974) believed that early recollections were retained because of a selective factor in memory; that they show a consistency with the individual's attitudinal frame of reference, the individual lifestyle; that they also reveal a perceptual framework within which the individual person interprets life experience. Adler defined an "early recollection" as one which can be visualized, which is a single incident, and which is a prototype of an attitude. In this Adler shares belief with those students of perception whom Krech (1949) has labeled the "New Look" psychologists, "who feel that perception and memory are both related to the individual's frame of reference or attitudinal set, that is, to his personal values and needs."

Harold Mosak has offered an excellent overview of Adler's theories and therapy. He discusses the "early recollections" technique as a method for "life-style investigation" and he comments that "an *early recollection* occurs in the period before continuous memory and may be inaccurate or a complete fiction. It represents a single event . . . rather than a group of events. . . . Recollections are treated as a projective technique. If one understands the early recollections, one understands the patient's 'Story of My Life' since people selectively recollect from their past incidents consonant with their life-styles" (Mosak, 1979, p. 67). Thus, these single, isolated events are usually recollected within the context of self-image and lifestyle, and can offer unique understanding of how the client has cognitively shaped his or her world.

In order to fully tap the rich material in early recollections, the therapist must elicit a number of them to create a picture of the varying themes and variations which are present. When used in this manner the technique can be a very effective tool for identifying the underlying patterns in family history and personal dynamics.

In Jana's case, the early recollections technique identified her whimsical differentness in a rather serious family which seemed unable to appreciate or understand their gifted, creative child.

I remember father bringing home a cardboard box which he set on my high chair. Mother was not too pleased when a little kitten popped out — and it was for me! (Age 3)

Dad was washing the car in the driveway and didn't see me and got me wet. When I took the hose and got him wet I got spanked.

I was drawing on the wall in the bathroom while sitting on the toilet. I put cards on the wall to cover it up. Later that night when Mom and Dad came in while I was in my crib I was laughing. He pulled the crib out and gave me another spanking.

I can remember saying to my Dad — he was watching bowling on TV — "What score do you get?" He said "200." Then I asked, "What scores do experts get?" He took it as hurtful. I didn't mean it that way. In the back of my mind I have this feeling that I hurt people without meaning to. I try to say things that are nice and they backfire.

I'd see my parents kiss and embrace. I'd want to talk about the bird's singing, but couldn't get out the words.

I used to feel so sad over an experience — trying to assimilate joy. I did it in a quiet way. I would file it away in my mind. (The seeds of her tendencies to hold private thoughts and feelings deep within her?)

As Jana and I talked about these early memories, she began to see herself in many new ways, coming to love her little child — the little girl with an offbeat way of seeing, doing, and saying things. With these images in mind she also came to understand how some of her current patterns of behavior had evolved (more about this in Chapter 9).

Other projective tools like the *Thematic Apperception Test* are useful for accessing unconsious thematic patterns not so readily accessible through direct questioning. In describing this test Anastasi writes, "In contrast to inkblot techniques, the Thematic apperception Test (TAT) presents more highly structured stimuli and requires more complex and meaningfully organized verbal responses. Interpretation of response by the examiner is usually based on content analysis of a rather qualitative nature" (1976, p. 565). Thus, Anastasi further comments, most clinicians rely heavily on "subjective norms" developed through personal use of the test. In my case I search for language and expression, vocabularies of emotion, perspectives on and identifications with significant others, cognitive style, beliefs and attitudes, hopes and fears, personal dilemmas, and alternative versions of the world and its problems. What I am seeking is insight into unconscious images, beliefs and cognitive/affective processes.

Vicky's TAT stories frequently consisted of two perspectives on the stimulus picture. For example, in responding to Card 1 which shows a little boy pondering his violin, Vicky said:

I see two things:

In the first one I see him practicing his violin . . . becoming very frustrated because he can't get the sequence right. He is wondering what he is doing and why . . . it's good to please his mother . . . he's not old enough to know different . . . he wonders if it will do any good. But he will eventually go back and practice.

He's composing a song . . . gotten to a point where he can't think what comes next . . . sitting and thinking . . . wondering what comes next . . . feeling perseverance . . . goes on and writes the rest of the song.

And, in response to Card 2 which shows a young woman standing in a field:

. . . Reminds me of *Fiddler on the Roof*. This can go two ways:

First one is that the girl with her books is the daughter of the other two . . . and she's looking forlorn. Mother is going to have a baby . . . doesn't know whether . . . [and then it faded away to be replaced by a second version]

She's in love with the guy who's plowing. His wife is pregnant—that distresses her. She's a school teacher, rather lost. He's a macho man, planting the field, experiencing the best of all worlds. Interesting that men don't have as cultivated feelings as women. Maybe it's all subjective . . . society's two cents that man is not to have as much feeling . . .

Certainly these could be interpreted in a number of differing ways, but what I saw reflected in Vicky's stories were her struggles between what mother wanted and what she wanted; between her artistic expressions and feelings of frustration at trying to please another; between her societal place as a woman and that of men; between the elements of a story and her analysis of that story; and between differing versions of love and relationship.

How did these simple stories help our therapy? They turned us in slightly new exploratory directions and gave further stimulus for discussion of her dynamics of creative expression vis-à-vis her family's evaluation of her as a person. For example, one aside that developed during the TAT session was, "People never give the advice I want to hear. Very few people are on the same wavelength." And as we talked further some of Vicky's deep feelings and reactions were revealed: a certain detached, observant loneliness; a frustration in the contrasts between fantasy and reality; and an accompanying anger and fear when she had to juxtapose a dream with the here-and-now difficulties of life experience.

The *Myers-Briggs Type Indicator* is another tool which has proved help-ful as clients start to name themselves. Based on Jung's theory of types, this self-report inventory is designed to measure personality dispositions and interests within four dimensions: extraversion/introversion; sensing/intui-tion; thinking/feeling; and judging/perceiving. The results of the inventory show the person as one of 16 different types with a cluster of characteristics which can reveal values and needs, styles of thought and feeling, as well as dominant approaches to problem-solving, relationship, and decision-mak-ing. The Myers-Briggs Type Indicator is particularly useful because it is a brief test, relatively nonthreatening, and easy to understand. Most clients find it interesting and useful although many will discuss and argue with some of its questions (and that is actually a very helpful reaction for learn-ing more about their cognitive styles). (See Myers, 1980, and Keirsey & Bates, 1978, for in-depth discussion.)

Whatever the reported style, the Myers-Briggs test results are offered in the spirit of health rather than pathology, with emphasis upon the accep-tance of oneself and of others rather than the rejection of particular person-al qualities. In my feedback I always emphasize that every one of us has qualities from both sides of the continuum, and that every quality can represent both a vulnerability and a strength. I also share a thought which I garnered from some wise person now forgotten—that any strength carried too far can become a vulnerability. Thus, to be a thinking person to the extreme is to lose one's emotional sensitivity; to be an intuitive too far is to leap from possibility to possibility; to be a perceptive person too far is to lack a certain discipline and structure in life.

Sometimes the identification of personal style can be threatening if a client judges his or her particular style as dull or uninteresting. Sometimes, too, people don't see their type operating well within a particular career context. For example, I once worked with a woman lawyer who was quite upset that the test showed her as a strongly intuitive and feeling person. Adamant that the portrait was simply not suitable for her chosen profession, she protested any identification with those qualities. Her protest simmered and then subsided as continuing discussion brought her to an appreciation and acceptance of herself which had never been present before. She also came to see how valuable warmth, intuition, and sensitivity could be in her analytical, logical work in the legal field.

On the other hand, most people find the mini-portraits (and I emphasize that they are just that) reassuring and interesting—another facet of the diamond which is themselves. Frequently, too, they begin to understand personal quirks in themselves and in others. The introvert, for example, who begins to understand why he "wears out" at a party, or the extravert who begins to understand a partner who simply does not want to be so involved in social activity; the "judging" person who begins to see personal needs for plan, closure, and predictability vis-à-vis his partner who wants to remain open to the spontaneity of the moment. Since such contrasts are present in almost any relationship, the identification of personal characteristics can also be particularly helpful in marital therapy, as partners gain new understanding of themselves and each other. They then become more able to identify and work with sources of the "sandpaper effect" in couple relationships. The purpose is not to judge a style, but simply to open and encourage understanding and mutual acceptance in order to negotiate personal differences.

The one danger, of course, is that people use this test indiscriminately, labeling self and others in a simplistic, inappropriate fashion. As a matter of fact, some companies use this test to assign employees to particular work roles. To a certain extent that may be helpful, but what is all too frequently forgotten is that every person is a synergy of qualities and tendencies which can *never* be revealed in a test, and every job is a synergy which requires a diversity of type and approach.

On occasion I also use the Sixteen Personality Factor Test, or the Minnesota Multiphasic Inventory, though I find these tests more difficult to interpret and feed back in the spirit of constructive dialogue. It is all to easy to be caught by diagnostic language or psychological stereotype, losing the free thinking and the gullibility which is so essential for creative self-discovery. Obviously, the use of these tests depends to a great extent on the severity of my client's disturbance and on my need for particular clarifications of the presenting problem.

Narrative Process

The information gained from testing feeds and supports another very important approach to self-discovery—that of narrative process.

Words "represent a decision as to what aspect of the world to disclose. Our understanding of reality is constituted by the language we use to express it" (Charme, 1984). Accepting Charme's ideas as valuable in a meaning-making therapy I turn now to techniques which pay attention to the use of language in the naming of self.

Writing. For a motivated client writing can bring rich results in the articulation of values, of that which is significant, of that which is closest to the client's intuition and feeling. Why is this so? First of all, writing touches and translates what Arieti calls the "endoceptual" experience. From his perspective, people gather a large body of inner experience and impression which has never been put into concept—"That which we know but which we don't know we know," in other words. This may be particularly true for sensitive, intuitive observers. For these people, who may have a hard time explaining their intuitions or their emotional reactions, writing becomes an effective means for translating preconscious, nonverbal experience (what

Arieti calls "endocept") into objective material available for analysis and thought.

Writing is also a stimulus for patterning as the person joins words and ideas into some sort of order. To write is to categorize, to compare and contrast, to select one word or idea over another. To write is to evaluate, to stand back, to become the more objective observer. To write is to join one body of memories with another, one place in personal history with the experience of the moment. Thus, in these many ways, writing is a stimulus to dialectical thinking and creative synthesis as pieces of experience become joined in new ways.

Assignments for writing arise quite naturally from the content of particular therapy sessions. Jennifer wrote about her emerging terror; Sonny questioned his change; and Natalie poured out her emotional reactions to her struggles with her father and mother. For people in the middle of grieving, a letter to the deceased can bring powerful release of anger and protest. And for people struggling with identity, the "Who am I?" exercises can lead to a fresh naming of self. This simple exercise, which has been used extensively in career development, translates effectively into the depth work of psychotherapy. A client is asked to first give herself ten titles (and I explain that these can be descriptive phrases as well as discrete titles). For example:

WHO AM I? I am:

- mother's daughter
- a teacher
- a person who procrastinates
- very fearful
- a shy person
- a wife
- creative
- in need of direction
- a sister
- a woman

After this list is completed the client is asked to put each title at the top of a separate sheet of paper and then to write a little piece about it. Something like this might result:

I Am A Sister

Who is out in the world earning my way as an accountant. Hoping to achieve a worthy, transferable, marketable skill, hoping I'm not wasting my time.

I don't want to sell out.

I used to think I couldn't do much. I hope it's okay to feel I'm smart and can accomplish things.

I'd like to earn some money, make some friends, finish my BA, and go back to school.

I'd like to be witty and pretty and interesting and older and have a lot of fun stories to tell you. But I'm just hardworking and sometimes bitchy, but mostly tired. Scared when I'm not doing the right thing.

Clients find these exercises interesting, revealing, at times troubling, as they come to realize how complex they really are. Certainly these writings are helpful to therapeutic process as they stimulate new discussion and as they help the clients to distance themselves from particular dimensions of their problems.

Building a Personal Story. The gathering of the bits and pieces of personal history and identity leads quite naturally into the development of a personal narrative. This can be accomplished either through written exercise or through verbal exploration. Whichever method is adopted, I encourage my clients to create a personal story as they begin to get a sense of their unique human capacity to join the past, the present and the future, and as they gain new capacity to name and understand some of the significant moments and the significant people in their history. In this we look for the childhood patterns which continue to repeat themselves in adult form. These can include powerful programmings of family edict and ideology, patterns and temperamental styles of a culture, or dualistic paradigms which hold them to limited constructions of their world. As varying elements are identified, the creative "catching of similarities" takes place as the client builds increasingly complex networks of self-understanding. A quote from Robert Glaser is pertinent:

Our research suggests that the knowledge of novices is organized around the literal objects explicitly given in a problem statement. Experts' knowledge, on the other hand, is organized around principles and abstractions that subsume these objects. (1984, pp. 98–99)

The client, then, is learning what theories he or she holds—facing them, debugging them, testing them, and comparing them with alternative theories which the therapist may suggest. Additionally, the client is building personal knowledge as he or she moves from the more concrete experience of being *in* the problem, to the more abstract, sophisticated attitudes of *having* the problem—being outside it, able to talk about it, and to put the problem within the contexts of past and present experience. In such manner, the client is building a larger base of knowledge about self and is moving from being a novice of self to an expert on self.

There are a number of ways to categorize one's story, but Jerome Bruner suggests that a "story must construct two landscapes simultaneously":

One is the landscape of action, where the constituents are the arguments of action: agent, intention or goal, situation, instrument, something corresponding to a "story grammar." The other landscape is the landscape of consciousness: what those involved in the action know, think, or feel, or do not know, think, or feel. The two landscapes are essential and distinct: it is the difference between Oedipus sharing

Jocasta's bed before and after he learns from the messenger that she is his mother. (1986, p. 14)

Bruner's two landscapes are certainly the landscapes of therapy, as we deal with the person as actor/agent who is also the person with consciousness who is continually shaping personal reality and meaning through thought and feeling. To touch these parallel streams through the writing of a personal narrative is to touch the streams of self.

But there are so many differing ways to categorize a history! A class on autobiography stimulated me to the following ideas:

- Look for the authentic story uncluttered by the stories of others.
- Look for the patterns of self—that which constitutes one's personal "myth."
- Seek the language which describes who and what we are.
- Consider this experience a "gathering, grasping, and ordering of personal meanings" in order to make sense of our life.
- We can categorize the patterns in our stories in many different ways: for example, thought, emotion, behavior, meaning, hope and doubt, interaction, interpretation, our names and their meanings.
- We can tell many kinds of story: of personal deed, of experience (whether explicit and concrete, or introspective and symbolic), of trying on roles for size, of the search for authentic self.

But writing is not for everyone. Some clients are either unwilling or unable to do these writing exercises. They may lack writing skills or they may be threatened by the thought of revealing themselves on paper. Or, yet again, some people have so much emotion around given topics that they are not yet ready to touch the areas of pain. Obviously, these varying reasons must be honored, but I do sometimes introduce a simpler alternative which draws on traditional free association techniques.

Semantic Free Association Exercise. I have used this semantic exercise for years, but have only recently named its value as a cognitive technique as I have come to recognize that one word can be the cognitive/affective center of a complex network of related words and feelings. Thus, every word seems to organize some sort of system. In a graphic approach to this free association I have the client put a key word or phrase in a circle. Then, as the free association progresses, each new word is put in overlapping circles around the central circle (see Figure 2). I frequently illustrate this technique in a therapy session as I draw the circles on my pad or the whiteboard. Then, I ask my client to join me as we allow a spontaneous flow of associations triggered by the original stimulus word. Frequently this exercise triggers emotion as a particular word or associative sequence floods the client with emotional memories which may have been ignored or forgotten. In fact,

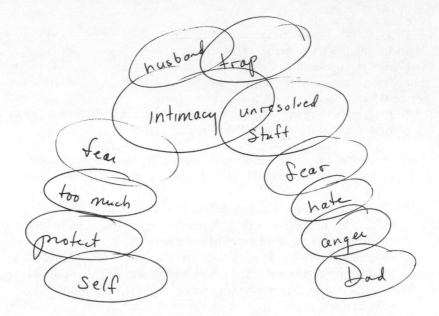

FIGURE 2   Free association exercise

some very important breakthroughs have come by tracking a series of words which at first may have seemed totally unconnected.

I have also used this semantic free association technique at workshops where participants deal with their associations with such key words as "retirement," "aging," "self," "career," and "love." For example, the word "retirement" brought the following contrasting responses from a preretirement group: "value, travel, broke, time, grandchildren, in the way, mind and growth, opportunity, self-exploration, writing, leisure, sailing, friends." And with a married couple the word "sex" brought these very contrasting responses. From her: "pain, fatigue, used, frightened, helpless, repulsive, angry." From him: "tenderness, caring, close, touch, feeling, wanting, excitement." Obviously, these people had a lot of work ahead of them if these perceptual differences were to be transformed and integrated into a workable, loving relationship.

The message in all this is that no word stands alone, no word is discrete; every word is an amazing system of correlated meanings. As I have just shown, "love" is not just love; love is a constellation of learnings, experiences, memories, images, ideologies, gender lenses — and more. "Aging" is not just aging; aging is a mix of all the forces of chronology, biology, relationship, learning, ascent and decline which can bring a wide range of associations from "frightening, unknown, disabling" to "challenge, wisdom, grandchildren, rest and relaxation." Because of the huge range of responses and associations (*and emotions!* There have been some significant emotional breakthroughs with this simple exercise), this is a powerful tool for tracking the cognitive networks of the mind, as well as the hidden images, ideals, attitudes, and beliefs which shape personal reaction. This free association technique is a brainstorming exercise, an evaluative tool for cognitive style, a stimulation exercise for creativity, and certainly, a data-gathering tool for learning more about my client.

To approach free association from another direction I may use an adaptation of a meditation technique suggested by Lawrence LeShan in *How to Meditate* (1974). Becoming relaxed, with eyes closed, and possibly with some light trance induction, a key word is chosen, and then any word which comes to mind is allowed to emerge. The person then returns to the initial word. For example, *love*-joy, *love*-fear, *love*-respect, *love*-hope, and so on. This exercise can be done as a written exercise in the manner described above, or with a tape recorder so that there is no interruption of the meditation process.

But even these semantic free association exercises can be difficult or threatening if clients are inhibited, fearful, or rigid in their thinking. Rather than discard them completely, I usually reintroduce them from time to time as clients become more comfortable with themselves, with me, and with therapeutic process. In fact, increasing willingness to make themselves vulnerable in these ways is a positive sign that growth is taking place.

Attention to Words. In all these exercises there is an attention to the meanings of words. Because language is important as mediator and guide, as organizer and stimulus, I am always listening for the semantics of my client. And I am continually questioning words as I ask, "Tell me what you mean by that," or "Go with that a little bit more. I'm not sure I understand that word." Thus, I don't take definitions for granted, believing (as well illustrated by the semantic free association exercise) that words have multiple meanings.

I challenge my clients to be specific with language because what they tell themselves they often do. Here I frequently incorporate some of the cognitive techniques of Albert Ellis or Aaron Beck as I pay attention not only to the larger statements of belief and personal premise but as I also attend to the semantic fine-tunings within these larger statements. I am alert to any generalizations, simplistic labels, or blunt obscenities which close cognitive process. These types of expression become fuel for questioning as I challenge the kinds of language which can close creative thought. In this I am indebted to Arnold Lazarus for his insightful discussion of cognitive retructuring in *Behavior Therapy and Beyond*. Reading that book fueled many ideas, turning my thinking and my therapy in creative new directions.

THE SHARING AND EXPRESSION OF FEELINGS

Throughout therapy I frequently turn to clients and ask, "How are you feeling right now?" If they start off on an abstract, intellectual tack, I bring them back by repeating, "How are you feeling right now?" To aid this process I often illustrate with an exercise from my acting teacher, Anne Graham, who suggested that I sit quietly and identify every kind of feeling in a given moment in time. Thus, within the context of the above exercise, I have described the tickle in my toe, the growling in my stomach, the tension in my shoulders, the hovering anxiety about my book, the fatigue which is only barely masked, and the mental rehearsal of fear which may be taking place. This exercise has worked for me in touching many areas of awareness, and I have found it useful in helping my clients to get more in touch with their feelings.

I continually check out emotions, therefore, asking my clients to share their fears, anxieties, disappointments, griefs, angers — whatever is going on at the moment. Though I may not encourage the use of roaring catharsis of Gestalt therapy, I do encourage weeping, talking, breathing, sighing, and shouting if that what is needed. But, in tune with Carol Tavris' (1982) ideas that anger can be a habit, I more frequently suggest new ways to identify and express anger as we spend time looking for the connections between the underlying feelings of fear, hurt, and guilt which create the hot-burner effect in stimulating anger. By understanding these more unconscious processes anger is frequently diffused.

In working with the expression of anger, I frequently return to ideas of Michael Mahoney, who has criticized those cognitive therapists who ignore both the unconscious and the meanings of emotional expression. From his perspective emotional expression may become the completion of a previously interrupted sequence of life experience. If the sequence involved a strong affect element, and if this was orginally unexpressed, it is possible that expression is both subjectively satisfying and therapeutic.

I also carefully reconsider the ideas of Lazarus and Folkman (1984), who remind us that when information is appraised as significant to our sense of well-being it becomes "hot information" or information that is laden with emotion. Indeed, these ideas mesh well with my own that emotions are "barometers of change" or "barometers of meaning" very much at the heart of our shifting "knowings." Because this is so, I encourage my clients to reduce their resistance to feelings, to tune to the messages which emotions are constantly giving. Thus, I often ask clients to sort their "hot burners" to discover those influences which affect their sense of well-being. Or I may ask what an anxiety is saying while I also offer clinical hypotheses about what anxiety can mean: the fear of the loss of intimacy, resistance to change, the avoidance of new, creative expression. I may suggest that my client read books and articles which talk about emotions — Tavris' *Anger*, for example;

Lerner's *Dance of Anger*; May's *Courage to Create* (1975); David Viscott's *The Language of Feelings* (1976) — all according to level of education and cognitive sophistication. But, again, what I am trying to allow and to encourage is the opening of the feelings which have so frequently been repressed and anesthetized.

What I emphasize, furthermore, is that some of the greatest "mileage" in therapy has been achieved by the simple question, *"What are you feeling right now?"*

GENOGRAMS

The self-discovery, meaning-making process continues, then, through dialogue, through questioning, through writing, through attention to personal systems of semantics, through the sharing of feelings, and now, through the developmental examinations of personal and family history.

In creating a personal narrative, the use of genograms can be very helpful. Monica McGoldrick and Randy Gerson, whose book *Genograms in Family Assessment* is an important addition to current family literature, define this technique's usefulness:

A genogram is a format for drawing a family tree that records information about family members and their relationships over at least three generations. Genograms display family information graphically in a way that provides a quick gestalt of complex family patterns and a rich source of hypotheses about how a clinical problem may be connected to the family context and the evolution of both problem and context over time. (1985, p. 1)

For the clinician the genogram is an "efficient clinical summary," providing a quick, graphic overview of emerging patterns. These can be easily updated and enlarged as new information is revealed. For the client it is new means for visualizing interconnections within the family and coming to see more clearly those patterns which are maintaining themselves. Certainly, with the use of a genogram, one assumes a developmental perspective:

By scanning the family system historically and assessing previous life cycle transitions, one can place present issues in the context of the family's evolutionary patterns. Thus, the genogram usually includes at least three generations of family members, as well as nodal and critical events in the family's history, particularly as related to the life cycle. When family members are questioned about the present situation in relations to the themes, myths, rules and emotionally charged issues of previous generations, repetitive patterns become clear. (McGoldrick & Gerson, 1985, p. 3)

Family history also includes attention to family ideology. "What did your family believe about religion? About divorce and relationship? How did your family show affection or anger?" These are questions which stimulate the comparing and contrasting of oneself with one's parents and siblings — a comparing and contrasting which facilitates the naming of self vis-à-vis family and significant others.

A therapist is a teacher as he or she offers thoughts and ideas, shares learning materials and models, and stimulates the client to think, feel and act in entirely new ways. In this role the therapist can intervene in a number of different ways which need to be identified, for it is all too easy for a therapist/teacher to slip into coercion or exploitation, rather than maintaining the supportive facilitation which is the mark of effective therapy. Dean Barnlund has written a little piece about this which I think is highly significant for the therapist:

Meaning, in my opinion, is a private preserve and trespassers always run a risk. To speak of personal integrity at all is to acknowledge this. Any exchange of words is an invasion of the privacy of the listener which is aimed at preventing, restricting, or stimulating the cultivation of meaning. Briefly, three types of interference may be distinguished. First, there are messages whose intent is to coerce. Meaning is controlled by choosing symbols that so threaten the interpreter that he becomes incapable of, and blind to, alternative meanings; second, there are messages of an exploitative sort in which words are arranged to filter the information, narrow the choices, obscure the consequences, so that only one meaning becomes attractive or appropriate; third, there is facilitative communication in which words are used to inform, to enlarge perspectives, to deepen sensitivity, to remove external threat, to encourage independence of meaning. The values of the listener are, in the first case, ignored, in the second, subverted, in the third respected. While some qualification of this principle is needed, it appears that only facilitative communication is entirely consistent with the protection and improvement of man's symbolic experience. Unless a teacher [or therapist] is aware of these possibilities and appreciates the differences in these kinds of communication, it is unlikely that he will communicate responsibly in the classroom [or therapy room]. (Barnlund, 1982, p. 52)

With these words as a caution and a guide I share now some ways that I teach — methods which enhance and continue the meaning-making process:

I teach by sharing anecdotes. By opening personal experience I often have a story to tell which reframes a problem in a novel way. In marital therapy, particularly, I can draw in humorous bits and pieces of history which show how my husband and I have faced comparable difficulties and worked them through to resolution — or, in contrast, how we have *not* found resolution but manage to maintain a satisfying and important relationship. For instance, I might tell about the time when we went to the ocean, where I expected to spend my time sitting on a rock, reading a book and absorbing the ocean spray, and my husband expected me to tend to his needs for companionship. Or the time we had our first fight over who was to cook dinner and how that fight resonated through our housing unit. I keep these stories to a minimum, but at suitable points in therapy they have lifted the dilemma from confrontational tightness to a humorous, open perspective on the problem.

Or I may teach by sharing dilemmas of life transition. Sometimes, for example, I share the drama of my career crisis at the age of 38, when I decided to leave a career as a professional pipe organist to return to school for a degree in psychology. Clients often do a double take when I tell them that I earned my Ph.D. at 45 and entered private practice at 50. Suddenly they see aging and life opportunity in different ways. The "impossible" becomes possible as they reframe their perspectives.

At other times I have offered a phrase, or an idea, or a word, that I have collected from a variety of sources — a book, a friend, a wise teacher. And it is sometimes these offhand comments which come back in later weeks of therapy to resonate as an important moment in the meaning-making journey.

Often I teach by drawing graphic models of stress curves, for example, or of developmental models, or of Rollo May's "pause" between the stimulus and response. Or I may share ideas from Richard Bedrosian and Aaron Beck (1980) about negative thoughts and self-statements which influence depression. Sometimes I draw my model of "process and ideal" as I demonstrate how a disintegrating life plan can bring accompanying grief, stress, and disruption to how one makes meaning. In all of these forms of teaching I treat the client as an informed participant in the learning process, as someone who is intelligent and capable of such learning. I have had many clients tell me later that this respect for their capabilities was an important ingredient in their resolution of the therapeutic dilemma.

Sometimes I have been torn between my role of facilitative therapist and a teacher of specifics. Thus, when one of my clients challenged me to "teach her" I found myself puzzled as I pondered what directions to take.

My client was the one who gave me answers. She said she wanted to learn about relationships, about being with people, about finding herself in interaction with others. She pointed clearly and correctly to the fact that her parents had so neglected her that she had no mirror on herself. Thus she never had them as the early models and teachers she needed so badly. In all of this, she commented, "I feel an awful sense of a void of identity at the center of my being." During therapy, certainly, we had been filling the void bit by bit, but we had come to an impasse. She needed content, ideas, suggestions, theories, models.

Together, then, we moved into new gear as I actively taught ideas and content, shared important books on personal dynamics and even etiquette, and as I continued to offer alternative ways of learning, feeling, and behaving. But in this, I insisted that she be active by practicing new behaviors, by arguing with me if something was not appropriate for her, and by making this a dialogue of learning rather than a passive acceptance of someone's lecture on life. Here I was walking the ragged edge between my roles as therapist/facilitator and teacher. Indeed if our therapeutic goal is the facilitation of client meaning rather than our own meaning, then we need to continually check the interface between our values and those of our client. In the words of Barnlund, the challenges are "to inform, to enlarge perspectives, to deepen sensitivity, to remove external threat, *to encourage independence of meaning*" (emphasis mine). It is that last bit which is most important.

As I teach, then, I continue the dialogue and dialectical questioning which is so much a part of a meaning-making therapy. This means the continuing comparing and contrasting, naming the past in juxtaposition to the present, thinking about differing points of view.

Using my whiteboard as a tool, I may also introduce graphics which highlight the contrasts between dualistic and dialectical forms of thinking. To do this I may write a set of words such as "black/white; yes/no; good/bad; success/failure" and then draw a series of continua between the opposing polarities. Using those models we begin to talk about the in-betweens, the "third alternatives," the approximations within these dualistic perspectives. As I draw a scale from 1 to 10, I ask at what point along the particular continuum success turns to failure, or goodness to badness. Or, drawing a percentage scale, I may ask what level of success is required to make an experience or an effort worthwhile. "Are you willing to accept a 75% success rate in a new experience? Or does it have to be a resounding 100%? Are you willing to let experiences like a class or an attempt at new friendship have less than that perfect score?" By playing with such questions and throwing ideas back and forth, clients frequently begin to see how they have locked themselves into perfectionistic thinking. Often, as a result of these cognitive challenges, clients begin to move their dualistic constructions in the direction of the dialectical. Others, of course, refuse to consider the in-betweens or the grays, particularly if such new thinking represents a real break with their belief systems. Here I don't push but usually return in more subtle ways to attempt to free patterns which are holding my client to a restricted, inhibiting way of thinking.

Behavioral assignment is also a part of this teaching as I send clients home with tasks to perform—exercise programs to break depression, for example; successive approximations in approaching the threats of "cold calling" in career search; attendance at a class in assertiveness training to sharpen communication skills. Which brings another point: I make full use of community learning resources as adjuncts to therapy—college and university classes, experimental learning programs, recreational offerings, journal writing classes, private lessons in speech or acting—whatever will work, in other words, in widening a client's perspectives on the world and in giving him or her a larger repertoire of skills, interests, and contacts.

Teaching continues within all the techniques and dialogues of therapy as both confirmation and disconfirmation, agreement and disagreement, stimulate therapeutic dialoque. Though a wide variety of techniques are joined under the constructive umbrella of cognitive developmental meaning-making, none is chosen which creates confusion, putdown, or the negation of client reality (and I am disturbed to hear of colleagues who actively practice "confusional techniques"). To reinforce this statement of attitude and principle I close this section by reviewing once again the goals for therapy which I named in Chapter 4:

- To join each client where he or she is.
- To create a genuine therapeutic dialogue.
- To fully explore the feelings within the crisis experience.
- To face and use crisis experience as the energy for constructive change.
- To help the individual face basic "existential fears" without building neurotic defenses.
- To teach, facilitate, and reinforce creative thinking processes.
- To model, stimulate, and encourage dialectical thinking patterns.
- To facilitate the "subject/object transition" (Kegan's words).
- To facilitate creative aging (see Chapter 13).
- To foster meaning-making.
- To facilitate a sense of sameness, continuity, and the "real me" in creating a life that is meaningful.

What I have hoped to stimulate in you is an appreciation and respect for a systemic eclecticism which honors and interacts with the broad spectrum of human thinking, feeling, and behavior—an eclecticism which is *aiming for system* within the concepts of cognitive developmental process.

In the next three chapters I share case material from my therapeutic work with Vicky, Jana, Jennifer, Nick, and Sonny. This material will be integrated in varying ways—sometimes featured, sometimes only touched upon. What I will be illustrating will be the progressive movements through "steps to meaning-making."

What I will also be illustrating are some *standards for knowing* that developmental movement is taking place. These are not necessarily dramatic turning points (though they may well be); more likely they are subtleties, hints, suggestions that a transformation of cognitive processing and emotional expression is taking place within the contexts of therapy.

But what are the kinds of evidence, the kinds of "awakenings" which let us know that some transformational step has taken place? What are our measuring points, our cognitive developmental "standards for knowing"?

Erikson has suggested the movements from trust and hope, to identity and faith, to generativity and care, to integrity and wisdom. Kegan has offered his model of the evolutionary growth of one's capacity to step back from personal experience with a new capacity to see into that experience, of one's capacity to incorporate the dialectic of differentiation and embeddedness, of separateness and intimacy. And, even further, Basseches has given us a set of four categories of dialectical thinking which become guides for questioning and evaluation:

(1) *Motion-oriented schemata:* These describe "moves in thought which function either to preserve fluidity in thought, to draw the attention of the thinker to processes of change, or to describe such processes" (1984, p. 73). When you read the material ahead you will find much dialogue about the processes of change as I keep teaching and encouraging my clients to recognize, interpret, and name these processes.

(2) *Form-oriented schemata:* This is thinking that acknowledges the idea of transformation or motion through forms which can be defined as organized or patterned wholes. These can include *"systems, structures, contexts, processes, sets of connections, wholes, forms"* (1984, p. 107). In this set of schemata an element or phenomenon is seen within the context of the whole, and it is assumed that this contextual relativism influences our forms of thinking as we construct personal reality systems. Take note as you read the material ahead that I ask many questions which deal with the client's elements of self which combine to make new patterns or a new sense of personal wholeness.

(3) *Relationship-oriented schemata:* These "serve to direct the thinker's attention to relationships and to enable the thinker to conceptualize relationships in ways which emphasize their constitutive and interactive nature and thereby permit them to be related to the idea of dialectic" (1984, p. 75). Certainly, within these forms of dialectical thinking is the capacity to compare and contrast one's position with another, the past with the present, or one's former state with how one is at the present time.

(4) *Meta-formal schemata:* These are the schemata of contradiction and synthesis, of the tensions of the dialectic. Here are increasing capacities to step back from self in movements of what Kegan calls the "subject/object" transition. Here are the meta-positions of therapeutic closure as one is able to accept ambiguity and conflict in a growing acceptance of the human fact of being in process throughout life. Within these forms are the concepts of the "revolving door," with acceptance that problems are not neatly fixed and tied once and for all.

With these concepts in mind I bring you to my primary sources—my clients—whose words, thoughts, feelings, and wisdoms give examples of what our therapeutic work is all about. In their words are the tellings of pain and anger, the tellings of insight and change, the tellings of emerging hope and love, the tellings of meaning and intention. It is with profound respect that I share their words.

Although I have named these next three chapters "Beginnings," "In Process," and "Revolving Door," all the chapters contain a mix of that material. In the three steps forward, two steps back, there will be many mini-illustrations of all the stages. But what I have tried to do is track the forward motions of my clients as they have moved through progressive sequences of constructive meaning-making.

. . . when things are most contradictory, absurd, difficult, and
frustrating, then, *just then*, life really makes sense; as a mechanism
provoking and almost forcing us to develop toward higher levels of
Being.

—E. F. Schumacher, 1977, p. 135

[The therapist] must recognize that he cannot go faster than his
patient, and that by calling attention to painful topics too
insistently he will arouse his patient's fear and earn his anger or
deep resentment. Finally, he must never forget that, plausible—
even convincing—though his own surmises may seem to him,
compared to the patient he is ill-placed to know the facts.

— John Bowlby, 1977, p. 426

CHAPTER 8

Beginnings

As THERAPISTS WE have all heard opening lines such as these:

"I feel like I can't act like the self I want to act like."
"I'm feeling 'freaked out'—age 30, wanting a divorce, not having an identity, no
longer able to hang onto the label of wife and I am not a mother. I want to grow and
to have grown."
"I hate my mother and father for lying to me. By telling untruths, they lied. Why did
they lie to me?"
"Everything has been going wrong. Somewhere I believe I've failed."
"Thrashing, wondering, talking, verbalizing, suffering, always in pain, constantly
unhappy, nothing can make me happy. I don't like myself very much. Life is almost
worthless."

Words of presenting concern, these only begin to touch the accompanying
feelings of fear, anxiety, depression, confusion, disappointment which are so
often present when people walk through the therapy door. Certainly, in these
words are the times and places in the dark wood, with all the elements of the
crisis experience pressuring the client to rework old meanings in the service
of the new.

132

This chapter is about these presenting concerns, about individual decisions to pay the money required, to reveal oneself, and to commit to one or two hours of therapy a week. Here are the stories of crisis, of the necessary turning points, the crucial moments when development must move one way or another—the time, in Erikson's words, for "marshalling resources of growth, recovery, and further differentiation" (1968, p. 16).

Here, too, are the experiences of a few of my clients who have had the motivation and courage to face their concerns directly and honestly, clients who have graciously granted me permission to tell their stories. You've met some of them in previous chapters and will be meeting them more particularly in this and the next two chapters, as I identify and consider the "beginnings, middles, and endings" of therapy.

Because I offer a mix of therapeutic specializations—marital and career as well as short-term and long-term psychotherapy—I deal with a broad diversity of clients. Most of my people represent a cross section of ordinary folks (in the best sense of those terms) who are basically intact but facing overwhelming shifts in personal life. They bring a great variety of presenting problems ranging from the concrete crisis event to the more abstract realms of personal meaning-making. I like it that way. But in my mix of specialties I am less likely to work with adolescents and children. This choice results from training, personal style, and temperament, as well as my strong focus on adult development. I am comfortable with this and feel it is one of the ways I am able to remain congruent with clients and self.

I do not advertise myself as either a "short-term" or "long-term" therapist or analyst, and I am not in the business of telling my clients in what manner and for how long they should continue therapy. In fact, my style of allowing them to name their purposes and name their pacing gives them lots of freedom to engage me in a wide variety of ways. But, interestingly, this very allowing is what often brings them to commit to the more in-depth processes of developmental therapy. I have seen this happen with clients who are quite uncertain to begin with—an uncertainty revealed in erratic appointments and in a questioning of my approaches. These same clients may leave therapy only to return at a later date to more fully invest in the process.

Others, who have completed well-rounded sequences of therapy, rejoin the process according to developmental need and readiness. This occurred with all the clients whose stories I tell in this chapter and the next two. With Sonny, Jennifer and Jana, the follow-up was brief and specific; with Vicky and Nick the follow-up therapies continued for longer periods of time. This flexibility of movement in and out of therapy demonstrates what I call "the revolving door."

What has impressed me in all the follow-up therapies is that we moved together so naturally from earlier work. Though the new presenting problems could be severe, the way these clients viewed the problems was not the same as when they first came to therapy. Returning with awarenesses maintained and perspectives developed, these individuals were able to move very quickly to the heart of new issues and new transformations of thought and feeling. Thus, I am more than ever convinced of the value of the developmental perspective in therapy.

I find that the majority of my clients complete their therapy within six months to one year. Thus, the long-term clients whose stories I detail below represent the exception rather than the rule. I use their stories, however, because the work they did gives a rich picture of the transformational processes of developmental meaning-making—processes which illustrate the shifts in cognitive construction which can move people from one way of shaping personal reality to another.

What this says, therefore, is that many clients do not invest in the long-term therapy required to make major developmental change. This is not to fault their process. They have their needs and their readiness which combine to shape the therapy. This can be important work but it may not be the same as long-term developmental work which brings about the cognitive, affective transformations which I have been describing.

As I write this I return to Basseches' concern that the word development has taken on a "public relations" aspect in which it loses the depth of its meaning. It is being applied in every way, at every angle, in the writings of today, and it is fashionable to attach it to the titles of almost anything— from workshops and therapies to management styles. Thus, as I describe developmental change I emphasize that not all people who come for therapy go through *development*. People "may either shift commitments in response to life-crises, or make new commitments which transform and reintegrate old commitments" (Basseches, 1984, p. 327). It is the latter transformation which is made possible through dialectical thinking and which "characterizes a developmental response to a life-crisis, as opposed to a merely adaptive response" (Basseches, 1984, p. 327).

What I have found important to acknowledge in my naming of contrasts is that the short-term work is frequently preparatory for the in-depth therapy which can occur at a later time. I also have to acknowledge that I don't always *know* what results have occurred during even the briefest of therapies. Letters years later, or a phone call, or a comment from a friend who has been referred to me, let me know that I can be fooled into too easily judging the kinds of personal change which either have or have not taken place during therapy.

What I discover time and time again is that I can't predict in advance how therapy will go. Clients have a way of surprising both me and themselves. For example, I have had people ask for *long-term* therapy, expecting that it would be a difficult, arduous, and extended experience. They rather settle back in their chairs for the long winter experience. And then it doesn't happen! Because they are relatively intact and have a perspective on themselves and their relationships, and because their self-search has already been initiated in many ways, the energy for therapy dwindles rather soon and they find it appropriate to go on their way. This interruption of a planned long-term therapy could not be predicted in advance.

At other times what appears to be a long-term case turns into a brief sequence, as the person makes a cognitive developmental leap which transforms the character of the problem. With people like this the developmental transformation may already be underway: in private work such as reading and journal writing; in therapy with another therapist; in the natural therapeutic work of relationship and support from others; or in exposure to ideas and challenges within a new learning experience. Thus, when clients present themselves they may be coming at the high points of other developmental processes. With these people who are primed for change it may take only a few sessions to create the cognitive leap which takes them into new ways of knowing and being in their world. Obviously, these are exciting clients, and it is gratifying to be present at their birth as a kind of celebrant of process.

In my career work I find examples of these leaps with clients who have done much research, much thinking, much agonizing in trying to determine who they are and what they want to do with their life. I am the catalyst, the feedback person, the brainstormer, who provides some spark to catalyze the process. In personal work this may not happen as often. People usually come when they are in pain and severely confused, and their problems may not be as defined as career problems (although career problems can also be extremely diffused and intangible). Therefore, it is less common to have this transformational event within the early weeks of general psychotherapy.

One kind of short-term client is the one who wants a "quick fix." Often this person wants a way to return to the safety of previous patterns of living and previous conceptions of the world. He or she may be frightened by the changes which are occurring but not willing to step into the unknown. To face feelings and attitudes about self is difficult. She or he is not yet ready to face the disruption of personal structures which accompanies major change. Frequently this lack of readiness reflects a fear of emotion, of craziness, of anything that smacks of being "out of control."

I think our culture and our profession unwittingly foster these fears, often avoiding emotional depth and expression in hurrying for the gratification of the "quick fix." We have often internalized a therapeutic language rife with the metaphors of the mind as somehow fragile and easily destroyed. Lakoff and Johnson (1980, p. 28) have assembled a few of these under the category of the "mind as a brittle object:"

Her ego is very *fragile*.
You have to *handle him with care* since his wife's death.
He *broke* under cross-examination.
She is *easily crushed*.
The experience *shattered* him.
I'm *going to pieces*.
His mind *snapped*.

In cognitive developmental therapy I find it important to bring these metaphors to attention in reframing feelings as barometers of meaning, as indicators of change, and as the natural energy and fuel for the change process. Cognitive work with semantics is helpful: "I can't handle it" becomes "I don't want to handle it." "I'm cracking up" becomes "I am desperately afraid of what is happening to me." "My ego is fragile" becomes "I am in a time when I don't feel very good about myself." All these statements can lead the client to understand and reshape the metaphors, thus coming to recognition of personal capacities for the hard work of change. With such reframings the client is put more in charge of choices rather than at the mercy of mysterious, uncontrollable forces. Again, this is not to deny the intensity of feeling or to negate the usefulness of medications when appropriate; it simply says, "Let's look at these emotional manifestations in a new way, a way which respects your strength to handle deep, profound emotions without 'falling apart.'"

Short-term therapy may well be the appropriate process for those whose readiness for change has not been established and for those whose inner sense of pacing and personal integrity says, "This is not yet right for me." But here are sticky questions for the therapist. We cannot be totally accepting of the old way or totally unwilling to contradict. But we can be sensitive, open to the possibilities for change, and cognizant of all that is implied in a major cognitive reconstruction.

Short-term therapy is often the choice of individuals caught in rigid patterns of thinking. In fact, in my experience these individuals seldom come for therapy except for career purposes or for marital counseling. And then, they are the ones who are often very difficult to help. They are people who illustrate the folk metaphors of being "closed minded," "hard-headed," "opinionated." They are black/white thinkers, closed to new ideas and caught in generalizations about what is right and wrong. They may be authoritarian personalities (as described by Gordon Allport and Jane Loevinger) caught in dualistic levels of cognitive develpment.

How to help these people? I'm not sure. If they are not moved by emotional distress or by an increasing awareness that life is not simple, they will probably not stay in therapy very long and they may well continue to point to individuals and circumstances outside of themselves for the sources of their problems. Unfortunately, these people are more likely to be the ones to blame the therapist if the problems are not resolved neatly and tidily once and for all.

Long-term Therapy

In contrast to those who choose the shorter therapies, some people engage in the serious, painful work of genuine developmental change. Though these shifts can happen quickly, as in the stories of Sonny and

Jennifer which I tell below, they more generally occur with long-term clients. These people usually arrive in a time of intense crisis, establish the relationship with the therapist, do their crisis work, and engage in the kinds of creative thinking and exploration which enable them to reconceptualize their lives historically in a more sophisticated and dialectical way. Usually this is not easy or quick work; the change must come from within the client as he or she becomes better able to incorporate and reconcile the past with the present and as personal realities are reshaped into new forms.

James Fowler (Fowler & Keen, 1979, p. 138) states the case for this hard therapeutic work:

If you follow me in my contention that stages which I describe are structural wholes, or ways of constructing a world, then you can imagine what it is like to move from one stage to another. In rare instances it is a smooth, gradual, incremental transformation. In most cases stage transition comes with pain. It involves enduring the dissolution of your world. You must be able to endure the falling apart of that which is held together . . . decentering and disintegration . . . are necessary for a new creation.

I honor this hard work as I tell the following stories. What will become evident as I proceed is that there are no discrete lines of demarcation between the "beginnings, middles and endings" of therapy — the establishment, data gathering, patterning, closing stages — but the use of the taxonomy enables me to point to movements through shifting vocabulary, shifting technique, shifting thought, shifting reality, and shifting meaning, which gain increasing definition and objectivity as the client continues through therapy. And even as I do this I emphasize that this is not a neat and tidy process. As each of us must know who has worked in this field, therapy is unpredictable, occasionally messy, dramatic, and surprising. "A mysterious process," I tell my clients, "with a life of its own."

I introduce you now to some selected clients. They share some common variables: (1) They all closed therapy and returned at a later time; (2) they illustrated developmental change; (3) they all experienced their crises as painful and difficult; (4) they developed a strong relationship with me; (5) they worked hard on their therapy; and (6) they were able to cognitively and emotionally move outside their problems and their relationships with new ability to interrupt negative cycles of thought, behavior and emotion. In their stories they also give us a kind of ideal of the creative, active, motivated client who is developmentally ready for the kinds of therapeutic work which they accomplished. But that is not to say that we always had easy times. Within therapy we had blocks, dilemmas, frustrating plateaus, "contractions" into old systems of thought, affect, and behavior, and angers and misunderstandings. Thus, as I said above, these therapies were not always tidy or neatly resolved.

I introduce Jennifer, Sonny, Vicky, Jana, and Nick with brief statements of the presenting problem, a description of our initial sharing, and a summary of early data gathering. What you will not find in these mini-portraits are diagnostic labels from *DSM-III*. My bias is to avoid these, keeping my mind clear to question and speculate in as free a manner as possible. That does not mean that my mind doesn't occasionally track a diagnosis, but does imply that I work hard to avoid stigma in thinking of my clients — particularly in the early stages of therapy. It also means that I prefer the language of description to the language of evaluation (a bias named for me in the writings of John Stewart in his *Bridges not Walls*).

JENNIFER

Jennifer, an attractive young woman in her twenties, brought a number of concerns: "terrible problems" at work, getting used to marriage, some sexual difficulties, feelings of resentment, tension, a fear of being out of control, and a struggle with intimacy. (This struggle with intimacy took on extra significance as I learned that our first session was taking place just four days away from her first wedding anniversary.) I found Jennifer open and ready to work, making it relatively easy to establish rapport. My initial impression was of someone who was highly intelligent, capable, and faintly critical if results did not meet her expectations. These early impressions were borne out in later sessions.

As I gathered Jennifer's "facts," she described herself as an only child, "never deprived," "pretty shy," a person who finds it difficult to talk to people. "I tend to be moody and have swings." She felt her motivation in her relationships with others was guilt as she described a belief that "achievement is to please others" and her struggle to "be the best or the most that I can do." It was not surprising, therefore, when she reported that her parents held high expectations and taught perfectionist ideals.

An early focus, therefore, was her strong achievement motivation which was closely linked to her feelings of self-worth — "I feel embarrassed and ashamed if I am just a failure." Related beliefs were stated strongly: "I need a tangible product to be worthwhile," for example, and "I enjoy responsibility, I crave it." She said she was looking for the rewards of a feeling of competence, of being "master of destiny," in control, safe, and with a sense of self-worth and self-esteem. (Already her semantic leitmotifs were evident, suggesting future exploration into "achievement," "self-worth," and "guilt.")

When I asked, "Are you a feeling person?" she replied, "I'd rather not." But tears welled in her eyes, making it evident that Jennifer had many feelings which were beginning to surface, but that it was difficult to share them and to talk about them. An illustration of this struggle with feelings comes from my rough notes from a therapy session three weeks into our therapy:

Very frightening to express feelings. At a moment of rejection also rejected feelings as "childish." Get angry at self for being "weak and emotional" if frustrated. If need somebody that is being weak, will lose a sense of self.

Age 12 was a time of discoveries and philosophical discussion. Father frequently asking "Who are you? — a little game — unsettled me."

In high school planned clothing as a theatrical wardrobe. Lived a role.

Learned early what pleased parents. "An obligation to myself to do the best." "Forced" to take on responsibility.

"Should" be objective.

From this discussion I began to understand her struggle with closeness, with the exposure of self, with her "shoulds" and "oughts." These are themes you will find developed in the next chapter.

SONNY

In severe turmoil and very unhappy, Sonny came for divorce counseling after having been separated from his wife for four weeks. Married six years, these people had no children. Thus, the presenting problem was fairly clear; it seemed like a straightforward case of grief management, self-definition in order to plan for the future, and some conjoint work with his wife to come to greater understanding of what had gone wrong in the marriage.

But this therapy of slightly less than four months also exposed deeper areas of concern in Sonny's relationships to his parents, his brothers, and himself. Very quickly, therefore, we moved into a psychotherapy which made him face himself and his relationships with others. In this he identified personality qualities which had had a negative impact on his marriage: "I pick on people, tease, and she doesn't like it." In painful self-examination he asked, "Was I listening? . . . There was an issue of feelings. My wife says we have different temperaments; she says I am set in choices, rigid, hard to deal with, that I have a temper, am volatile, am driven." Although Sonny acknowledged these tendencies in himself, he also argued that he was changing and had changed. Sadly he commented, "I would have liked her to be happier married to me."

In further data gathering I used the Myers-Briggs test and found Sonny an extraverted, highly intuitive, thinking, perceptive person. Here also was indication of his creativity (which has already been shown in the pieces I quoted in Chapter 1), *and* his strong thinking style, which sometimes led him to be insensitive to the feelings of others. This became a topic for our conjoint marital therapy and for later work when he brought his new woman friend (and later wife) for premarital counseling.

Although Sonny's therapy was relatively brief, I consider his story an illustration of developmental therapy because he moved rapidly to combine and integrate old perceptions and feelings into new perspectives on himself and his abilities to love. He thus seemed to be moving from an earlier stage of self-absorption to increasing capacity to share intimacy and to understand the feelings and reactions of another.

In his words:

I need to love. I cannot be whole without that sharing, without that caring and concern and respnsibility that go with love. I cannot love just anyone. So, losing my wife threatened my basis for existence. Here was someone who meant more to me than anyone else. Yet I knew deep down that she did not love me. So we learned that love must be a mutual process.

VICKY

A complex, powerful, delightful personality, Vicky presented many challenges for me as a therapist. And in the process I presented many for her as we acted out many varying forms of confirmation, continuity, and contradiction. I learned much from her and, as her letter in Chapter 5 demonstrates, I am continuing to learn from her.

Vicky first came to see me when she was in her early twenties, married for one year, and working both as an artist and a model. She came on the recommendation of her mother, who had somehow picked me from the ranks of an agency staff as the person who could help her daughter. Whatever the reasons for her choice, mother's intuitions were accurate and Vicky and I had rapport almost from the beginning.

But those early hours of therapy were difficult because she was seriously depressed and troubled. In her words, "I'm here to clear up unknown problems." A first step, therefore, was to establish some sort of bridge for communication. Because she so often sat silent, looking out the window, I encouraged her to bring her art work. Together we would sit on the floor studying her drawings and searching for new ways to talk about their meaning and intent. It was obvious from these samples of her work that Vicky was a serious and talented artist who used her creative abilities to express herself. And in our early hours together it also became obvious that here was a young woman who was engaged in a very profound struggle with her interpretations of self, her art, her marriage, and her family.

In establishing our work together, I encouraged Vicky to verbalize her life experience and her feelings in whatever way she could. In this she was sometimes very passive, other times excited and animated as she shared her story. She described the awfulness of her parent's divorce when she was seven, and her helplessness and grief when a year later she was adopted by her stepfather and given his name. She also told the story of grandmother whose personal disturbances had created dilemmas for the entire family, and which planted seeds of fear in Vicky when she remembered her own fleeting moments of disturbance. Though they were brief, transient episodes when she seemed detached from current reality, they stood in her memory as fearsome events which continued to haunt her. In this it was all too easy for her to incorporate the family image as the sick one.

Vicky's appearance changed from session to session as she alternately arrived as a little girl with pigtails who came cuddling her puppy; as a relatively traditional looking young woman, neatly groomed and conservatively dressed; as the high fashion model with sophisticated hairstyle and makeup (and she was a modeling teacher at the time); and, occasionally, in avant garde clothing which touched on the fashionably bizarre. These alternating styles were there throughout therapy, seemingly a reflection of her differing versions of self — what we later identified as the young woman struggling to separate from family and tradition, the young woman conforming to the standards handed to her, and the young woman who had arrived at an integration of the two. Within her differing styles were also the alternating currents of impulsivity and passivity, of rebellion and acquiescence, of intensity and withdrawal, of euphoria and depression.

As she worked with me Vicky reached for support and a reality check on the perceptions of her family. She came from a highly intelligent, verbally articulate family, where members liked to discuss ideas and issues, and where family gatherings often became intense arenas for debate. On one particular night everyone was debating a current psychological self-help bestseller. Mom and Vicky's husband liked the book but Vicky did not. She felt the family siding against her point of view until a cousin joined her in fighting to be heard. As Vicky reported this she became very animated: "She understood what I was saying — it was the first time anyone was on my side." (At this stage Vicky tended to speak in black/white terms.)

The struggle for acknowledgment, for understanding, for being heard, was evident from the beginning. In her words, "I feel like I have to win if I am right. If I feel I can't win I either cry or hit somebody." These alternative ways of responding to disagreement later became a major theme of therapy as we examined patterns of reaction. And some of the strongest moments of our dialogue occurred as I struggled for a way into her logic system. What she had a hard time learning was that she, too, made others feel unheard and unacknowledged.

Vicky observed, "I listen to the tone of voice rather than the words," and, "When I'm trying to get across my ideas I feel threatened." (Again, this was a major theme which helped to explain the intensity of her emotional response when confronted or contradicted. This emotional intensity made it difficult to raise alternative points of view in the early stages of therapy, but, as her later letter so poignantly illustrated, this was one of the very important parts of her psychological, emotional growth.)

Married for one year when she first came to me, Vicky talked not only about herself and her family, but about this new relationship, which was difficult for her in many ways. Facing a crisis of identity and self-definition, Vicky was also facing crises of trust, intimacy and love. Therefore, I invited her husband to join us for conjoint therapy. That was helpful as I saw these two very attractive, creative young people share a mutual struggle for emancipation from their families, from more superficial models of relationship, and from the negative communication patterns which had already crept into their marriage. Alternately, Vicky and her husband presented their concerns and their dilemmas, their differing hopes and fears, their career goals, their needs for particular kinds of love and affection from the other. This therapy became quite dramatic at times, as they explored options for an open marriage, and as they debated the merits and the timing for having a child.

Vicky's struggle to work through her developmental processes later brought her into a genuine adolescent crisis, as she acted out her needs for dating, sexual exploration, and for identity clarification in the contexts of relationship. The marriage simply couldn't handle the strain and blew up in a sequence of sexual impulse and abusive response. These endings were the impetus for some important therapeutic work in Vicky's final sessions with me.

During the initial data gathering I gave Vicky the Sixteen Personality Factor test, the MMPI, the Wechsler Adult Intelligence Scale, and the Strong-Campbell Interest Inventory. I had two purposes: (1) to gain some measure of her tendencies towards depression, emotional lability, and impulsivity (although the tests confirmed these tendencies they did not show alarming exaggeration of the patterns); and (2) to begin the self-discovery process that could lead Vicky to an increasing sense of her own strengths, uniqueness and value vis-à-vis a powerful family which had a tendency to interrupt her search for self. Certainly, what was shown was her strong artistic interest and her intelligence.

In the eyes of the family Vicky was the deviant one, the bizarre one. Because I could see her glimmers of change, and because I believed she was growing, I often had to argue this growth with her mother who challenged me when she didn't see evidence of change. And we did have some heated discussions. This highlighted a perceptual problem which Charles Hampden-Turner (1981, p. 132) has poignantly identified: "Once a child is out of phase, its needs are seen as illegitimate and the odds against the deviant multiply."

Vicky was out of phase with her developmental process, for her behaviors were those of the impulsive child—the child who reacts with emotional intensity, who acts out, and whose logic includes the little man who pulls the strings—who operates in a complex system of God, the Board of People, the script writers, the guardian angels, and the little man who intervenes on behalf of people like Vicky. I did not challenge this model for I saw these mental images joined by a very sensible logic which seemed to help Vicky, the little girl, to survive the confusions of her parents' divorce, the remarriage of her mother, and the loss of her name. The need to use this configuration of reality faded away as our therapy developed.

As Vicky's initial therapy deepened and developed, I continued both individual and marital therapy as well as some family work which included mother, stepfather, and sister. But the focus and therapeutic emphasis remained in-depth, individual psychotherapy. We will return to Vicky in the next chapter when we join her in the middle processes of therapy.

JANA

Jana came to me when she was 34 years old, single, never married, and working as a bank teller in a nearby suburban community. Her purpose in coming to therapy was: "Learning to be stronger, happier with myself, more sure of myself." Her crisis was that of self-image and self-esteem, of relationship with the important people in her life—mother and stepfather, boss, and a close male friend—and of the major transitions of deciding to leave aspects of a child/adolescent world to be an adult in ways she had rejected before.

Bright, alert, and verbal, Jana had had previous therapy and so entered into the therapeutic process quite easily. Feeling very lonely and in a lot of pain, she described a tight family system where "barbed messages and mean things" were not uncommon; it was a matriarchal family system where great aunts influenced family style and dynamics of power. Struggling with this she stated, "I feel very close to Mom—too close," and "I feel angry at my mother and stepfather but I feel very guilty about that."

Jana manifested a mannerism in which she ducked her head and pulled in her chin when she felt challenged or unsure. "I want to cringe away and get smaller and smaller." The child in a powerful family, Jana found this a way to avoid attention but it also represented a pulling away from personal autonomy and control. Not only did she cringe behaviorally, but psychologically and emotionally as well. And, as her transcript in the next chapter will show, this was very much tied to an inner image of "the turtle" which she had taken as a symbol of who and what she was. To begin to break this deep-seated habit, I asked her to practice cringing in front of the mirror—to paradoxically perform her "symptom." I also worked with her on relaxation exercises so that she would be more aware of the tension in her jaw and neck when she started to cringe. The further work in this was in the cognitive domain, as we talked of her beliefs and attitudes about Jana, the person who cringed. As we talked she asked:

JANA What goes in its place? If I don't cringe what is there?
THERAPIST You know you're sharp, don't you? You ask wonderful questions.
So, when you give up the cringe, you're asking what on earth will you do

in replacing it? What would you like to put in place of it? I think here is where you can begin to create a choice.

JANA Well, it seems like the more positive response may be if someone is sitting there and I am cringing . . . it seems like some kind of different response . . . but I don't know . . . that's a whole change in attitude and gesture and everything . . .

THERAPIST And thinking . . .

Which raised, of course, the whole problem of the total *construction* of a way of acting, responding, thinking — of the attitudes, the gestures "and everything."

Jana's talent and ability as a musician — singing, playing violin and guitar, and dancing — provided wonderful resources for our work together. In fact, I encouraged her to start singing lessons as a way of reducing tension in her neck, developing confidence, and widening her circle of friends and activity. She acted on this and I continued to use her music as a stimulus for her growing sense of identity.

In our beginnings together Jana began to describe other roles: She was the listener who was taught not to interrupt. She was the child who fended off emotional blows — "I came through childhood trying to keep out of the way. I never knew." At the same time she was trying to keep out of the way, however, there were little bursts of the imagination and adventure which were very much a part of this creative, gifted child. (Return again to her "early recollections" in Chapter 7, p. 115, which illustrate her struggle with differentness.)

Jana is one of the clients who effectively used writing as a therapeutic tool. To use this skill to good advantage I taught her to dialogue with her feelings. Here are my instructions from the original transcript:

Okay. This is what I would do if I were feeling a jumble of feelings. I would sit down with my tablet in a quiet place. I would probably breathe quietly, bringing my body down — feeling in tune with my body. And then I'd write down just what I was feeling: "I am feeling a jumble of feelings," or "I am confused by my feelings." And then I might do a question and answer dialogue on paper. Question: "What feelings are you feeling right now?" Answer: "Well, I'm not very sure, but let's see if I can figure them out." And, then, question again: "Why don't you start by telling me what your body is doing?" And you might say, "Well, right now I have a lump in my throat," or "I'm tense in my chest," or "I feel fidgety." Often that's a beginning for getting in touch with the feelings. You just keep writing "question and answer" like this, not pondering it, just letting it flow. It's amazing what can come out on paper. I have had a lot of breakthroughs by writing. And when I feel depressed I'll say, "I'm really feeling down. What's going on?" And then I dialogue with my depression. I might say, "Depression? What are you trying to tell me?"

How well Jana learned this technique is illustrated by the written materials in the next chapter.

NICK

Nick had worked with me in career development several years before, but when he came to me for this new beginning it was our first intensive focus on depth psychotherapy. My intake writeup stated:

Nick is currently working on relationships with his boss as well as patterns of relationship with others. His reactions to his father (an alcoholic) and his mother have fed his response patterns. My tentative hypothesis is that his "hypervigilance" plus fears of confrontation and avoidance of the anger of others have combined to create cognitive blocking in his processing of information.

Nick's 16 PF test shows a pattern of reserve, shyness, suspiciousness, and a tendency to carry guilt. In addition there is a lack of focus of energy and control at the same time he carries considerable tension and anxiety. His abstraction level (8) shows that he does have the ability to use his mind. The challenge is to free his anxiety and "mental garbage" (Nick's metaphor).

During this intake interview Nick talked of his "attic clogged with stuff" — an apt metaphor for his cognitive blocking. He does psychic checking. He described his boss as like a father "who is still keeping his son under his finger." This relationship is stirring up a great deal of emotion, probably triggering old patterns with his parents.

In describing history, Nick reported his father's dramatic personality changes when he was drunk — changes which were "really scary — I was afraid he would hurt me." And, yes, father did hurt mother by breaking her tailbone. "There was yelling and screaming and his eyes were violent. My heart was beating, I was hiding, running from him, not knowing what was going to happen." These experiences of fear and unpredictable reactions no doubt influenced his avoidance patterns. "I was trained to be a good child . . . didn't know how to deal with anger . . . somewhat passive . . . low self-confidence and great self-doubt."

In talking about fears we did a free association exercise which brought these responses: "unknowing, unpredictable, not knowing what to expect" — all threats to Nick's sense of security and equilibrium. And when he named specific fears from childhood he named "fear for life, for protection, Dad, his violence. With my father we couldn't ask questions or raise a doubt if I wanted him to define more. He gets angry . . . makes me shake . . . nervous about doing the right thing . . mixed messages. I didn't know if he were serious or kidding so I didn't know how to take it." (I saw much important work to be done in developing verbal and emotional congruence so that Nick knew what he thought and felt at a given moment.)

Nick described his loneliness in a family that "doesn't know me." He has been a nonconformist in a number of ways — going to a different college from the rest of his brothers, being "different." "I am the rebellious one but it doesn't show. I have different kinds of friends."

During this initial work with Nick I described his tendencies to move his eyes from side to side in a rapid scanning of his environment. This seemed to come from his constant response to external stimuli and his ceaseless hyper-vigilance. As we talked about possible sources for this he also shared his difficulty in expressing "heavier, deeper feelings. I feel badly about the friend with whom I share the burden." The naming of these tendencies seemed helpful as Nick gradually began to assess his behaviors and his responses. Although my early questionings often made him uncomfortable (and because he did not talk a great deal my questions were not always natural and spontaneous), these questions stimulated his thinking, bringing him increasingly to his own questioning.

Nick had a hard time remembering the content of our sessions and asked for help in establishing themes from session to session. To help this process I began transcribing my notes for him. Although at times this was painful for him, the notes provided an anchor for his thinking and remembering, and helped him to do some cognitive work between sessions. He also began to gather articles and to make graphic models of his ideas because his mind very naturally created visual images. Tapping this visual aptitude proved very important in bringing increasing understanding and a loosening of his cognitive blocking.

Nick's story is a complex one, as the next chapters will reveal. As is so typical of many children of alcoholics, he was very confused about his own identity, had few anchors of personal interests and hopes, and did not have a solid base for comparing and contrasting his own thoughts, feelings, and behaviors — in other words, he didn't have many models of people who shared healthy intimacy and had a strong sense of themselves. Thus, one challenge was to keep teaching, modeling, stimulating, so that his knowl-edge of life would grow from that of the inhibited, frightened, constricted child to that of the more cognitively, emotionally sophisticated adult. In spite of the deep pain of loneliness, rejection, and differentness which fre-quently kept him close to tears, he continued to search and to grow as he struggled to know himself.

Here you have had introductions to those courageous clients who were willing to probe themselves in the service of growth and development. In these introductions I have pointed to presenting problems, the establishment of their relationship with me, and the developing body of information which began to collect during the early stages of therapy. In the next chapter these people begin to name and make sense of themselves.

Sensations do not come to us, sorted and labeled, as if we were visitors in a vast, but ordered, museum. Each of us, instead, is his own curator. We learn to look with a selective eye, to classify, to assign significance.

—John Stewart, 1982, p. 49

Indeed, we must recognize that the very process of describing the human experience changes that experience and that the more such a description approaches completeness, the more it is apt to be a basis for change in the very experience it describes. This is probably true for all science, but it is particularly true for the sciences that deal with man. Man's awareness about himself acts as a constantly "recycling" agency to produce changes in himself.

—James Bugental, 1967, p. 7

CHAPTER 9

In Process

IN THEIR WISDOM clients sometimes name their processes of growth in a manner quite astonishing. Jana was one of those people. To introduce this chapter, then, I use her words to provide a sample of the sorting and patterning of thought, feeling and experience which characterizes much of the hard work in the middle stages of therapy. (This was Jana's writing so all the "therapist" questions and responses were her own as she imitated my style and reaction.)

THERAPIST Jana, I'd like to hear about what you've learned from our sessions so far.

JANA Well, it's sort of hard to sort out. But one thing I've learned is, when something is hard to sort out, sit down and write about it. It takes a lot of time, but it helps to unravel everything from the tangled ball it gets into in my brain, to be able to write it down and then look at it on paper. The very act of having to get it from my brain onto paper helps me clarify things because I have to slow down and put general thoughts and feelings that are whirling around into actual words. And I try to put them into some coherent order, which is far superior to the willy-nilly way they are sailing around in my brain.

THERAPIST So what else can you sort out?

JANA It was very helpful and revealing to me to go back over my childhood the way we did. I thought I had thought it through, but somehow the way we did it, it was different. I saw things in a different perspective. I saw a little child that had a lot of gumption and love of life and joy in living, who was also very intelligent, sensitive, and confident. And I saw that she, although no doubt with the best of intentions, was not allowed to or supported in or encouraged to blossom in her own way. She was not very well understood. She was suppressed. She was sheltered. She was criticized. She was loved, true, but not in a way that could help her to grow into autonomous adulthood. *And she grew up to not be grown up at all.* (Emphasis mine)

THERAPIST What else was different to you after we talked about your childhood?

JANA Well, I felt that I *grieved* over my dad's death and dealt with that for the first time. I got to talk out my feelings, my thoughts, my awful feelings and thoughts. And I got to cry. And it seemed to put things into perspective somehow. The sadness and thoughts and feelings are still there, but they have been sorted through now. I've looked at them, acknowledged them, and filed them away in a drawer that I'm no longer afraid to open. I know what's there now, and it feels more settled and assimilated.

THERAPIST What else did you find different?

JANA Maybe this goes into the first part of my answer, but I found that you stood up for me. All this time, when I've been blaming myself for everything, and putting myself down . . . and then you come along and say: "I see a gutsy girl who wasn't listened to." And suddenly I'm not the one who was wrong all along. Suddenly, my judgment is not so faulty. Suddenly, my feelings are right-on instead of off-base. Suddenly, with you believing in me, I can believe in myself. And that frees me to say: "If it wasn't all me that was wrong, then what was going on?" And I can look around at the different figures in my life and see them as human beings with things going on of their own. And I can begin to see how the whole picture fits together, with me getting caught somewhere in the family knot.

THERAPIST I'm really glad to hear all these things. Is there anything else that you handle differently now?

JANA Yes. I was just thinking about my superstitions. There were those superstitious thoughts that I would get that would drive me up the wall. I'd think: "If I go through this door, something awful will happen to me." . . . But you helped me to see that those thoughts were an effort on my part, however ineffectual it might be, to control the unknown future.

"If I wait to eat this apple 'til I get to a certain street, then I'll have a good time at the dance tonight." It was an attempt to make certain the un-makc-certain-able. Once you helped me to recognize that, I could, when those thoughts came around, realize there was no point in trying to control the uncontrollable. Once again, you helped me take that extra step that would get me out of a no-exit circle. You showed me where the exit door is, and I can use it now.

THERAPIST How about the spunky Jana?

JANA I'm discovering that there's a lot more fire and fun in me than I'd realized. I've been so busy being quiet and retiring that I haven't realized that I'm more vital and bouncy and fun-loving than that.

THERAPIST Sounds like you're on the right track to me.

But let us move back from such positive summary statements into the actual processes of therapy where frustration and confusion are more the rule, and where the client is still *in* the problem and has not yet learned to stand *outside* that problem. Certainly, Jana's summary did not come easily. Here, for example, is an earlier session when we were struggling with her superstitious thinking, when she was still unwilling to acknowledge many of the good parts of herself because her thoughts and feelings were so tightly tangled with guilt and fear. Challenging her reluctance to name the positive, I asked her to make a "glad list," hoping the whimsical title would help her to get past some of her fear. She completed the task with a mixture of emotions which we discussed in the following session:

JANA I made a glad list.

THERAPIST All right, what was that like for you?

JANA Actually, it brought a lot of anxiety listing things I'm glad about, but it was also fun to see how many things I'm glad about.

THERAPIST (After reading the list and returning it to Jana) I like that. As you reread that what does it feel like?

JANA Some of them, like this one, "I'm happy to have people who like me and care about me," . . . I still don't think I believe that. Intellectually I think they do, but I'm not real convinced.

THERAPIST Are you hard to convince?

JANA I guess so. It feels not a 100%, sort of like I'm mouthing words more than believing them.

THERAPIST Well, you might be practicing a new feeling or belief that you didn't have before . . .

JANA Phew! [*a reaction which Jana has when she feels something deeply or sees something in a new way*]

THERAPIST The anxiety, though, is interesting. Do you know? Do you have any feeling about that?

JANA Well, I figure it goes back to what we talked about, just my feeling that

I don't deserve to be happy and that anytime I am happy that it will be taken away from me. [a guiding belief]

THERAPIST And also it might be a little dangerous, then, to acknowledge having this?

JANA Right. If you're miserable and something bad happens, you don't fall as far.

THERAPIST It's almost like tempting the gods if you say "I'm happy"?

JANA Hm-mmm. It was real hard for me to write this.

THERAPIST What? To put it out on paper in black and white?

JANA Right. I just sort of gritted my teeth and went for it. Isn't that something!

THERAPIST So there's a fear somewhere down deep? What's the fear?

JANA That if I get happy it will just be taken away; that I'll be punished for being happy.

THERAPIST So there's a theme of punishment?

About this same time in therapy Jana was writing about her angers:

What am I angry about? I don't want to delve into this because it will stir up a lot of things that I have safely tamped down under a closed lid. I am angry about lots and lots of things. Things from long ago . . .

She named her anger at self:

I am angry at myself for being so fearful. I am angry at myself for getting in my own way. I am angry at myself for not being more giving, loving, unselfish. I am angry at myself for being so tied up with must's, ought's, and shouldn't's that I can hardly breathe. I am angry at myself for not trusting in myself and having confidence in myself. (But how could I, given all the above "I'm angry at myselfs?")

And her anger towards her family and her upbringing:

I'm really angry at the upbringing I had. I grew up with so much criticism, so many cruel remarks, so much "protection," so much "shaping," so much being told what to do, what to eat, when to speak, what to say, etc., so much negativism, so much fear, so much loneliness. I guess it's a wonder I'm not worse off than I am. *And now I feel really sad . . .*

Naming all these angers was frightening because to share anger was to challenge "the Gods"; to be angry was "a big 'no-no'." But she said she was helped in this *because I told her* to do these writing assignments. In her words, "When you say 'write out your angers and don't be afraid of the Gods,' I can do that because *you* said it. It came from an authority figure, *not* from *me*."

To sort the progress of our therapy Jana taped each of our sessions. And after careful listening she would sometimes write a set of questions to share in our next therapy session. For example:

Do you think I laugh too much? Inappropriately? I hear myself laughing a lot on the tape. Some of it might be a nervous laugh. Or even another way of apologizing for myself. But some of it *is* genuine laughter. [*Jana sorting her responses, gaining a perspective*]

At one place in the tape we speak almost together, describing qualities of mine. You refer to them as "an interesting blend." I refer to them as "a weird mixture." It occurs to me what a much nicer feeling about myself is conveyed by "interesting blend" rather than "weird mixture." You were painting "fun-loving Jana" while I was giving another rendition of "Yucky Jana" it seems to me. [*"Yucky Jana" was a title she gave to herself during a previous session.*]

You were talking about the effects of being forgiven. "It makes us more flexible. We don't pay as much attention to our mistakes. It doesn't assume an importance." I, on the other hand, was taught to worry over my mistakes instead of letting them go by. I found myself, at this part of the tape, striding around the room exclaiming: "That's true! That's true!"

When I listen to the tape I feel embarrassed about crying. When I'm there, talking, I'm very involved with it and go with the emotion. It disturbed me that I felt embarrassed, because I felt I shouldn't feel embarrassed. Complicated, huh?

The material above is only a small sample from the rich resource of material which developed during Jana's time with me. She illustrates a highly motivated, active client, who fully engaged in her therapy. She illustrates further the cognitive processes of naming, reframing, and reordering. Through these processes she gradually defused tendencies to cringe, to hide her angers, to worry, to turn pleasure into negatives, to feel guilty when she didn't respond to mother in certain ways. She also reframed her self-identity in quite dramatic ways as she responded to therapeutic reinforcement of the positive, intriguing, creative aspects of herself. In the next chapter I will review her closure and her later return for brief therapy.

JENNIFER

Jennifer was another client whose therapeutic work included considerable writing; she was also a client who rapidly made cognitive/affective leaps from one version of the world to another. As she painfully faced herself, her verbal and written dialogues were with feelings, with terror, with ambition, with intimacy and its accompanying dependency. Here is a sample as she assembles a definition, "facts," and assumptions in her consideration of dependency:

Definition of Dependency

Requirement that some vital factor needed for survival be supplied by someone or something outside oneself.

Facts

(1) Dependency removes power from the dependent person and gives it to the object of dependence.
(2) Some dependencies are unavoidable. All people are dependent upon sources of

food, air, water and shelter for physical survival. Some dependencies are avoidable—dependency on drugs, flattery, parents, charity, love.

(3) Dependency makes one vulnerable. Withdrawal of the object of dependence can cause death, pain, unhappiness.

(4) Vulnerability to dependencies can be minimized by recognizing the general dependency and avoiding specific psychological dependencies. Because we are a monetary society people need money obtained through employment to survive. You don't *need* one particular job in one particular company. Flexibiity is important to overcoming the vulnerability of being dependent.

Assumptions

(1) All dependencies that can be avoided should be avoided in order to reduce vulnerability and maintain personal power.

(2) Happiness and security derive from within. Any happiness derived from without is a dangerous dependency and is doomed.

And further:

Writing this I have felt very defensive—just waiting for you to poke holes in it. I can hear the suggestion that it is not necessary to avoid *all* dependency. My response to that suggestion is identical to what I'd think and feel if my M.D. told me I shouldn't be afraid of using heroin.

Up to this point I have been able to look at some of the gut beliefs we've uncovered in an objective way. I can see that tangible results shouldn't be a criterion for the worth of *everything*. Perhaps I still believe it, but I recognize it as a faulty belief and I believe I can change it. But this is different. I feel—and I can't afford to be different. I know I'm right (no matter what the facts indicate) and I can't risk too much investigation. It would be heresy. And the fact I could feel this way about *anything* really troubles me.

During this time of struggling with the logic of dependency vis-à-vis the feelings of dependency Jennifer followed my instructions to write a "dialogue with terror":

Terrified of becoming dependent, being unable to exert my will, submerged, suppressed. At the time of marriage I felt as though I were going crazy. I wanted to run away, never see any of these people again. I felt as though I was being swallowed whole. I got through it by thinking to myself that it was possible to get divorced if things became too horrible.

I can't seem to get beyond the idea that dependency is a terrifying state and that emotional involvement causes a self- destructive dependency. I'm not sure why this is true; rather, why I believe it to be true [*Nice bit of distancing*]

In these writings Jennifer kept going deeper into feelings and logics which had influenced her fear. She began to wonder at her capacity to love as she stated, "I don't ever want to be 'in love'—it strikes me as a self-destructive state—something to be avoided. Perhaps I fear expressing love because it might cause me to 'fall in love'—something to avoid at all costs. My final question and an earnest one—is my distinction a real distinction or purely semantical? This bothers me a great deal."

Jennifer was at last facing herself as she named the question which she had never dared to express before—the question, she wrote, that made her frightened of seeing a therapist. "I feel that I am not a giving or a warm person. I would like to be if only it weren't so frightening." With these statements and questions Jennifer moved into new domains of sharing as she lost some of her fear of emotion and self-disclosure. Finally, she began to work through her deepest concerns about her capacities to love and to give.

Jennifer, like Jana, was special in the power of her writing. But this was not the only technique which was used in her therapy. We spent time with feelings, with history, with current behaviors in work and marriage, with her relationship with her husband, and with her dreams. Again, because of her intelligence and effort, our work progressed very rapidly and it was not long until Jennifer had worked through to new perspectives on herself. And she seemed also to have rearranged and reformed many of her attitudes, feelings and beliefs. In describing some of her adolescent behaviors, for example, Jennifer was able to identify her former strategies for handling shyness and for protecting herself against embarrassment and criticism. As she described these she was also able to compare and contrast present behaviors and attitudes with the past.

JENNIFER I would always love to play devil's advocate, always loved to take the unpopular side, because usually I was good enough to just wipe out the opposition. It's kind of perverse, in a way. I love to get people totally confused about me . . . .

THERAPIST Was there a value in keeping them confused about you?

JENNIFER Mostly what I got out of it at the time was a sense of being different.

THERAPIST But was it also a protection? Did it keep them away?

JENNIFER Yeah. Because some of the things that I would do and say certainly did keep them away. I used to love to get into religious arguments—that's terrible—'cause this was at the time I was reading everything. . . . I think I scared a lot of people with some of the things I would say. It took me a long time really to grow out of that, liking to tromp people.

THERAPIST Kind of got a pleasure out of it?

JENNIFER Yeah, I think I really did. I felt superior, that I'm smart and you're stupid and I'm going to give it to you.

THERAPIST So what elements of that are in you now, do you think? [*An attempt to reconcile the past with the present in a comparing and contrasting of patterns.*]

JENNIFER I think I still secretly believe that I'm right and that the rest of the world is wrong in a lot of ways.

THERAPIST Do you think you ever fail to take into consideration another point of view? [*A pointing to the dialectic.*]

JENNIFER I think that I looked at all these attitudes about religion and politics and whatever, and think I felt that the attitude that the person held *was* the person, and that I couldn't allow for different people having different needs, and that what's appropriate for one person is not appropriate for another, that some people have different needs.

THERAPIST You say you couldn't allow it or you could?

JENNIFER I couldn't, at that time. I think when I finally grew out of doing this to people, making them uncomfortable in the things that I would say about religion and politics, social issues, it finally came with the realization that the beliefs that were harmless to other people could very well be very helpful and necessary to them; that I didn't have to accept it or believe it, but I had to respect insofar as it had importance to them, and it's not doing anybody else any harm. I think that was my criterion . . .

THERAPIST So I hear a broadening viewpoint. Is that right?

JENNIFER More tolerant. I think it boils down to also being not so easily threatened myself. I don't need to be so constantly on the offensive because I don't feel so defensive.

THERAPIST What a lovely relief from a constant monitoring, giving up that monitoring of the environment or of the input.

JENNIFER I still do it, but it's not, it's more like a hobby.

This last bit of humor certainly gave an indication that Jennifer could take a meta-position towards herself, a position which is illustrated even more fully in our next chapter.

As a client is more able to take a meta-position on personal problems, thoughts, feelings, and history, other signs give hope for genuine development. With questions widening in their range, some clients move from a kind of reductionist attitude to widening awareness which enables them to frame more abstract, overarching questions about the universals of life experience. For others, the movement will be from tendencies to always be "in their heads" — in vague abstraction or fantasy — to new ability to question and reframe the here-and-now, to savor sensory experience, and to translate the abstract conceptions into practical steps for change. To develop both types of thinking and behavior is to learn important repertoires for change.

As therapy develops the way I question changes. Becoming more involved with my client — and I think this cannot help but happen as the intensity of therapy increases — I may become more confrontive as my client becomes more comfortable with pointed, probing questions. Certainly, as I begin to join the bits and pieces of my client's experience, my questions will be more directly framed out of emerging, interconnected hypotheses. And, for that very reason, I must guard against the stereotyping of my client or against too easily losing creative openness to the other directions therapy can take. To shake my therapy at this time I often introduce a greater variety of technique — imaging, Gestalt work, relaxation techniques, assigned reading, behavioral tasks—all to interrupt the sequence a bit and to introduce novelty and a fresh approach to what is being asked and experienced.

The therapist-client relationship shifts as clients join the therapist as more equal partners in the process; as they get to know more; as they more fully name their own assumptions and patterns of thought and emotion. To bring clients to this position of mutual trust the therapist must believe in them and help them to name themselves in ways that will enhance self-esteem and new abilities to make meaningful choices. Here the kinds of feedback we offer are significant. In the words of Andras Angyal: "To react to the healthy aspect of the patient rather than his neurosis is one of the many ways available to the therapist for stimulating and furthering the patient's growth without falling into didacticism" (1965, p. 194).

Now I do use the didactic approach with my clients, because I believe I am a teacher as well as a supporter and facilitator. But I use this cautiously, for I don't want therapy to turn into a time of *my* interpretations and *my* pronouncements. As a teacher/therapist, therefore, my task is to affirm my client's health and capacity for growth, to recognize, acknowledge, and affirm while contributing new ideas and new pieces of information which can feed back into new cognitive connections of thought and idea.

The therapist's *belief* in the client is essential here. If you think back to Vicky's words in Chapter 5, you will remember that she considered my belief the significant element in her emerging sense of wholeness and health. Jana says something similar in this summary of her process:

Insecurity. Low self-esteem. Depression. But underneath it all there was still the spark of gumption and love of life and joy in living and confidence in self that she was born with. *And she felt like crying when you discovered that she was still there, imprisoned and denied, but waiting hopefully, all the same, to show herself again.*

. . . Suddenly, with you believing in me, I can believe in myself. And that frees me to say: "If it wasn't all me that was wrong, then what was going on?" And I can look around at the different figures in my life and see them as human beings with things going on of their own. And I can begin to see how the whole picture fits together, with me getting caught somewhere in the family knot.

In working with client philosophies, ideals, and models I seek to maintain an attitude of respect for the integrity of these constructions. Indeed, most client philosophies, ideals and models do make sense: They fit together, they are quite well reasoned, and they really aren't "irrational." But they may not be functional, or they may not fit changes in the client's life. Furthermore, these cognitive constructions may not be open to the feedback/feedforward systems of new experience and insight as they keep cycling back on themselves. Not adaptive in the service of growth, they are closed systems of thinking—cognitive circularities which clients have not yet learned to interrupt—circularities such as Jana's superstitious thinking or

Jennifer's hook into achievement motivations which kept her separate from genuine care and intimacy. Nick, too, has his circularities, as we see below.

NICK

Nick was struggling with issues of hope and trust. Indeed, he was caught in a *basic mistrust* — of the intentions of others, of his own version of reality and reaction, of his emotions and his mind, and of his capacity to grow into a mature adulthood. At the earliest stages of his life his father's alcoholism and the fear it engendered had created severe avoidance patterns, which brought cognitive/affective blocking and a withdrawal from intimacy and social outreach. Much of our early work, therefore, had to do with the building of trust: of himself, of others, and of the possibilities for change. Much of our work was also about thinking and feeling as I questioned him, taught him, and challenged him to share thoughts and feelings. And, in a third major effort, we worked together to identify and name him in order to create a more anchored integration of personal identity. In developmental terms, therefore, we were simultaneously tackling many levels of Erikson's "psychosocial tasks," of Kegan's stages of differentiation and embeddedness, and Basseches' schemata for dialectical thinking. What made much of this easier was that Nick and I already had a mutual trust because of my previous consultations with him in career development. We also started with the encouragement and support of his previous therapist, whom we both knew and liked.

Sharing my written transcripts with Nick proved very helpful in bridging the themes of one session to another. That seemed particularly important to him in making sense of what was happening and helping him to remember what we had said. Little by little the cognitive interconnections did begin to occur; little by little he was able to identify and share his feelings; and little by little, he began to translate some of the more abstract learnings of therapy into new behaviors and explorations outside the therapy room. For example:

NICK I started doing things for myself. Yesterday I was kind of listing them — things I'm doing for myself. I had started smoking about a month and a half ago again — and so I said "enough of that." So I haven't smoked since Saturday. I feel good about that.

THERAPIST That's a positive . . .

NICK I'm taking more vitamins, doing more exercise, and I've been getting sleep . . . so just things like that — things that I can do for myself.

THERAPIST These are really self-care, then, aren't they?

NICK Yeah . . .

THERAPIST Still doing the TM? [*And I had previously encouraged him in this to slow down his hyperactivity.*]

NICK I'm doing that on a regular basis now. Before it was kind of hard. . . . I'm finding time to get that second time in each day. So I feel good about that. I still . . . everything I do, I think, I want it accomplished, I want it done now. I don't want to have to wait. *It should come natural.* [*And here we have moved into a very important new theme which demonstrates a circularity of thinking.*]

THERAPIST To come natural?

NICK It should happen for me that way.

THERAPIST You believe that?

NICK Right now talking to you I can see I don't believe that.

THERAPIST But that's sort of a natural thought? That it should come natural? [*I didn't want him to adapt too quickly to the disbelief I had just signaled to him. I wanted to really go into this belief to explore its ramifications.*]

NICK That it should come natural. . . . I shouldn't have to exert much effort or . . .

THERAPIST Why is that?

NICK Because I think I'm a natural—or I should be a natural.

THERAPIST You should be a natural?

NICK Everything I do I should be able to accomplish when I put my mind to it. . . . I should be able to do it with little effort. [*Another belief.*]

Our session continued as this theme brought us into his perfectionistic tendencies, which caused him to abandon projects or relationships if they weren't going just right. This thinking fed back, then, into the discussion of "being natural."

THERAPIST There's part of you that says, "If it doesn't come easy I give it up." And I'm also kind of hearing a should—it *should* be easier, it *should* be . . .

NICK Kind of natural . . .

THERAPIST I shouldn't have to exert . . .

NICK Uh, huh . . .

THERAPIST Now, let's play with that a little bit. [*A sign that I'm starting to interrupt the thought, to confront a bit, to challenge Nick to think in slightly different ways.*] If you *shouldn't* have to exert . . . but what if you *do* have to exert?

NICK Then I feel as if there's something wrong with me.

THERAPIST Really? If you have to exert?

NICK I shouldn't . . . as far as making friends . . . it shouldn't be such an effort to make friends . . .

THERAPIST I see. So it's in the area of friendship that you might think this way?

NICK I can . . . comparatively . . . yeah . . .

THERAPIST Uh huh. Any other areas where you *should* be able to do it, and you shouldn't have to exert?

NICK Well . . . I think about school. But I had to work pretty hard . . .

Here we have started to touch Nick's feelings of being stupid. That led to a discussion of how he covered up his so-called "stupidity" by being silent. "I think a lot of times I've felt if I kept silent and didn't open my mouth that would hide a lot of it." Other ideas developed as we freewheeled a bit, but Nick brought me back to center by asking, "Where is this leading us?" *Good question!* I scrambled for a moment as I tracked my notes and then offered the following summation and interpretation.

THERAPIST Well, I think all we're saying is that some habits of thinking and responding got reinforced early on. So let's back up to your initial idea, which I think is the real important one: "I shouldn't have to exert; it should be natural; and there is something wrong with me if I have to exert — like in friendships or in learning." Questions of friendship and questions of learning? Those seem to be two big areas, don't they, Nick?

NICK Those things should come . . . they should come natural for a person, it seems. [*And here Nick has modified his original statement somewhat. I then move in to challenge.*]

THERAPIST But what if they don't?

NICK They don't for me.

THERAPIST But what if they don't for a lot of people?

NICK Well . . . (laughter) . . . I guess you just keep working on them.

Our discussion had now tapped Nick's humor, which I felt was very positive in indicating that Nick could step outside the problem a little bit. We continued our discussion in this vein, although we moved into other related topics. These belief systems would recur from time to time and I would continue to probe, question, and challenge in the manner above. At no time did I tell Nick that he was being "irrational" or that he *should* give up his beliefs.

In another session we contrasted early reactions to his father with his current dynamics with a woman friend. Here is illustration of Nick's growing ability to connect thoughts, feelings and new behaviors.

THERAPIST You've told me your father sent very mixed messages, depending on his state of alcohol.

NICK That's true.

THERAPIST Did you check him out pretty carefully? To see what kind of response you were going to get?

NICK I think I chose the words pretty carefully. Yes, I think I did.

THERAPIST Depending on what signals he was sending?

NICK With some people I have to be very careful. [*Here he starts to generalize to other people and other contexts.*]

THERAPIST Because if you're not careful what might happen?

NICK I may get that negative response.

* * * * *

THERAPIST What we're trying to do is "unhide" your messages. Kind of like a little circle here. If you look for acceptance from other people and you don't get it you're not going to be very open. Right? You're going to hide the messages. Now if you get a clear message of acceptance then maybe you'll share the messages.

NICK Is that a good way to look at it? [*A perking of interest — a shift in posture and voice.*]

THERAPIST I don't think it's real good. What do you think? Let me ask you that question.

NICK My way is to depend on those messages.

THERAPIST Yeah, I think you're right.

NICK And I call that rejection. Rejection is the lack of positive response. If that directs me, those responses make my decisions for me.

THERAPIST I like how you're saying it. "Those responses make my decisions for me" — I think that's the most significant thing you're saying. You've let those response make your decisions for you?

NICK Uh huh . . .

THERAPIST And that's the part you're kind of challenging here?

NICK Do I need those? Do I need to do that?

THERAPIST What do you say?

NICK I've been attempting this last week to kind of observe how I respond to those messages. It's kind of interesting to see what you get. I think yesterday . . . this last week Jean has been really kind of distant. Not someone I could relate to this week . . .

THERAPIST Just not so available?

NICK And she was kind of bitchy and, uh, before I would allow her to show that part of her because I would tend to back away. Not knowing how to react to that kind of response. And this week I didn't care.

THERAPIST How did that feel?

NICK It was really testing . . . it forced our friendship.

THERAPIST Why? Because you were being different in that way?

NICK She was trying to question my motives. I didn't back away . . . I pursued it.

THERAPIST You just weren't willing to let it ride?

NICK Just because you're in a really foul mood doesn't mean that I'll put off wanting to know until you get in a better mood.

THERAPIST OK. That's great! So you made a decision "I don't need to base everything I do on how she's reacting . . . " What happened?

NICK Last night she gave me a call and asked if I would like to meet her for a glass of wine. I told her I was ready to go home and she kept pursuing it. So we went out and had some wine and some clams and had a good time. It was kind of neat.

THERAPIST So what happened to the friendship?
NICK We still have it.
THERAPIST And maybe it's in better shape than it was before?
NICK Could be . . .

So much of Nick's hard work involved recognizing and breaking loose
from the powerful negative learnings of childhood: from the fending off of
the unexpected angers and harsh behaviors of an alcoholic father; from his
tendencies to hide behind adaptability and quietness so others wouldn't
know him; from his fearful avoidance of the explorations of friendships;
and from his hyperactive vigilance in the scanning of his environment. In
this, part of the challenge was to express and allow the emotions which were
held so tightly from his own view and from the view of others. Thus, this
therapeutic sequence showed an important breakthrough in his willingness
to risk.

Another big part of his work, moreover, was about the naming of self —
about the sorting of the pieces so he could make sense of himself. Without
this translation of the parts into some sort of identity whole, he would not
be able to create a meaning of self. Here is a sequence where we struggled
with this. Nick was pondering a dilemma of self: He saw how he needed and
wanted friendships but also was recognizing his need for aloneness.

NICK This week I was doing very well with people, to the point I needed to
    be away from people.
THERAPIST Uh huh . . .
NICK That seemed strange. So many times you need people around and you
    don't choose to be alone. And this time I chose to be alone.
THERAPIST Is that a little puzzling to you?
NICK It isn't because I think I am tired — I just need to have some time to
    myself.
THERAPIST The idea of balance is kind of important here, isn't it? It sounds
    like you are a person who needs this time alone.
NICK I love to be alone — it's not that I'm really alone. It's just that I want to
    be at home to do some of the things I want to do and I want to put things
    in their place.
THERAPIST Order them a little bit?
NICK Order them! It's just great — I really enjoy it.
THERAPIST Great. Kind of order it then. [*And I had an insight which
    brought me to the next question.*] Umm . . . do you feel you are kind of
    in a new stage here? The way you are? [*I was sensing new abilities to
    compare and contrast intimacy with aloneness without fear and a des-
    perate return to the search for connection.*]
NICK I feel different — I think I'm becoming more aware of myself. Ummm.
    I think some of the pieces are starting to come together — they're starting
    to make sense. Umm . . . a while back I came to you and I wanted you

to tell me how I related to people—what is Nick like—because I can't observe that. I'm starting to realize . . . very slowly, very slowly . . .

THERAPIST But you've got some glimmers . . . I'm hearing pictures . . . you're getting some pictures of what Nick is like. It's not all such a great fog in there . . . [*Rereading Nick's transcript, I regret the direction I took here. I should have explored his words, "I'm starting to realize . . . very slowly, very slowly." I assumed too much in my reflection and questioning.*]

NICK It's becoming a little clearer . . .

THERAPIST You say they're beginning to come together a little bit? Do you ever imagine the portrait of Nick? [*Nick had done some study of art and was a very visual person.*] If you were going to paint a portrait of Nick how would you paint it? [*A question to take him outside himself.*]

NICK In pieces . . .

THERAPIST In pieces?

NICK Yeah.

THERAPIST Do you know what the pieces are? Can you name the pieces?

NICK (Big sigh) Uh . . . I haven't . . . [*And then a discouraged silence because Nick blocked almost completely when I asked him to describe himself. That's why I shifted to an affirmation of what he had said.*]

THERAPIST That's a wonderful image, though. At least you see the pieces don't you? Are they just floating pieces or are they coming together?

NICK Floating. I think they are all over.

THERAPIST All over?

NICK All over. And now they are starting to come together—you can see there is an image—it's really like there are all these little pieces and there are blocks and they are starting to come together. I'm starting to see an image. They're not touching yet.

THERAPIST Getting close?

NICK Getting close but they are not touching.

THERAPIST It would be interesting if we could name those pieces.

NICK [*Nick's response was unintelligible—usually a sign that he was blocked or was feeling strong emotions.*]

THERAPIST Oh, you mean there are that many . . . many pieces? But it's encouraging to know there are pieces.

NICK Uh huh . . . that's a good way to look at it.

To help Nick describe himself I started summarizing some of the things I knew about Nick: his work, his colleagues, his friends, his customers, his feelings, his father and mother, his brothers. "You've got your home and your book that you put your words into (kind of journal which he had recently started). These are nice pieces. Do these sound genuine? Do they sound like you?" With a soft "uh huh" Nick responded. This closed our session but what I had hoped to affirm and to plant as seeds of thought were

both the *process* of self-search and connection and the *contents* of personal
identity which needed to be shaped in creating the continuity of self-naming
and self-understanding. Though this session was very encouraging, Nick
faced much discouragement in working through his feelings and perspectives. Thus, with Nick I probably did more teaching and modeling than I
typically do, and I was continually working to plant ideas of hope and
direction.

VICKY

To sort Vicky's material is difficult because she was changing in many
differing ways within the contexts of many differing relationships. But three
themes seemed to order her search—those of trust, love, and personal identity and meaning. And further subdivisions of this material can be ordered
around her relationships with friends, with her first and second husbands,
with her family, and with her art. Certainly, too, there was her relationship
with me where I offered confirmation, continuity, and differing forms of
confrontation so that her circularities of thought and emotion could take
some new turns.

My work with Vicky bridged not only her developmental changes but
mine as well. In our first sequence of two years I was still feeling my way in
certain areas of therapy, but when she returned after a three-year absence I
was reframing my cases through the theoretical lenses of cognitive developmental theory. I think that made a great difference in my approaches to her.
I began to understand her dilemmas in new ways and to point her in new
directions. I talked more of love and care and I used more dialectical thinking in my questioning and responding. More in tune with the philosophy
and language of Martin Buber's dialogue, I had also become more skilled as
I maintained a very active therapeutic role. As this was happening I also
became quite close to her. This closeness was both a strength and a vulnerability: a strength in the kinds of work we could accomplish; a vulnerability if
I backed away from confrontation or allowed my biases and feelings to
interfere. Certainly, this closeness did not work for our later therapy with
her new husband.

Vicky's early dialogues had much to do with the feelings and outlooks of
the child. Then she moved through a kind of delayed adolescence as she
experimented with relationships and new images of self. Finally, in our later
work she moved into the identity and intimacy issues of young adulthood as
she framed questions which may be tracked through Erikson's sequencing of
hope, will, competence, fidelity, and love. Consider these themes as we
continue. I quote here from our early sessions:

"I have to talk myself out of feeling guilty, as though everything is my fault."
"I want to be okay in the eyes of the other person but I also want them to

understand I'm different." (Here she described two differing Vicky's: the conforming Vicky who is law-abiding, not drinking, and with morals. And then the one who is insecure, not sure of herself, wants attention and love, wants to act, gets upset. This struggle is between the dumb, the smart; the wrong, the right; the no, the yes; the heard, the not heard.)

"I do what I am told but don't get any rewards. I can't please anybody. I'm not heard." [*These words were expressed in a conjoint session where her husband also felt unheard and rejected. They both expressed tears and anger.*]

"If I love someone they will leave." "Is it worth it to learn to trust my own judgment? To care for myself? What is my reward? What is my evidence?"

Vicky and her husband alternated conjoint therapy with Vicky's individual therapy and occasionally I worked with her husband alone. After a year and half of this work Vicky and her husband seemed to have worked through some serious questions of extramarital exploration, of growing intimacy and love, and of new steps in their respective careers. Both of them seemed more able to take the other's position, to be sensitive, to listen—in other words, they both seemed to have grown in many different ways. Based on all those signs it appeared appropriate to replace weekly therapy sessions with intermittent follow-up. Certainly, this was what they wanted and I agreed.

But then, after about three months, the marriage blew up in an explosion of impulse and violence and Vicky left her husband. (To protect the privacy of all who were involved in this blowup I have chosen not to share that story here.) Both Vicky and her husband did some therapeutic work together but it appeared that the marriage was beyond repair. Thus, very quickly the therapy returned to focused individual work with Vicky, with some family members, and, for a few sessions, with a new friend who became her live-in partner for a new time of exploration. Our therapy closed when Vicky left the city for another state. But from time to time I would hear from her as she shared the progress of her life.

Three years later I received a call from Vicky saying she was back in the area, terribly depressed and needed to see me. With that we moved into an entire new dynamic of therapy as we worked with intimacy questions, the challenges of her art, and continuing explorations of personal identity. But this was a different Vicky from the young woman who had first come to see me several years before. Now she could protest, speak up, and declare herself with intensity and increasing clarity of expression.

Vicky's statements during this time gave evidence of her widening outlook as she moved from being in her problems to having the problems:

"Body used to be just a vehicle—a thing. Therefore, sex was almost purely physical. Now I see the big difference between making love and sex. This difference emerged before I was able to articulate it."

"I make a theory; test it from different angles; then I revise."

"People stuck me in boxes. I want to be sure the box has an open end."

"It's hard to feel worthwhile without a man's love."

"I feel ashamed that I would confine and manipulate someone." (Feelings about her former husband).

"If all I know is what I am in then I don't have the information or the belief." [*Ponder that in the light of the contrasts between being in a problem and having a problem.*]

"If we are strong enough in ourselves then we can start hearing other people."

[In speaking of her former marriage] "We were both insecure so we couldn't hear other people."

During this time Vicky was writing in her journal as well as doing written assignments for me. One of these was a free association around the word "reaction"—an exercise which helped her understand the contrasts between positive and negative reaction between that which was helpful to growth and that which was not (Figure 3).

She continued to compare and contrast herself with her family and its images and ideologies: "The person inside logically shouldn't be allowed according to the rules with which I was brought up. I have been a 'pseudo-Vicky' in opposition to my family." She felt that as she was in touch with her genuine qualities she could release some of her reactions to other. In this she felt she was not "sharing the 'outrageous part' so much," that she was becoming more creative rather than more reactive. "I react negatively to challenge on one level—challenge to my rightness, my freedom to be me. . . . Intuitively I have to remove myself from people who aren't helpful to me." And, "I'm building myself doing self-oriented things. I'm saying 'no' in contrast to being in a 'selfless' place. It's where I want to be—like an

FIGURE 3 Vicky's free association around "reaction" (her notes)

opening, elevating—going to a place without constraints—totally free—unconditional love."

This was a time of many mood shifts for Vicky, as she went from euphoric highs to serious, depressive lows. These shifts made relationships with her mother and sister very difficult and raised concerns for all of us. Once again we did a free association exercise during one of our sessions giving some new insight into this intense time of identity struggle (Figure 4). My intuition was that Vicky was going through a very difficult but impor-

FIGURE 4 Vicky's free association around "identity" and her former husband (taken directly from case notes)

tant developmental transition as she moved from dependency on others and from impulsive reaction to a greater trust of herself and an increasing ability to hold another person's point of view.

What was heightening some of Vicky's emotional intensity was a new and very important relationship, which was to lead very quickly into her second marriage. This emerging friendship raised many new questions about intimacy, love, and sensuality. Within these thematic contexts Vicky named the contrasts between the processes of searching and exploring: "Search is desperate—negatively motivated. Exploration is a choice, not a compulsion. It's more relaxed and curious as well as positively motivated." On this optimistic note Vicky felt that she was in a transition stage "redirecting energy from sexual searching to sexual sharing as two persons explore together. I'm influenced by my environment. My new friend is supportive and nonchallenging. I don't have to set him up to get my own way. I don't have to pretend or offer little white lies or selective truth. Before I had to prove my case over and over again. Now I don't have to come up with excuses and reasons for what I am doing. It is no longer required; it is now a choice."

With Vicky's "gathering of choice" within the contexts of a new and important relationship our therapy rapidly came to a close. When we attempted marital therapy it did not work well because I was too close to Vicky to maintain the dispassionate perspective which was necessary. During our final sessions, however, we had some dramatic "fits and spurts" as Vicky moved back and forth between her differing ways of constructing the world. But her reversals were brief and important because they were occurring within her developmental transition into a new kind of adulthood. I will cite some of this final material in the next chapter.

. . . the developmental approach truly captures the spirit of
Freud's suggestion in *Analysis Terminable and Interminable* of the
consideration of ongoing treatment at different stages of life. The
door to the consulting room is never finally closed; rather,
termination is more flexible and open-ended.

—Colarusso and Nemiroff, 1981, p. 240

A growth spurt. They have occurred before. A new awareness and
new appreciation of what life is about. Small successes supplanting
earlier disasters. I am confronted with a devastating event that
tears my heart and soul apart. But somewhere within me there is
something. I feel as if I am touched; that out of all that happens I
seem to regain and go on. I feel as if I am blessed with boundless
enthusiasm and optimism and that in the long run I really do
enjoy life. I know more now than I did before. But it is not
something easy to articulate. So we prepare to leave the nest. A
valuable friend gained but what now? Having taken so much; now
a desire to give. How do I say goodbye when I do not want to
leave? Knowing that I must part. Very, very melancholy.

—Sonny

CHAPTER 10

The Revolving Door

THIS CHAPTER IS about moments of therapeutic closure. It is about the
"revolving door" of the therapy room which swings open and shut according
to client need. It is about the view from the side of the mountain when client
and therapist sit together to describe and unite perspectives from the past
within the perspectives of the moment.

To take a postion on the side of the mountain is to see therapeutic closure
in some very particular ways. As I have suggested previously, therapy is
never really *finished*. If we consider therapy a *process* of learning, of working-through, of a "making of meaning" within evolving, shifting contexts of
time and place, we probably could never say "this is it." But the relationship
with a therapist does come to an end — appropriately so — as the client moves
into his or her own world. And if we have done our work properly, the client
leaves with an increasing sense of his or her own story, of the motions and
processes of living, and of new abilities to interrupt the cyclings of thought
and feeling which may limit the individual capacity for flexible, adaptive
response in the service of developmental growth.

The stories which I now tell, then, are not *finished*. Rather, there is the latent energy of continuing change as these clients name and examine their processes, as they step back to tell a personal story, or to share their excitements, or to come to terms with that which they will never change. And you will soon discover that these so-called "terminations" or "closures" may be far from closed. These people leave knowing there will always be work to be done, habits to be altered, forms of thinking to be reframed. My purpose, of course, is to teach them the skills and lead them to the understandings which will enable them to do this work on their own — I don't want them to continue to *need* me as therapist. But they find some assurance in knowing that I will be available for a "tune-up" if needed.

In addition to those clients who have arrived at new forms of "evolutionary truce" within altered forms of thinking, feeling and doing, there are those clients whose closures are less satisfactory, less complete, less clear. Of these latter types, some leave because of a job change or a move to another city. Or they may leave because they need more focused work with another therapist. They may be tired of the entire therapeutic experience and want to give it a try on their own. And certainly, on occasion, they may feel I have failed them or frustrated them in their efforts to grow. Those times, few though they may be, always give me great pause and force me to reevaluate my approaches to therapy. Whatever the cause for what I consider premature closure, I work to let my clients' wisdom be my guide. If I try to hang on or tell them what's best for them (as if I could know that!), I inevitably lose them. But if I keep loose and open to client reaction and suggestion, they feel less awkward about returning for follow-up. And if they have internalized a developmental perspective which allows them to be "in process" for the rest of their lives, they won't feel like failures if later circumstances bring new crises in their lives.

In emerging closure it is essential that the client continue to name and shape new understandings to bring about the orderings which make new sense of things. As I have stated before, to ignore this vital step is to lose the power of cognitive/affective meaning-making. Thus, the final sessions of therapy become a time for clients to name their changes, to share their feelings, and to describe as fully as possible what the time of closure means to them. Dialogue intensifies and then begins to taper off as we share final questions:

- What are you feeling as we close this therapy?
- How do you *think* you are different?
- What is unfinished for you? What remains to be resolved?
- What possible problems will arise in the future? How will you deal with them?

And so do we question, discuss, compare and contrast, as we reinforce and anchor the emotional and cognitive learnings of therapy. We also consider and reflect on shifts in habits, behavior, and outlook in the active, practical experiences of love, play, and work. By doing all this we are continuing the naming, narrative processes which are so vital in making sense of oneself and one's world—in other words, the processes which comprise the constructive, constitutive workings of meaning-making.

In the namings of these experiences and in their tellings of change lie the meanings within therapeutic closure. Here can be found new organizing principles, new world constructions, new comparisons and contrasts which unite within ever-enlarging categorizations of life. Here, too, are the shiftings of the dynamics of feeling as the individual releases the grip of constricting fear and emotional circularity through new abilities to face, name, and defuse negative feeling. At the same time the individual is becoming more in touch with the rich variations of personal emotional life. To describe these transitions and achievements I turn to my clients, whose closing words, thoughts, feelings, and wisdoms give examples of what constructive meaning-making is about.

VICKY

With Vicky there was never one neat ending where we sat down together and named all the good steps which had been taken. (Her letter in Chapter 5 is probably the most complete statement of closure.) Rather, there were many mini-closures as we tied one idea or one new behavior into a new form of thinking, feeling or doing.

Thus, to neatly summarize Vicky's material is impossible. Indeed, within the constraints of space her material is much too complex for simplistic statement. But as her therapeutic work progressed during her second two-year sequence, several themes gained ascendance, illustrating her increasing capacity to name and rework her descriptors of self as well as her interactions with her art and her intimate friends and family. These themes included:

- the capacity to validate herself;
- insight into negative tendencies to protest so loudly that others felt shut out;
- realizations of the contrasts between physical sex and the love and care which goes beyond the purely physical.
- increasing ability to think about her own thinking and feeling.

In our dialogues and in her writing these themes kept recurring as Vicky continued to make sense of herself.

Self-validation. This passage from Vicky's diary names and validates her differences in thought, emotion, and verbal style:

This book on Georgia O'Keeffe is just incredible. I keep finding validation of myself through its pages. Not necessarily in the specific ways of O'Keeffe, but in the rights of belief. Things like "She thought in color the way others thought in words." Change the word "color" to emotion/feeling and I see myself.

It struck me as odd that people think in words. They're so limited. Images and emotion are so much more specific and therefore varied. In that thought I was able to more clearly understand my pausing in answering questions. I have had complaints to me by others (including family) that I must not be there if it takes me so long to answer a simple question. The accusation is not fair. Nor is it true. I had thought that the problem might be in my having to remember specific instances to connect with. More closely is this—*it's as if there are two languages being spoken. The pause comes from my taking the words and translating them into emotions. Answering the question and trying to put it into words again* (emphasis mine). "Emotions" referring to this images-reactions way in which I think. I suppose you think it strange that I should be so excited and validated by this new-found fact. What can I say? It's lonely out here . . . . [*Every time I read this passage I am moved by the poignancy of Vicky's insight and by her statement of loneliness. I am also moved to consider the ease with which we as therapists might label someone irrational or disturbed when really what the problem is is that there are two languages.*]

Art and Conviction. These words came from Vicky's "Subject/Object Interview," which I was using in a rather loose form to probe some of our movements in therapy. She is exploring questions of "conviction" and "strong stand":

VICKY It seems like I am constantly losing my convictions—or what I believe in or . . . I have to keep going to look for it—it's not there constantly.

THERAPIST So there's almost a fear of loss—rather than the actual loss? [*I missed the essence of what she was saying but she nicely corrected me in the next statement.*]

VICKY I don't think there's a fear of loss. I think at this point I've finally convinced myself that it can never be lost—it's my choice to either make it go away for good, or . . . you know, it's more of a connecting with it again. I know it's always there, but the bridge gets lost.

THERAPIST And why does the bridge get lost?

VICKY The best thing I can give is it's the emotions. I get distracted. It's interesting . . . we went to a festival this weekend, and at this bed and breakfast place where we stayed this guy who runs this place and is also an artist had discovered in himself that it takes him about three days after people have been around—it takes three days of soli tude to find himself with no distractions—to be able to get into the mood, so to speak, to sculpt again. And I thought—it just went "ding"—because it was like I keep telling myself that that's what I need, but I never—I don't do that—because I have so many other sources telling me "that's unreasonable and unreal"—to be wanting that kind of solitude. And I repeat it to myself very often that I've chosen to live with a part of society . . .

therefore, it's not feasible for me to recluse like that. Oh, a weekend away, or something like that—often the idea has come into my head that if I lived alone in the desert then I would probably be a lot more productive because there wouldn't be much other choice . . . because there really wouldn't be much other choice and there wouldn't be distractions from my art.

THERAPIST So what are you saying? It's your choices?

VICKY I guess I'm not making choices yet that are basically "Screw you guys—I know what works!" I still try to follow other people's rules, so that's where I lose the conviction. I lose sight of the fact that I do know what's best for me, and I start living by other people's standards, and it doesn't work.

THERAPIST Do you see that more clearly?

VICKY I'm seeing it more quickly.

THERAPIST More quickly?

VICKY At the same time, I'm seeing distractions as well. so it's like I've opened my eyes, but I've opened them in all ways not just one. [*Nice statement of a shift in personal construction.*]

After following a number of streams of thought which included a discussion of her passion, we moved into a consideration of "strong stand" as it related to her art and her conviction:

THERAPIST So you are a passionate person?

VICKY Ah, yeah. [*We laugh together because both of us know that Vicky is a very passionate person.*]

THERAPIST Does that fit in with the card on a "strong stand"? What's important?

VICKY Yeah. Because when there are things I believe in I strongly stand on them. As soon as I've presented the logical things that I believe in—when it all fits and I feel comfortable with it—then I can be real passionate and aggressive and "strong standish" about it. I'm getting more and more like that with my art or what I believe is the preferred path for my art to follow. And, hopefully, I will be able to allow a freedom to other people that want to follow the same path. [*Vicky's growing ability to hold her own position at the same time she allows other to hold theirs.*]

But sometimes Vicky's growing ability to hold her own position shut other people out of their positions. She didn't really process this until the day I challenged her. This confrontation grew out of a rather innocuous discussion, but somehow I was ready to move in on an aspect of Vicky where I felt she was blind to herself, where she made it very difficult for others to argue with her.

THERAPIST If you'd come across real strong to me I'm not sure how I would react. I might feel as though you're not just playing with different ideas. . . . I might feel you have really, really made up your mind because you're coming on so passionately.

VICKY Oh yeah. Aggressively, even. It looks like I'm attacking. I can see . . . I mean . . . my challenge is backing off quickly enough before they get their wall completely built.

THERAPIST Yes. I've learned in here, for instance . . . I might feel strongly about something, but I'd say, "Hey, let's play with this idea," or "I'm going to throw something out for you to consider . . . " [*Teaching and modeling*]

VICKY It makes it a lot easier . . .

THERAPIST Well, it says to the other person, "We may not agree, but we can kind of play with these ideas." I think it was Einstein who used the term "play with ideas," and I like that—the playing with ideas. That's what creativity is all about, playing with ideas. [*Some more teaching as well as my technique of almost overnaming a concept to make it sink in.*]

VICKY [*Vicky starts to argue and to defend her position.*] Yeah! See, I'm not . . . it's that they react and they tell me that I am a certain way . . . but I'm not!

THERAPIST See, Vicky. You still have to be aware that people can only read what they're hearing. And if you really want them to know you've not locked in, you've got to let them know. You can't assume . . .

VICKY I know. But I tried. The problem is that, darn it, it's all happened so quickly that they're defending way too hard for what I'm . . . because now I've stepped back and they've got this *big rock* in here. I mean, I don't think they can even barely hear me through the wall.

THERAPIST Yeah. And people are really good at shutting, aren't they?

VICKY Protective . . . because the attack has been perceived as a huge one so they've made this big *huge* wall, bomb shelter.

THERAPIST Now your mother, on occasion, has sounded as though she's attacking. I mean, she makes a strong statement that's really hard to deal with.

VICKY It's not just a statement. I mean, they personalize theirs. *Oh, God. I guess mine look personalized, too.* [*Vicky's breakthrough of thinking was quite dramatic here.*] . . . because the way I was defending my stance—or the stance I was taking . . . I think I said it like this: "How can anybody with any brains at all defend that law!"

THERAPIST So what have you said? In essence . . . ?

VICKY That you're stupid!

THERAPIST That's right. So . . . ?

VICKY Which isn't what I mean . . . it's like, what I'm really asking for is "show me why this would be a good idea . . . I mean . . . show why

they're even. . ." [*And here was a long pause as Vicky struggled for words.*]
THERAPIST What are you feeling, Vicky?
VICKY I'm trying to figure out how to say this without giving up my beliefs . . .

This was an important session as Vicky and I worked on ways she could take a stand without putting other people on the defensive and without losing her passion and her conviction. She puzzled still why people couldn't understand where she was coming from — why they couldn't know that she wasn't attacking. I replied, "Because of the way you're saying it, Vicky. It's strong. And if they don't know you they will misunderstand you."

Love and care. During her final sessions Vicky was sorting reactions to intimacy and to contrasts between physical sexuality and more abstract concepts of love. In her diary she wrote:

My reactions are changing. Let's start with *sex.* I cannot recall any time during the past ten years that sex wasn't a high priority on my needs list. The word "compulsion" comes to mind. In the past months that has been different. Anyway, I have become removed. Objective. Not needing to fulfill my curiosity of "anything on two legs."

Over the past year and a half I have been seeing the seemingly infinite gap between "sex" and "making love."

I'm becoming more selective in personal sharing.

And so the changes collected, mounted, and came together in new syntheses as Vicky formed and reformed her constructions of personal reality. In all this Vicky had certainly been demonstrating my developmental concept of the "revolving door," for when she returned for this second major round of therapy she was dealing with her concerns in new ways — ways that demonstrated an increasing capacity to talk about herself with frankness and openness, and to see the contrasts between her current developing outlooks and behaviors and those which had occurred before.

About six months into our second sequence, our therapy accelerated when Vicky met Alan, whom she would soon marry. Her sudden marriage plans created new drama as relationships with her mother and sister took new turns, as many old questions took on new salience, as feelings became more sensitive and erratic within new struggles with intimacy. Indeed, unresolved questions and feelings from her former marriage surged to the fore with insistent demands for attention. Thus, turning points developed rapidly from week to week as I was never quite sure where Vicky would be coming from. But this was an extremely valuable time, as crisis made Vicky more willing to face important issues. And as I have already told you, my attempted premarital and marital therapy did not work. My relationship with Vicky was just too strong for effective conjoint therapy to take place. At their suggestion they were referred to a new therapist whose practical, direct approaches meshed well with Alan's style—and, fortunately, who was accepting and reinforcing of Vicky's continuing challenge to grow in intimacy and love.

As I have also indicated, there was no neat and tidy close to Vicky's therapy. Her new marriage, a need for marital therapy, and a planned move to a new home—all these joined to close our work together. But, as I have read her words, and as I have heard from her at intervals, Vicky's transformations are well established, laying a firm foundation for her new abilities to deal with her marriage, with her family, and with her growing sense of self. Her final words in her last letter say it nicely:

I've realized more growth and gotten more comfortable with that already done . . . fascinating—this life!

NICK

Nick's first closure with me came when emotions escalated in an alarming way. What seemed needed was the insight and perspective of a man with whom Nick could identify in sorting through male identity issues. Nick was ready for this and moved very quickly into this new therapy, which lasted the greater part of one year. From time to time Nick would touch base with me but there was no sense of dependence on me or of continuing necessity to maintain the connection.

And then, about nine months after his termination with the other therapist, Nick returned to me to resume work on cognitive developmental questions—primarily his struggle to work through the unfinished business of trust and love which involved some serious tensions with an important friend. I felt much was happening which picked up on our earlier work. Certainly the work with the other therapist was extremely valuable and very complementary to my own approach. So, although Nick was in crisis when he returned, we were able to address old questions of love and relationship, self-definition and self-esteem, negative habits of thought and behavior from a new base of interpretation and perception.

This current therapy has been a gratifying illustration of Nick's growing capability to declare himself rather strongly, to name and express his feelings, to begin to sort further career questions, to share with a brother in more intimate ways, and to explore autonomous growth. At this writing, Nick is emerging from the crisis which brought him back to therapy—the crisis which intensified old separation anxieties, residuals from the uncertainties and traumas of his childhood. With broadening perspectives and motivation Nick is looking around for new activities and interests which will widen his network of friends as he moves from old fears and constrictions to new constructions of hope and confidence.

My sharing of Nick's materials in this book came at the close of an insightful session which very naturally brought us to the discussion of *meaning-making*. In that session he raised questions of "forgetting or forgiving" in speaking of letting go of the painful experiences with his friend. He commented that he could now talk about the friendship without getting overwhelmed by hurt and anger—that it all seemed more distant somehow. And what he also came to was that it didn't have to be an either-or of forgetting or forgiving, that he could hold in memory some important pieces of information about his friend at the same time that he forgave that friend.

This discussion led quite naturally into a discussion of differing kinds of awarenesses—of the front-and-center kinds of thoughts, feelings, and behaviors, in contrast to those which had slipped back into a kind of unconsciousness. Though I lightly touched the terminology of "tacit dimension" and the "things we know that we don't know we know," the emergent purpose of this session was to reinforce Nick's newfound attitudes and perspectives on his friendship.

Thus, after we had closed that session, when I finally handed my book material to Nick for him to review, we were approaching our review with this discussion of "awareness" fresh in our minds. And I had a few diagrams on the board which remained while he did his reading. It was he who pointed to the juxtapositions of ideas—of how he could see the peripheral awarenesses, recognize the memories of feelings, acknowledge how he had been in contrast to how he is now. Words like, "I answer my questions differently now. I take the question, interpret it, and then respond. Before it was a question of the either-or, the right or the wrong. Now I can reflect on it." He also noted that he could read my notes about his childhood, about his father, about his struggles without feeling bad, that it was like "the view down the side of the mountain" (Einstein's metaphor which I had shared before). Just six months after a crisis entry, therefore, Nick is almost ready to move on again. I will reinforce a few things, do some more comparing and contrasting, develop the narrative with him, and encourage him in his new ventures into boating, golfing, and friendship.

SONNY

Sonny's therapy closed off rather quickly as his crisis emotions softened, as he gained a perspective on the closure of his marriage, and as he moved rather quickly into a new and important friendship which was to lead to his second marriage. Though this closing was somewhat premature, and though many questions were unresolved, I still felt that Sonny had formed new cognitive constructions—new cognitive lenses, in other words—which were shaping his perspectives on self and relationship in new ways. As he wrote in his journal explorations, "I know more now than I did before. But it is not something easy to articulate."

Sonny's "revolving door" experiences in therapy came when he brought his new friend Elaine for conjoint therapy. Both of them had been battered by the traumas of divorce and were concerned they not go through its griefs and losses again. Thus, the two of them were very committed to making their relationship as close and constructive as possible, so we used both individual and couple sessions to explore personal issues as well as the more global concerns of marriage. This therapy continued both before and after their marriage until the time they moved to a new home across the country. And although these therapeutic contacts were somewhat erratic at times, the work which we did together maintained a sense of developmental momentum as Sonny and Elaine both came to new understandings and widening perspectives on the meanings and challenges of intimacy and love.

In contrast to Sonny who never rounded out an individual therapy, to Vicky whose closure was somewhat diffused, and to Nick whose closure is yet to come, I write now of Jana and Jennifer whose terminations can be described in more definite terms.

JANA

Jana's closing phase lasted about three months because she was going through rather dramatic changes in her job. These required some intensive career work and supportive feedback in her new job search.

But I felt that her constructions of self and relationship had changed a great deal before this last phase. Here are a couple illustrative quotes:

Mother's and my relationship is changing and I need to hold onto the maturity I have and realize that she is having a hard time and I would like to reach out to her, adult to adult, and to help her to feel better. Hopefully not with any strings attached.

I felt like I sort of felt something click into place this week and I don't know quite how to put words to it. But I liked what you said when you said, "I am bigger than that." We were talking about my different facets and how we can put those together. And that anything I face I can be bigger than that. [*I had used an illustrative story from a local actress who gave a delightful talk on "I can be bigger than that" in describing how she surmounted some large blocks to her career.*] And that has helped and I don't know . . . I don't know how to put it into words . . . the things about I am a separate person and I am bigger than that and (sigh) what else? There's something in there, that I've felt that my confidence has grown and that . . . see that you can say those words and they don't ring true, or you can say them and they do. And people before have told me, "Have self confidence" and all that stuff. Well, I can say that to myself, "I am self-confident." I can say that'til I'm blue in the face and if I don't feel that way, then it hasn't done any good. Or, lately I've felt, or when I said, "I am self-confident," it has had a truer ring. It's like, somewhere in there I have felt like I flopped over.

In our final session we did not do so much of this comparing and contrasting but spent time contemplating some of the feelings and memories about her mother and father that were still percolating as griefs and dilemmas.

JANA Hmmm . . . there's something else . . . I'm talking sort of "detached" today . . . not getting at the emotion, but talking intellectually . . .

THERAPIST How does that feel?

JANA It feels like I am talking it out in a way . . .

THERAPIST Go with it where you're at. I think . . . maybe you are able to look at things a little more dispassionately. What would that mean?

JANA That I've put things into perspective.

But then we touched base with feelings as she talked of her father's death and some of the grief which was still unexpressed.

THERAPIST There are really feelings there, aren't there?

JANA (Crying, hardly able to speak . . . exchange of Kleenex, nonverbal support . . . after a long silence) You know that wasn't the easiest thing [referring to her father's death, her mother finding a new relationship, and Jana staying alone in the old home]. Here I've been sort of hard on myself, but . . . gosh, to lose my Dad, and then sort of lose my Mom and all of a sudden I was just on my own.

THERAPIST Uh huh . . .

JANA When, really, the kind of upbringing I had had didn't prepare me for that. "Be our little girl, be our little girl, you're on your own." WHEW! Oof! [Varying little exclamations . . . her seeing something she had not seen before.]

THERAPIST So what did the little girl do on her own?

JANA I felt lonely . . . and I felt alone . . like other people had people but I didn't have anybody . . .

THERAPIST Uh huh . . .

JANA I did have some fun, though, and I went dancing . . . ummm . . . a mixture . . .

THERAPIST A mixture . . . sure! Certainly you were getting on with your life in some other real ways . . . you went back to school?

JANA Yeah, I went back to school and to college. Hmmm . . . trying to sort it out from back then . . . but I feel like something happened . . . and it took it a long time to have its fruition.

THERAPIST Any other thoughts before we close our session?

JANA Oh . . . probably lots . . . but I was thinking that I have come to appreciate my Dad in a lot of new ways—that I guess I understand more of who he was . . . that it wasn't so easy for him. Somehow that helps . . .

THERAPIST Thank you, Jana. I'm glad you said that. It kind of rounds out our time together.

Eighteen months later Jana returned for a few more sessions. I quote from a session near the end of that second sequence:

THERAPIST Okay. If we could name the issue you are dealing with . . . how would you characterize the issue we're dealing with here?

JANA The only thing I can say . . . is taking charge of my own life and taking responsibility . . . that seems too trite.

THERAPIST Doesn't quite have the flavor of what you're feeling? Well, okay . . . let's start playing with words. The words you were using were . . . responsibility? What's another word?

JANA Control . . .

THERAPIST Control . . . what else? [*writing on the board*]

JANA (Sigh) . . . Somehow being the power person instead of the victim. Of course, that's the same thing as control.

THERAPIST Well, let's put it in those words. Being the power person instead of the victim. Okay? [*Writing all this on the board*] Any other way of saying that?

JANA Here again it sounds trite, but I almost get the picture of the worm that's gone into the cocoon trying to figure out how to come out a butterfly . . . (little laugh).

THERAPIST I like that . . . the worm that's gone into the cocoon and is trying to figure out the next stage . . . how to get out there and be the butterfly . . .

JANA And, really butterfly to me could fit very nicely if you think of the colorful . . . just free floating around. I think of springtime and flowers and that sort of thing . . .

THERAPIST Uh huh . . . what else does a butterfly . . .

JANA The trouble with a butterfly is that doesn't connote — or denote — whatever word — much responsibility and the difficulty for me.

THERAPIST Is there another metaphor? Or image that would work?

JANA Do you have something in mind?

THERAPIST I like the idea of development. Do you know what the metaphor for development is . . . where it came from? It's the seed, the kernel of the seed, and opening . . . so there is the idea of the seed and the uncovering of the seed . . .

JANA Like the acorn and the oak tree . . .

THERAPIST Yeah, whatever it is . . . the butterfly comes from the cocoon, right? So that is one image of coming free . . . uh, an oak comes from the acorn . . . what else?

JANA Hmmm . . . can't think of anything . . .

THERAPIST I can't help but think of music . . . all the parts that come together to create a whole . . . we're something like that . . . we have our parts that come together . . . something happens to bring it to life . . . . So what if all this stuff you are doing . . . so if we put our little magnet here at a different point along the helix . . . [*All this is illustrative of board work when I might use a model such as the helix; where I tap metaphors and images of my client; and where I do modeling and teaching about ideas from adult development.*] Could you say these are stages of awareness? New awarenesses?

JANA That could be . . . an emotional acceptance and understanding of something I may have finally intellectually known . . . but it's different to hear the words and to finally have it lock into place.

Jana's words "have it lock into place" have a similar ring to Natalie's words in Chapter 6 (p. 107) when she described newfound abilities to name and order her emotions:

THERAPIST And this feeling of being able to rearrange, what does that do for you?

NATALIE Well, it gives me some hope . . . After a while that makes me feel like, "Hey, I'm in charge here . . . I'm in charge here and I really can reorder things, reorder my decisions, or my behavior, or whatever. . . . "

And now, you will read Jennifer's words as she compares and contrasts, organizes and names, and also "locks into place" her new thoughts and ideas. Of all my clients, Jennifer probably has offered the most nicely framed statements on closure.

JENNIFER

In my final session with Jennifer I encouraged her to compare and contrast current outlooks and reactions with those of the past. Her resulting dialogue with me showed her dialectical abilities well established. Though she returned for one session several years later, there was no need for new therapy. Still married and reasonably content with how it was going, she felt good about what was happening with herself in terms of job and career direction. That brief follow-up showed that she had continued to grow, building on the outlooks which are reflected below.

JENNIFER I think I remember the ways that I felt about certain situations, and ways that I felt that I don't feel now. And it's really hard for me to believe it . . . I guess . . . it seems sort of ridiculous.

THERAPIST So you're realizing that you've left behind attitudes and beliefs, or softened them, or whatever, and yet it is very hard because they're intangible?

JENNIFER I think it's a matter of perspective. And in some ways it feels strange. I feel like in some ways I'm almost not willing myself anymore.

THERAPIST How do you mean that?

JENNIFER That somehow that was a unique aspect, even though I was probably so negative—in a way I miss it, 'cause I think it was a crutch in a lot of ways.

THERAPIST It was a lot of things for you, wasn't it? How a crutch, do you think?

JENNIFER Either a crutch or an escape valve. When things got too much I would go off and go into these little fits, and everything was bad and it was all because of things external to me, or some internal flaw that I had no control over. I'm just basically lazy or basically weak, and in a way I'd have this kind of fit, get terribly upset, and then I'd end up by saying well it's not really my fault but . . . (inaudible). It was an excuse for things that I felt were wrong with me.

THERAPIST So first it started out with some sort of basic thinking that there were some things wrong with you, or . . . ?

JENNIFER Well, I would, it always seemed to happen that things would all of a sudden pile up on me. It was a combination of housework, school-work, things that weren't right, feeling guilty about my parents not being happy—just all these things that for some reason at some point all seemed to close in on me. And then I'd get terribly depressed and I'd have fits and I'd cry a lot and at the end it would all kind of go away and I'd be left with the feeling of "well, I can't help it because I'm just too lazy to get my schoolwork done on time and I'm just not as neat a person as I should be." Instead of doing something about these things, I'd just explain it away by my being lacking in some way. And then I'd kind of ignore it all for a while until it got all built up again.

THERAPIST And would it make you feel better, then, to be able to explain it away?

JENNIFER Well, it would calm me down so that it just resumed until it all built up again.

THERAPIST So it served a real purpose for you, didn't it? Well, we've been changing around a whole system of behavior and belief—the two go together. So how is that for you—I like to think of it as a journey here. [*I bring the discussion back to center again to continue the process of comparison and contrast.*]

JENNIFER I think it's made me feel more responsible for all these things, and I think along with it I'm more realistic in my expectations of what I can really do, of what a human being can really do.

THERAPIST It's a paradoxical thing, isn't it? As you soften your denial of flaws, at the same time you allow room for them; it's no longer a big deal, in other words. Is that what you feel?

JENNIFER Yeah—it's working in two directions. Things don't seem to build up to the point of total frustration as they used to. I think, one, because I realize . . . I can see a little more clearly what are reasonable goals, what are reasonable expectations. I see that I can deal with them instead of trying to do too much, and maybe I'm not going to overcome that, but I can realize and accept the fact that if you want to go to school and work and do all these other things, the house is not going to look really good. So that makes it easier, and things don't get to the point — I don't get so frustrated as I used to. But at the same time I don't have to get as frustrated because I think I actually do more . . by not being as frustrated I get more done.

THERAPIST [*Here I do a little summarizing of my own as I refer back to earlier issues and to the differences I see in Jennifer. I also name the stages we have been going through.*] There are stages of therapy . . . it's like the initial stage is where you come in and we're working it through. And then there's a kind of reinforcement of the new pattern. Now I really think that once you've changed around an attitude or a belief system and are aware of it, that sure, there will be some ebb and flow, but I don't think you'll ever go completely back. Because once you are aware you're already different. But I thought it would be fun to go through and think about some of the things that you've stated clearly, strongly in the past . . . that that would be helpful because it's those statements that were influencing you when you first came in. Like, "if it's easy for me it's not worthwhile." That's a pretty strong belief. "If I'm capable of more I'd better do more. People like me better than I like them. You can't have happiness without achievement." Those are heavy statements and you were making those in July (seven months before). So the thing is that I've found you have turned around. [*And then I check this out*] I don't know, have you turned around those beliefs?

JENNIFER There are aspects of that that I still . . . I think that I'm still very achievement-oriented, and I do like challenging myself, but I don't look as that as central like breathing.

I found that one of the most interesting statements that Jennifer made in our final session was that she was almost missing the epic quality of her therapeutic struggle — that it was almost too easy for her now — that there ought to be more difficulty in her life. She described how she liked to grapple — how she created struggles to feel better about herself. She said that she has not been used to extended periods of happiness, and that she's almost grieving the loss of her childish qualities, which include the peaks and valleys of the emotional, artistic temperament.

I asked Jennifer where she could get her epic quality now that some of the old issues were resolved. She said she could get it through her writing and through her work. She enjoyed enjoyable "difficulties," such as homework for school, deadlines, the sense of accomplishment, the feeling of confidence, having a focus and being in touch and having a specialized purpose. I said this would probably be her challenge — to stir up life in a creative way in order to keep on being involved. Plans for the future included being an author, earning a Ph.D., and continuing to probe the "machinations of politics and business"—a kind of grappling which she wants to explore.

As I look back at the work completed with Vicky, Nick, Jana, Jennifer, and Sonny it seems appropriate to summarize a few of the passages of meaning-making which took place during our time together.

These were all relatively young people—in their twenties and thirties—who were still very much involved with separations from family, the forming of intimate relationships, and the continuing search for personal identity. Coming at times of crisis, they were facing many versions of the developmental challenges of trust, autonomy, initiative, industry, identity, and intimacy; the alternating currents of embeddedness and differentiation; the finding, sorting, and reforming of internalized images and ideologies; and the identification of patterns of thinking which needed to be opened, freed, and enlarged if they were to move towards more enlightened understandings of their personal stories and their constructions of personal reality.

What these clients were only beginning to glimpse were the more global, abstract, spiritual forms of meaning-making which come as people begin to touch their own sense of mortality. This emerging awareness heightens concerns of choice and commitment in all areas of life, particularly those of career, marriage and relationship, contributions to one's community and world, and coming to terms with aging and death. These more overarching concerns are now addressed within the topics of career development, marital meaning-making, and creative aging. And within this material you will be meeting clients who represent an older group of people and who bring a new salience to the developmental questions we are exploring here.

SECTION IV

Some Specific Therapies

Human work lies at the intersection where man confronts creation.

—Louis Savary, 1967, p. 9

It is about a search . . . for daily meaning as well as daily bread, for recognition as well as cash, for astonishment rather than torpor; in short, for a life rather than for a Monday through Friday sort of dying. Perhaps immortality, too, is part of the quest—to be remembered was the wish, spoken and unspoken, of the heroes and heroines of this book.

—Studs Terkel, 1972, p. xiii

. . . someday global theories of career development will be made up of refined, validated and well-assembled segments, cemented together by some synthesizing theory to constitute a whole which will be more powerful than the sum of its parts. It has been my view that self-concept theory, treating the individual as the socialized organizer of his or her experience, might be this cement.

—Donald Super, 1981, p. 39

CHAPTER 11

Career Development as Meaning-Making

M ANY OF MY IDEAS about a meaning-making therapy have been seeded and cultivated in the active engagement of career questions, for such questions go to the very center of larger questions of love and self. Clients who are without a career meaning—like clients without a love or self meaning—feel lost or in limbo. Their crises can be as severe as any I see, and they illustrate dramatically the pain of being lost in the wood.

Certainly, loss of career is tied to concrete issues of survival. To be without work is to be without money, or continuity, or an orienting structure for the activities of each day. But to be without a job is also to face personal questions of self-worth, of goal, and of meaning. In fact, questions of economic survival are often outweighed by questions of personal meaning, for it is a fact that people face career crisis who *do* have jobs, who *do* have excellent incomes and benefits, who *do* have a secure, definite structure for their lives. In fact, these very securities can become the "golden handcuffs" which lock them into self-defeating lives, lives hooked into all the accoutre-

185

ments of success, but without the elements of a sense of purpose and meaning.

I see this as I meet the young executive types, the stars, the "yuppies," many unhappy and insecure because they have risen so fast that they have not built a solid sense of self, often hanging their very identities on a frail, superficial structure called "job." On some intuitive level they sense that they have not yet faced and resolved identity questions of who and what they are. They are the ones who may say, "I'm only 28 but I feel 35," as they contemplate continuing such a rapid pace that they have little time for establishing friendships or family life. Frightened, they see life stretching out ahead of them with the possibility of another 40 years doing the same thing. The thought of such a future leaves them feeling helpless and caught.

Clients of this sort face an assault on their constructions of self. They built their goals, they followed their beliefs, and they set in motion plans of action — but the plans, so neatly and tidily laid out, are no longer working. With the shattering of systems of meaning comes pain, and, paradoxically, the "dangerous opportunity" for reshaping the elements of the old system into a new, more transcendent system of self — a self anchored within the cognitive structure of transformed ideals and meaning.

In these reframings, "career" is much more than simple job definition — it is a concept which builds on its original metaphors: "the way or route over which one passes," "path or street," or "chariot." These French and Latin roots open the conceptualizations of *career* as a carrier of meaning, or as a path which offers structure, direction, and significance to life. It is obvious, therefore, that when I use the term "career" I am not thinking just of a job — I am thinking of a guiding image or a concept of a personal path, a personal significance, a personal continuity and meaning in the order of things. When I discuss this metaphorical image with my clients most of them understand immediately what I am saying, and find this a helpful way to name the importance of career in their lives. They begin to understand why a career crisis can be such a serious challenge to identity and why they feel lost within a state of limbo.

If career is more than a job, if it is more than a place in the marketplace, if it is more than a salary which one brings home every month, the concept of "retirement" can also be addressed in new ways. How important this is, because the word *retirement* means "withdrawal" and can be defeating and humiliating in its implications.

To illustrate: In a preretirement workshop which I offered several years ago, a band director was considering her coming retirement feeling deeply concerned that she would miss the excitement and stimulation not only of her students but also of the performance experience. She knew herself well enough to know that being up in front of an audience was both great fun and an important ego stroke that would be hard to replace. She was acknowledging how much she needed that stimulation and feedback to keep herself feeling good about herself. Recognizing these elements of experience as vital to her sense of well-being, we played with new career titles suitable for her late-life activity. What we named were "leader," "performer," and "stimulator." Certainly, the title of "teacher" was still there but we began to envision that in new ways. These cognitive reframings opened her eyes to career possibilities after she officially retired from the school system as she imagined herself working with a band of amateur musicans or participating as a performer in a local community group. What she saw, also, was continuing outlet for her energy, her leadership initiative, and her performance capabilities. With those insights her mood shifted from anxiety and concern to increasing hope and enthusiasm.

What I am addressing here are passages of meaning-making — passages which move personal reality from more restricted constructions of self to more universal frames of reference. The challenge for the therapist is to facilitate these transitions in a manner which opens the vision of the client to something much larger than a single role or a specific job label.

A THERAPEUTIC STANCE

In the early years of career development theory, many of the developmental schemata followed normative chronological sequences as researchers postulated that career success was built on the vocational decisions made in the early twenties. These ideas have changed considerably, no doubt reflecting the complexity of contemporary culture, but also reflecting the growing appreciation of theorists for the unique twists and turns which people can take in the course of their work lives. Eli Ginzberg was one of those who reframed many of his central ideas, writing this revisionary statement in 1972:

(1) . . . we no longer consider the process of occupational decision-making as limited to a decade. We now believe that the process is open-ended, that it can coexist with the individual's working life.
(2) While we still feel that the multiple educational and occupational decisions that a young person makes between his childhood and his 21st or 25th year have a cumulative effect on his occupational prospects, we now feel that it is wrong to see these decisions as having an irreversible impact on his career.
(3) While we believe that no one ever makes an occupational choice that satisfies all of his principal needs and desires, therefore giving validity to the concept of compromise, we now believe that a more relevant formulation would be that of *optimization*. Men and women seek to find the best occupational fit between their changing desires and their changing circumstances. Their search is a continuing one. (pp. 169, 171)

Even more recently, in 1984, Ginzberg has added another revisionary statement: "Occupational choice is a lifelong process of decision-making for those who seek major satisfactions from their work. This leads them to reassess repeatedly how they can improve the fit between their changing career goals and the realities of the World of Work" (p. 180). It is this fit we are talking about: the optimal match between the person and the career path which is chosen. Thus, emphasis moves from the description of a particular sequence of vocational development to the differing kinds of environments that a person can choose, to differing sources of meaning and kinds of realities, and to the sets of variables which each person brings to the task of developing a fulfilling work life.

John Holland (1973, 1985) has given us a theory which is rich with potential for examining the fit between the person and the job, a theory which has been incorporated into the Strong-Campbell Interest Inventory, the Career Assessment Inventory, and his own test instruments—the Self-Directed Search, and the Vocational Preference Inventory. His delineation of six personality types—realistic, investigative, artistic, social, enterprising, and conventional—came out of hundreds of interviews with young military inductees during World War II. It was his task to assign these young people to an occupational specialty, and as he continued his interviews and assignments he recognized patterns of self-description, interests, and skills which he categorized within his six personality types.

In an overview of Holland's theory, Carole Minor (1986) shows that an "overwhelming body of research" has been generated to support the theory. "In general, individuals do seek environments similar to their personality types, and there is some evidence that adults changing occupations do seek more congruent environments" (p. 26). Certainly, these assumptions are central to my own approach to career development, and they complement ideas about meaning-making and about the diversity of opportunity which arises out of rather simple models for adult choice. Indeed, diversity is the key word in current career theory, as old models tied to the chronology of age give way to newer models which identify the variables within the individual which can create contrasting designs for career choice.

I turn to another theme which I think is very important in career development. Not only does each individual present some degree of continuity and consistency in personal traits, but he or she also offers the potential for multiple possibility within the living out of each of these qualities. Here lies the career dialectic of stability and change, of process and content, of the consistent and the unpredictable. In the words of Leona Tyler:

. . . an individual is not limited to one way of dealing with any of life's demands. Through encounters with a very large number of situations and persons exemplifying different possibilities for structuring reality, one puts together one's own repertoire of possibility-processing structures. If we need to predict a person's behavior in some situation and we are familiar with his or her repertoire, we can predict with some certainty what he or she will *not* do, but with much less certainty what he or she *will* do. (1978, p. 9)

The words *repertoire of possibility* are significant here, for, as will be shown more clearly below, the therapeutic challenge is to help the client sort and identify that repertoire, not to limit choice or limit vision, but to help the individual come to terms with what he or she *is* and what he or she *may* do.

CAREER THERAPY

Those of us who work with careers are in the business of taxonomics as we struggle to order the infinite number of jobs available. Accepting the challenge of this task, Neale Baxter (1982) offers suggestions for classifying the work experience:

Jobs can be classified in as many ways as the cheeses of France; but like ancient Gaul, the various systems for classifying jobs can be divided into three groups, each of which puts the same worker into a different context. First, we can look at the *tasks* performed by the worker; this yields a classification system for occupations. Second, we can look at the *product made or service rendered* by the worker's employer; this yields a classification system for industries. Third, we can look at the *training* the worker brings to the job; this yields a classification system for instructional programs. Crosswalks allow users to move from one taxonomy to another of the same kind — such as occupations — an important ability because the data collected or presented according to one system are often unavailable in another; after all, users want the information, not the taxonomy, which is merely a tool for organizing it. (p. 14, Italics mine)

The career counselor/therapist, then, spends time collecting information (in fact, being a bit of a human packrat is very helpful!), organizing, sorting, drawing on every possible resource to make sense of job possibility. Here the *Occupational Outlook Handbook*, the *Dictionary of Occupational Titles*, the *Occupational Outlook Quarterlies* (all United States government publications) are helpful, as they translate the more abstract classifications of Holland, for example, into programs for collecting and naming the data. But the therapist also has to be adroit in leaping barriers to help clients synthesize these discrete categories into creative, imaginative job descriptions tailored to their unique career portraits.

And this is where we must attend to a second set of taxonomies, which are those of the client. In fact, this attention must come first if effective career direction is to be achieved. This is where a person like myself offers a program to aid and challenge clients to name themselves as fully as possible so that they can create a working master plan for lifelong career development.

Here is the program I offer my clients:

Career Development Plan

I. *Identity Clarification*
The first and most important task is determining "who and what you are" in terms of skills, interests, values and needs. The following tools are used to facilitate the process:

Interview: The gathering of history in a search for patterns of vocation, interests, skills, needs and values. At this time attention is given to the presenting problem as well as any self-defeating attitudes which may be present.

Testing: Strong-Campbell Interest Inventory
Myers-Briggs Type Indicator
Career Assessment Inventory
Rokeach Values Test
Other tests as needed, for example: Sixteen Personality Factor Test, Word and Number Assessment Inventory, Wechsler Adult Intelligence Scale

Autobiographical Exercises: Review of Significant Experiences
"Who am I?"
Fantasy exercises of various kinds
Dialogue with self
Naming the "chapters" of life.

II. *Developing a Plan:*

Research: Through library research, interviewing for information, reading, collecting want ads, studying the yellow pages, attending professional workshops, possibilities are gathered and unique job roles are brainstormed and defined.

Resume: As job descriptions take shape, resume writing is begun. The goal is to mesh your personal identity profile with particular job descriptions.

Time Plan: A time plan is developed showing the "shape" of exploration. At this point there may be several types of plan according to varying job goals. Pros and cons are discussed using techniques of decision-making.

III. *Active Search:*
Much of this stage is in your hands but I am there to teach you interview techniques, decision-making, and job-searching skills. I will also be giving supportive feedback as we continue to brainstorm career possibilities.

Because terminology is significant I carefully explain my terms:

Interests: Our interests attract our attention and give us satisfaction and pleasure as we learn more about them and act upon them in work and play. Interests help determine vocational direction because we are more alive to life experience when we have a genuine interest. Interests also give a base for vocational connection with others.

Skills: These include the abilities which we have gained from learning, practice, and the specialized training of talents and aptitudes. A skill is not necessarily something we *like* to do. Skills may be developed and enjoyed at one stage of life and then become boring when we see no further hope for improvement or enjoyment.

Needs: These are the aspects of life which make us feel good about ourselves—a form of personal nourishment and a base for motivation. Examples of needs: space, solitude, human interaction, quiet, intimacy, and family time.

Values: The word comes from a Latin root, "to be worth, to be strong," and has come to mean that which is intrinsically valuable or desirable. Values are those qualities or goals which are important to us and in which we believe. "Instrumental values"—the ones which help us achieve our goals—include such qualities as wisdom, playfulness, sensitivity, spirituality. Our "end values"—the values which constitute our goals—include such achievements as the good life, harmony, peace, learning. They are values which can give intentionality, structure, and meaning to life.

While sharing my model and definitions, I explain that every career therapy is adapted to client need; that a "typical" career series can consist of four to six sessions, but that there are seldom "typical" sequences. I also emphasize that if depression or anxiety is present, of if relationship concerns are complicating decision-making, these will be examined within the context of career therapy. As I explain, "I am a psychologist, therefore I will be working with you as a 'whole person' rather than just a person seeking a job." Indeed, because career crises range from simple, fairly direct problems of job search to more profound questions of lifelong meaning, I feel I move along a continuum from a more directive counseling role to the in-depth processes of psychotherapy. And yet, at all times I maintain an approach that I call *therapy*, for I do not believe in simplistic advice-giving, and I am always working with the cognitive/affective constructions which may either interrupt or facilitate the creative career process.

Because internal meaning events do shade and merge with those more tangible and "external," I find it important to keep loose in defining what is happening in order to avoid premature closure on *the problem*. Maintaining a harmony between this perspective and client goals is essential to the process, and I continue to check with my clients to be sure that we agree on our goals and that I am not going beyond what they want for career work. Most clients are relieved to find that they can share feelings and confusions at the same time they work to make sense of career.

As I have already indicated, career development is often conceptualized as an advice-giving process. Many clients come to me with that expectation. They want a series of handouts, a set of answers, a quick solution, a prescription for steps to the future. In failing to meet their expectations I obviously lose some clients, but others come to respect and appreciate the challenge and opportunity for creative self-discovery. Furthermore, they begin to assimilate a knowledge of the creative process which gives keys to successful career development. This knowledge is essential if the client is to handle future career crises in an effective manner, for career development questions are never resolved completely; the contexts of life experience are constantly changing; the job that was created yesterday is gone tomorrow; the career solution which worked ten years ago is falling apart today. Thus, it is in the constructive process of ongoing, creative exploration that the client finds a structural backbone for the lifelong meaning-making called career development.

In doing career development I follow a truncated version of the same meaning-making steps which I have named before as I establish the relationship, begin the data gathering, stimulate clients to pattern personal knowledge in new ways, and join them in integrating and reconciling old versions of the "truth" with the new. Thus, even in career development I pay attention to both the rational and emotional aspects of self-exploration, decision-making and reality-testing. Within this framework I am freed to use a wide range of therapeutic styles as I combine Rogerian approaches with those which are more directive. Certainly, I include at all times the stance of the constructive, developmental therapist.

Developmental perspectives continue to shape my questioning and hypothesizing as I think of my client in terms of both love and work. Questions of generativity, of love, care and wisdom are continually present, affected by levels of insight and cognitive construction, as well as by the contexts of age and aging. The more knowledge of these developmental stages I can bring to the process, the more likely I am to raise the significant questions pertinent to a particular period of life or a particular context of meaning. Thus, I will often be dealing with so-called spiritual questions with someone in the early fifties, or questions of retirement planning with a 60-year-old, or the relationship problems of being a workaholic entrepreneur at the age of 32.

To summarize these stages and challenges of career development I turn to Donald Super (1957), whose descriptions of career process are complementary to my own. He describes the sequence as consisting of three parts: (1) *problem appraisal*, which is the defining of the experienced difficulty and expectations for career therapy; (2) a *personal appraisal*, when client and therapist work together to develop a personal portrait using demographic, psychometric data along with the interview process; and finally (3) *prognostic appraisal*, which comes with the client-therapist dialogue about predictions for probable success and satisfaction. The best appraisals are made collectively, with attention to the client's reaction to the data and to the therapist's tentative interpretations. By using creative questioning—"Could that mean . . . ? I wonder if you have considered it this way? What would you think of this possibility?" — the therapist can use client responses as a healthy corrective for the counselor's own biases. By actively involving the client in the process, the therapist can encourage the person towards a willingness to take the consequences which begin to lead him or her towards a goal which is based on a cooperative, realistic appraisal of the factors involved.

I point us, then, toward a career development therapy which draws on advanced therapeutic skills and which gives attention to the whole person. I call for a developmental perspective which looks at the long view, which encourages dialectical thinking and process, which prepares clients to work for themselves, and which seeks a balance between creative dreaming and practical reality. This is the mix encapsulated in Arieti's "ten creative attitudes and conditions" for creativity (see pp. 111–113).

CREATIVE PROCESS

It is the creative process which I find most interesting and most valuable in career development therapy. Building on all the ideas detailed in Chapter 7, I work to teach creative approaches, to unlock limiting fears, to retrain negative thinking habits, and to interrupt cognitive patterns which keep the client from opening his eyes to multiple possibilities. And, in addition, because most people are fascinated by personal identity search, I feature those exercises which not only define the person but add interest and impetus to this therapeutic experience.

A first task is to uncover client attitudes which interfere with creative thinking and planning. Here the therapist works to loosen cognitive structures in the service of the brainstorming and imaginative searching which make career development work successful. Among the blocks that are common is the "yes, but" sequence. "Yes, I could be a teacher but I really don't have the ability to discipline kids." "Yes, I could ask my friends about what they are doing, but that really wouldn't do any good." A second block is the "success/failure" concept, which makes life a series of either-ors. Perfectionists become locked into this, as well as people who are afraid of risk. A third block can be the "thou shalts and thou shalt nots" taught by family and culture. These can include gender prescriptions which have limited vocational choices for men and women, or they can include attitudes about status which scorn the role of the skilled trades person or the artist.

Very helpful in this therapeutic work on cognitive blocks is Roger von Oech's *A Whack on the Side of the Head*. As a consultant for the "high tech" industries of California's "Silicon Valley," he writes with humor and insight about the "mental locks" which can interfere with creative, innovative thinking. He lists ten of these, which include such statements as "That's not logical," "To err is wrong," "I'm not creative." To break these locks, he says, we sometimes need a "whack on the side of the head," which can interrupt and "dislodge the assumptions that keep us thinking 'more of the same'" (p. 12).

And what are "whacks on the side of the head"? They can be problems or failures, or a novel idea, or a joke, or a paradox. They can occur when a dream is shattered, when we are fired from a job, or when we lose a raise or a promotion. In such times of personal disruption, our cognitive/emotional *whacks* become the stimulus and energy for the creation of new meaning.

Von Oech uses the dichotomy of "soft" and "hard" thinking to name two phases in the development of new ideas: a germinal phase and a practical one. "In the germinal phase, ideas are generated and manipulated; in the practical phase, they are evaluated and executed. To use a biological meta-phor, the germinal phase sprouts new ideas and the practical phase harvests them" (1983, p. 31). He also describes soft thinking as trying "to find similarities and connections among things, while hard thinking focuses on their differences" (p. 31). He believes that while each of these types of thinking plays an important role in the creative process, they usually appear at different stages. Soft thinking is the type of thinking most useful in the global, brainstorming, data-gathering stage; and hard thinking is important as therapist and client begin to move into the practical, resume-writing, interviewing stage of job search.

Another first task is creative data gathering, as we search for the unique-ness of skills, interest, values and needs. In tune with the gathering of personal data and the breaking of cognitive sets, I cite the creative exercise of list making. Though lists may seem fixed and compulsive, they actually provide impetus for creative thinking. James Adams (1974), in his study of conceptual blockbusting, considers a list a springboard for the opening of imagination. A delightful quote from his book *Conceptual Blockbusting* effectively illustrates this (as he also incorporates a beautiful example of his own "Who am I?"):

The listing of attributes is a powerful way to rapidly get more insight into the possible usefulness of an object, which in turn is an advantage in conceptualizing. Let us briefly examine a typical object, namely me. I am a professor. Most of you, never having met me, can conclude quite a bit about me from that statement. However, let me list a few more of my attributes. I am also a husband, a father, an acceptable mechanic, machinist, and carpenter, poor tennis player, a better basketball player, and a piano player. I tend to be happier in rural environments than in cities. I like a great deal of contact with other people in my work but prefer a light and relaxed social schedule. I have a bad knee, a messy office, a Timex electric wristwatch, and a 1909 brown shingle house. I am 6'4", have brown eyes, and let my crew cut grow past my collar when I came to Stanford in 1966. Now, as I list these attributes, you should get a better feel for me as a person, and therefore be able to develop better "uses" for me. (1974, p. 81)

What methods do I use for the data-gathering process? Every approach I can possibly find that will stimulate my client to think in new ways. The

"Who am I?" exercise illustrated in Chapter 7 is one that has proved extremely valuable in naming the person in a wide variety of ways: personal themes, beliefs, values, hopes, fears, for example. What I often do with this material is use a highlighter to identify words which are used repeatedly, for in repeated vocabulary are road signs to the presenting problems and the kinds of issues the therapist will be dealing with. For example, if I keep finding "desperate, afraid, hopeless," I know I am probably dealing with a depression or deep fear. But if the language of writing keeps touching "warm, good, decided, possible," I can feel quite assured I am dealing with a person who is basically optimistic about the possibilities for career change.

The descriptive titles are often revealing from a developmental standpoint. If I find a list from an older woman who names herself entirely in terms of others, I become a little concerned that she has become fixed in reflective roles which do not stimulate the development of self. This was true of Eunice, who came at 59 in severe depression because her entire world had crashed around her when her husband's business went bankrupt, when they sold their home to move to the city, when one daughter was diagnosed as seriously ill. All of her reference points for meaning were gone. Growing in her ability to reflect on self, she offered astute commentary on her dilemma as a woman who lived her life as a "shadow of success" for husband and children: "It is the fracturing of a woman . . . the splitting of sections of self . . . a bracketing . . . not left to be a whole." And then she described herself as "absolutely incapable of anything in the work world," although she said she worked well with people.

Although one of her "Who am I's" was "I am me," she wrote: "Sometimes I don't know who I am for who I think I ought to be. It's hard to get over the notion that expectations are set in concrete—to be acted on as law. I can't keep on blaming others for that. The problem is that I don't know where my expectations for myself leave off and expectations of others for me begin. . . ."

What started as a therapy with depression began to move into a therapy of career as we both realized she had to find a sense of herself which would stimulate her and open her to new activity and learning. Here we were dealing with *career* in the largest sense of the metaphorical meanings which I described early in this chapter. Fortunately, Eunice took hold of behavioral planning for herself as she named her changes: "I'm becoming more attuned to self. . . . I am learning a vocabulary. . . . I am doing more."

Here is illustration again of the creative power of the written exercise called "Who am I?" But there are many more exercises to choose from—so many, in fact, that it is necessary to review them from time to time to stimulate new approaches to exploration. I find it helpful to read selectively from the very broad literature on career development. Certainly there are the classics written by Richard Bolles (1981), John Crystal and Richard Bolles (1974), and Bernard Haldane (1974), but then there are all the others which keep enriching this field. Tom Jackson's *Guerrila Tactics in the Job Market* (1978), for example, is filled with hard-hitting approaches to job search as well as a series of "tactics" for sorting personal attributes and intentions. The career counselor/therapist does well to keep informed and to continually search for new ideas to make this self-discovery stage as interesting and fruitful as possible.

Here are just a few of the exercises which I consistently use:

Exercise I: Imagine yourself having only one year to live. But during that year you would have your health and as much money as you needed for whatever you would want to do. Now, what would you do during that year? (Obviously, I would *not* use this exercise with a severely depressed person.)

The answers which come from this exercise may contain fairly common themes of wanting to travel or to spend time with family and friends. But frequently they are highly original, as they reveal a set of values uniquely significant to the person. For example:

- I would design and build a house. When it was finished I would throw a big party and invite all my friends to celebrate.
- I would quit my job and spend my year working with children who are dying.
- I wouldn't do a thing differently; I would keep on with what I am doing.
- I would go to school and take the classes I haven't had a chance to take.

Exercise II: Write the letters of the alphabet down the left side of a clean piece of paper. Then, beside each letter write interests which start with that letter. For example:

a. athletics, art, action . . .
b. books, boys, boxes, building . . .
c. calligraphy, calisthenics, camping . . .

This list is a stimulus for thinking and naming and is not to be taken too seriously. Encourage the client to have fun with it, to keep it handy so that ideas can be added as they occur. (I sometimes have couples do this so that they can brainstorm new shared activities, or so they understand contrasts and similarities in their individual interest patterns.)

Once the list is fairly complete I have my client look for patterns of interest, or for the themes which keep repeating themselves, or for interests which have been important in the past but which have been long neglected. The major purpose in these listings is to name varying interests which can be incorporated into a job description. To reinforce the multiple possibilities inherent in such lists, I often put these on the board. Then we play with differing combinations of these personal "ingredients" to see if we can find better "uses" for the person.

Occasionally I find someone who is completely blocked in this list-making. She may be seriously depressed or may have a background seriously impoverished in its cultivation of skills and talents. If this is the problem I often move therapy towards new activity and new exploration—through classes, for example, or a support group or an interest group. This is essential groundwork if any kind of effective career planning is to take place.

Exercise III: Who are your models? To answer this question, name people who have been very important to you because they are the way you would like to be, or because they are doing the kinds of things you would like to be doing. These can be people who are living or dead, famous or obscure, characters in books or neighbors next door. You may choose anyone.

Here again, the lists are fascinating as clients search and sort possible answers. John (whose story I tell below) named James Garner of the "Rockford File." Why? Because "he doesn't sell out, has adjusted to the enviroment, has changed his horizons, other people see him as a bum, is relatively free of outside reinforcements." This model was important in our therapy because John was struggling to free himself from family ideologies and conflicting demands. Here he began to see some of his own values and ideals in contrast to those which came from others.

The significant contrasts between people become evident as lists develop. For one client I find this package of needs, for example:

- to learn
- to find intellectual challenge
- to be a part of a team
- to find meaning
- to avoid repetitive, boring tasks
- to work with abstract ideas
- to keep control of work life

Actually, this is my package of needs. It is one reason I am a therapist/writer. It is why I have refused jobs at a lower level of abstraction or resisted job hunting in the university system. Of course, I am not getting that team need met, but I have built affiliations which give me some of that fulfillment on a psychological, emotional level.

Now, let's go with a contrasting package named by Joe:

- to have a routine which is consistent
- to have a plan for the future
- to earn a regular salary
- to have things organized

- to keep life on a pragmatic, factual level
- to know my place within the system

Joe's needs are being well met in the military. He has found a good place there and hopes that he will be promoted so he can stay in the system. I am a little concerned that if he ever gets "passed over" he will face a serious personal crisis. But crisis, after all, may be his moment of change, his moment of loosening some structural fetters. But—maybe not. It will depend on how flexible he is at that moment of crisis and whether he can find a context for continuing fulfillment of such needs.

Testing further stimulates list-making. The tests I most frequently use include: the Strong-Campbell Interest Inventory, the Career Assessment Inventory, the Myers-Briggs Type Indicator, the Holland Self-Directed Search, and more occasionally, the 16 Personality Factor Test, the Rokeach Values Test, and specific aptitude tests like the Words and Numbers Assessment Inventory. All of these have proved helpful in naming client variables, and in informing and stimulating further discussion and synthesis of career possibilities.

In using computer printouts for these tests my bias is for the colorful graphics of the visual profiles. These open thinking as my client and I cluster attributes and similarities in a number of different ways. And I find that the more global descriptors are more helpful than discrete job titles. I point to the reality that "psychologist" can mean many things—researcher, professor, clinician, business consultant—so the tight little title does not tell us much. But if we take that title and play values and needs against it, we often find many ideas for future exploration. Certainly, I do use the narrative printouts and find them helpful, but I usually save them until later in the process so that the language does not limit our thinking.

THE TIMING OF CAREER THERAPY

Career therapy can extend from one session to over a year. That does not mean decisions are complete when clients terminate their sequence with me, for, as Richard Bolles has noted, the process of career clarification and decision-making is not quick, often taking at least six months for answers to be defined. In spite of this, most clients move through my office in fairly typical sequences of from four to six sessions, often motivated to continue the specifics of the actual job search after they have defined a career model for themselves. With the emergence of some sense of perspective on choice, personal energy is often released and mobilized for the research and networking required to actually get a job. They have also learned methods for career decision-making which will help them to assume an active role in continuing the search.

That is the task of therapy. In the words of Richard Bolles:

There is an ancient saying: "Give me a fish, and I will eat for today; teach me to fish, and I will eat for the rest of my life." It is time in our society when we thought it worthwhile to try a noble experiment: to stop giving the job-hunter a fish, half a fish, or no fish at all; and instead to teach you how to fish. (1981, p. ix)

Without such teaching those who receive help usually haven't a clue "as to how you should go about your job-hunt the next time . . . and the next time . . . and the next next time; i.e., every 3.6 years, on an average" (Bolles, 1981, p. ix).

Many clients return at intervals for a morale boost or for feedback on their ideas and efforts. During these times I often feel like the coach or cheerleader who is rooting for a player from the sidelines.

In contrast to the relatively short-term career sequences, there are those cases which are ostensibly oriented to career but require attention to psychological issues, especially if the loss of career meaning has thrust the client into intense emotional conflict. At the moment of vulnerability, unresolved issues and ineffective personal patterns move to center stage and must be attended to. Thus, without losing sight of the original career goals, the therapist must use all possible means to reduce emotional stress, interrupt negative cognitive patterns, and rebuild self-esteem, to the point that the person can more actively pursue long-term career planning. These cases can be difficult and discouraging, because survival needs create pressure at the same time the person's emotional resources are so drained that he is unable to work on his own behalf.

If you recall, I introduced you to a lawyer in Chapter 2—a young man who tried to commit suicide at his moment of career crisis (see p. 24). His deep depression was so tightly tangled with career issues and problems of meaning that a number of approaches to therapy had to work hand in hand. As exploration of this man's career disillusionment was begun, medication was prescribed by a psychiatrist, suicide management was implemented, and attention was given to the anger and protest of his grief experience. Attention to these basic psychological dynamics was maintained at the same time that an intensive, ongoing dialogue addressed his personal philosophy of meaning and intention—a philosophy which included some very strong values which had collided with the occupation which he had chosen. What also seemed to be happening was a dramatic developmental shift from dependence on his parents to dependence on himself. The point I emphasize by telling his story is that a rich therapeutic repertoire is needed to attend to the presenting crisis. And what must be avoided is a simplistic set of answers, a quick solution, or a prescription for steps to the future.

Other clients whose career dilemmas were tightly involved with psychological issues include:

• A young career woman, Jane, who came to see me "to stabilize her goals, her self-perception, and to find new coping skills." She had a strong sense of being molded by others and not knowing who she was. We started the self-discovery process by developing this list of descriptors:

I'm a scholar, a freak, an eccentric, I'm needy, I'm jealous, I'm lonesome, curious, tired. Who am I? I am B's sister, father's little girl, L's roommate. I'm the Jane who vomits, I'm Jane the scholar, I feel like little Dorothy from Kansas. I avoid friction and change in my belief by stopping reading and thinking [she grew up in a strict religious background]. I'm afraid of adulthood; I'm afraid of growing up; I'm afraid of declaring myself.

- Jim, a high school senior with fairly definite interests, who said he needed career clarification and focus for entering college. What looked like a simple short-term process without heavy emotional overload turned into a time of resolving the emotional separations from parents as well as the dilemmas of career meaning. This young man made this a time for grieving the loss of old dependencies joined with the practical planning for new responsibility.

- Maria, a very angry woman in her mid-thirties, who was still carrying many of the "movement" philosophies of the '60s and wrestling to find a place in contemporary culture. She felt deep regret and guilt for the lifetime lost during her heavy drug usage, but she was not yet ready to face these conflicts. Very angry, in a self-defeating manner, she tried to throw the blame for her problems on her parents, on society, and on her former boy friend.

- Charles, a military man who was forced to retire from the service because he was "passed over." His crisis occurred when he leaped for the first job he could find after his discharge. Rather than define his career meaning he let salary and place make his decision for him. A year after he entered this job he walked into my office in serious depression because he had chosen too quickly without resolving the transition questions of what he really wanted in his life. He had also ignored the grief which was a part of his retirement, and the culture shock when he faced responsibilities and choices which the military had taken care of for so many years of his life (like buying light bulbs, and taking care of a garden, and signing up for a mortgage!).

- Edward who, at age 57, was facing the harshness of a negative management system which was forcing him to make hard decisions about his job. This decision-making was complicated by a diminishing energy level, his detachment from social contacts, and an increasing anxiety that his life was basically finished. Depression and apathy, therefore, were serious issues in his career development therapy.

All these clients needed interpretations and approaches which a cognitive developmental therapy can provide. And they illustrate the variety and complexity found in career development problems. This is the reason why this therapy offers unusual challenges to the flexibility and creativity of the therapist. Although every tool of psychotherapy must be used to relieve debilitating, defeating kinds of emotional distress, the primary goal is not symptom removal but symptom use, as the therapist supports the client in facing both cognitive and emotional conflicts in the service of growth. These are further illustrations, also, that a set time prescription for career therapy simply will not work.

THE STORY OF JOHN

To illustrate the varying aspects of career development therapy from the intial data gathering through the patterning and process to the times of closure, I cite now the story of John (see p. 24 for my earlier introduction). His was a case which went far beyond the simplistic notions of career development as a practical, tangible, advice-giving process.

John came into therapy "to deal with career frustrations and depression." It was evident from the beginning that these two problems fed on each other within complex patterns of high achievement motivation, negative cognition, family ideology and expectation, and current frustration with his failure to find an academic job.

Thirty-seven years old, a Ph.D. in political science, a successful writer with a second book under contract with a publisher, John was unable to find satisfaction in his career mixture of part-time teaching, research and writing. Certainly, this mix did not match his frustrated ideal of being a tenured professor in a college or university, and anything that did not meet that ideal was interpreted by John as a serious failure.

A major stream of our therapy, therefore, dealt with career, as we completed interview exploration, testing, and autobiographical work. This work moved quickly because John was intelligent, creative, and motivated. And, in spite of his depression, he was active in addressing his career questions.

In our initial interview I asked John what he would do if he were rich. He said he would write a book and travel "anywhere" doing his research and writing. Why? Because he didn't want regimentation. John's resistance to conformity and to hierarchical systems became further evident in his "early recollections," as he told stories of the little boy who was stubborn, standing apart, a nonconformist, "not normal," "different"—a little boy who felt "family type things were generally a waste of time" and who didn't like doing things he was "supposed to." In reporting these recollections John shared his impression that he tended to make himself feel bad on happy occasions. This seemed to be a resistance to the feeling of pressure that "I was supposed to do a certain thing or feel a certain way."

John's Strong-Campbell Interest Inventory profile was skewed towards the negative. I hypothesized two reasons for this: (1) He was definitely depressed, which would influence his interpretations considerably; and (2) he really was highly selective in what he liked or didn't like to do. In studying his material I came to believe that this man *was* on his vocational track — and a good one at that — but had not accepted and acknowledged it as his track because of his confusion in separating his goals (and independent, nonconformist style) from those of an angry, conflicted father.

In spite of the low SCII scores, John's profile showed his artistic, investigative interests, which no doubt brought him to his writing, research and teaching. And his introversion score of 60 showed that the aloneness of writing was comfortable to him. In fact, the themes of differentness, nonconformity, stubbornness, "standing apart," were revealed repeatedly in our dialogues and in an interesting list of common variables which he developed by studying his original SCII answers. The occupations and activities which he liked shared these qualities:

- work alone
- high status
- produce something on one's own
- set apart from others
- a free agent
- stand out within a group
- center of attention
- achieve maximum identity by what other people are saying
- need external reassurance
- feedback is an energy source
- active and doing
- independent
- separateness and togetherness
- creativity
- "expression of alienation" or a withdrawal from uncomfortable or confrontive situations.

He also developed a *needs* list:

- to see something tangible
- to find a symbol of accomplishment
- recognition of accomplishment
- security
- predictability for tomorrow

And a *skills* list

- writing, research, oral presentation
- ways of analyzing people, finding perspectives on characters
- an ability to detach self from writing material

I have already cited his wonderful little exercise on James Garner which confirmed again his rather off-beat, nonconformist, independent posture towards life.

Although career work continued, from the beginning much of our therapy dealt with John's depression. His negative cognitive processing was evident from the first session, when he commented that he continually saw himself anticipating bad things happening. In fact, he said, "I almost manipulate a situation into being bad, thus taking a very negative view of the world. . . if I get well it might take away my depression as a resource." When I asked if he were suicidal, he replied, "My curiosity about what might happen would keep me from killing myself." This relieved some of my concern about suicidal potential, but I never stopped evaluating his status and would have referred him for further consultation if I had felt it necessary. The fact that he continued to jog and to bicycle reassured me that he was still working on his own behalf.

His success-oriented, "black/white" thinking was revealed repeatedly in statements such as these:

- "I like doing things I've done when I can do them well."
- "If you don't like something, why do it?"
- "I tend not to do things that are a waste."
- "Winning is everything."
- "I don't enjoy things I can't do well."

John's depression deepened as he reported a "lowered resistance" to his emotions. In his words, "I feel really depressed. I could do something but it probably won't do any good."

In this time of depression (and what I later named as very important grieving), I saw an important therapeutic shift occur when John was able to name his father's model for men in general and for his son in particular:

- Men don't cry.
- Men don't have those kinds of problems.
- Men are strong and silent.
- Men are rugged and outdoors.
- Men shouldn't express anything sensitive.

With these statements John began to acknowledge and face a different kind of feeling as he examined more deeply his relationship with his father and his reactions to father's training and ideas. With these acknowledgments John's feelings intensified, as he reported lack of sleep, fatigue, and strong negatives. At the same time he was beginning to voice his anger about his father, he was identifying similar emotions in regard to his job, and the word "unfair" appeared frequently as he protested his failure to find an academic role. He also shared his embarrassment at asking people for letters of recommendation and having to acknowledge his lack of success.

Finally John's grief burst forth as he stated with great intensity how disappointing his life was, how disappointing people are, how he always felt like he was letting father down, how he never had much feeling for his family, and how he was now reaching out for intimacy with his wife in ways he had not done before.

Remarkably, after these powerful sessions of naming feelings, John's depression shifted towards a dejection which had an entirely different emotional character. He also began asking new questions: "Is my constant activity a way of avoiding central problems?" And, "What about my dilemmas and feelings of having to be working, satisfying people, meeting deadlines, feeling regimented, and under the pressure of standards and deadlines?" In all of this he felt discomfort, anger, "being obstreperous," and a guilt at "letting myself down." "What about my feeling of being alone, of being different, of being outside the family?"

The patterning of personal history and its relationship to current experience and feeling accelerated during this time, as he talked more about his father as a "strong, silent type with limited intellectual interest who stereotypes and deals in 'mental neuters.' Is this what I escaped from?" With such observations and questions he saw his father with new recognition and a more objective perspective. But this was also a painful time as he saw how "I've tended to laugh when I feel like crying — I became the comedian." In this he shared the feelings of emptiness which brought him to his comedian role. He also recognized the powerful influence of his mother, who had had a dream for her son, who understood and encouraged him, and who, too, "marched to a different drummer." (Thoreau's poem was one of mother's favorites). Unfortunately, some of mother's affirmation that John was "always right" added to his burden of having to be perfect.

With new insight and emotional expression, John's depression was relieved as his therapy came to rapid closure. But what seemed most remarkable in this six-month therapy was his dramatic cognitive shift. He no longer constructed the meaning of his world according to a dream which could not be achieved — and which, in so many ways, was not his dream at all. Rather, he took hold of his mixture of research, writing and part-time teaching with new energy and direction as he named himself in entirely new terms and as he broke the ideological connections to his family. Developmentally there are many ways we could interpret this: according to Erikson's identity/intimacy/generativity concepts; according to Kegan's embeddedess/differentiation model; or, yet again, according to enlarging dialectical construction. Whatever the model chosen, John's developmental leaps were profound and good.

Some Closing Thoughts

In active career process the client challenge is to objectify that which is subjective and to avoid premature closure or denial in the management of the crisis experience. These objectives are not always achieved. In fact, according to researchers Irving Janis and Dan Wheeler, many people "tend to short-circuit the essential stages of search and appraisal when they become aware of possible undesirable consequences of their choices. Even the most mature and the best educated can deceive themselves into believing they have complete information after brief contact with a so-called expert and perhaps a few informal discussions with friends" (1978, p. 67).

When people confront a complex problem of trying to satisfy many different objectives and foresee the consequences of various alternatives, they often come up against the limitations of their mental capabilities. Misjudgments also stem from pressures to conform and other social constraints. Above all, the stress of making crucial choices, with serious consequences that one might later regret, sometimes itself impairs critical judgment. (p. 67)

Janis and Wheeler have identified several patterns which contribute to ineffective career decision-making. One is *complacency*, as the individual ignores challenging information about possible choices. A second possible factor is *defensive avoidance*. Here the client doesn't believe there is an acceptable solution and closes considerations of creative possibility. Such thoughts as, "It can't happen to me," "Nothing needs to be done about it now," "I am not the one who needs to do anything about it," are typical in this type of avoidance. A third pattern of negative reaction is *hypervigilance*. This is a panic reaction. When this is the dominant pattern people search frantically for a way out of the dilemma and seize upon a hastily contrived solution. (That was certainly the case with the former military man I described above.)

The effective use of the crisis experience involves what Janis and Wheeler call *vigilance*. Vigilant decision-making occurs when anyone faced with a crucial choice believes that the threat is serious, that he can find a solution, and there is enough time. There are dilemmas in this, of course, because sometimes there is *not* enough time for the client to come to satisfactory solutions. Money is running out and survival is the front-and-center issue. When this is the case I encourage clients to think of the career discovery process in three stages: (1) the exploration stage which can be continued whether one is working or not; (2) a bridge stage when one begins to move towards a goal. This can include a compromise job either to provide apprenticeship or to provide food for the table while continuing the search. It can also include further academic study to prepare for the goal that is being defined; and (3) the achievement stage of the goal. In all this I emphasize process rather than product; I emphasize also that these stages may take one, two—even five—years to accomplish. With some sense of emerging plan and evolving process, however, much of the tension and fear can be relieved.

The therapeutic art in career development is to actively teach self-discovery process so that clients can manage their own crises and use their own techniques to arrive at new career decisions. In self-discovery we are not just tacking some quality on top of another—we are working for the discovery, synthesis, and transformation of qualities already present, Thus, it is a qualitative rather than a cumulative change. The final state is not simply a new one replacing the old. It is the old state transformed.

I suppose the most profound statement I could make about our marriage—and I can't explain it adequately—is that each has always been willing and eager for the other to *grow*. We have *grown* as individuals and in the process we have grown together.

I think that people normally talk about marriage as an institution, or they think of a marriage as a structure, and it's not, it's a *process*. It's a set of *processes* which people engage in and you never know where they're going to go.

—Carl Rogers, 1972, pp. 28–29, 190

CHAPTER 12

Marital Meaning-Making

T HE FOCUS SHIFTS here from the individual in process—the "being-in-the-process-of-becoming"—to *partners in process*, as we consider the combined meaning-makings within the ongoing, developing marital experience.

To tell the story and stories of partners in process a systems perspective is essential. There is really no other way to consider these two individuals with differing perceptions, differing constructions of reality, *and* differing perspectives on love, life and partnership—two individuals, therefore, who are in the business of creating systems of self at the same time they are building a marriage. To respect the individual systems is to acknowledge that the two marriage partners are irreducible to each other. If we lose one within the other we lose the rich potential of a mature, interdependent marriage with individuals capable of doing for themselves at the same time they are doing for each other.

Carl Rogers would call these marital processes a *"living* partnership [which] is composed of two people, each of whom owns, respects, and develops his or her own selfhood" (1972, p. 206). In pondering these active, often difficult, processes with a group of long-term married couples he searched for what he called "threads of permanence or enrichment"—those marriage experiences and qualities which contributed to the survival of the marital partnership in spite of some rather dramatic challenges to the fabric of the marriage. Dismissing the idea that such a thing as commitment to a structure would bring marital success, he came to the conclusion that "commitment to a process"—to the growing, the becoming, the emerging, to the not knowing in advance where the processes would go—that this was the critical variable in keeping a couple together.

And it was this same commitment to process which provided a further thread of permanence in offering a "safe harbor" for growth and development. In describing this Rogers wrote:

A marriage which is continually being transformed by the development of each spouse is without doubt one of the greatest sources of security a man [or woman] can know. From it he can venture into daring, innovating, challenging, behavior, can work freely to change his world, can take risks because he knows he can return to his secure relationship. Even this is security in change and process, not in something static. But a core of this continually blossoming security is, to me, marriage at its best. (1972, p. 198)

This *security* of a good marriage is like the ballast in a ship which keeps the ship afloat in times of stress—it is there to stabilize and free rather than simply to protect and constrain. It is Kegan's "holding environment" which provides confirmation and creative contradiction as it creates a continuity through the shifting developmental processes of life. This security gives meaning to Rollo May's (1981) idea that "freedom is born of limits," for within the commitments, the dedications and, yes, the structures and sacrifices of marriage, individuals actually gain in their freedom to be themselves, to experiment, to try on life in the manner which Rogers has described above. This marital security can foster, therefore, the dissolution of old roles as genuine interdependence allows people to shake up their traditional learnings as they reform themselves.

Contemporary marriage may be uniquely suited for the kinds of developmental processes I am describing. In thinking about this I have considered these words from Clifford Sager (1976):

In recent years the "style" of marital systems has been shifting from that of two closely intertwined persons with clearly designated, gender-determined roles to that of two "free" and independent people, each very much his or her own person. This is a trend, not a fait accompli. To the extent that it occurs the marital system tends to become more a system to which both spouses have a part-time commitment, similar to each partner's work system, school system, club system, or family of origin system. This concept of marriage as one of several systems for both spouses makes more understandable many of the changes now taking place in husband-wife relationships. Men have commonly had other sources of fulfillment and self-definition, whereas significant numbers of women are only now beginning to develop such extramarital and extrafamilial sources. For the person who has other significant areas that involve her or him creatively and emotionally, the marital system need not now represent survival importance; *it need not become the sole or major potential source of fulfillment or definition of self for the individual.* (p. 26)

Much of this statement fits my own conception, but I do struggle with the words "part-time commitment." I don't think so. I think an effective marriage is shaped within a cognitive umbrella of full-time commitment. It is a construction which influences choices of time, fidelity, career directions, fun. I would reframe Sager's words to eliminate the semantics of the either-or — it isn't a case of part-time versus full-time — it is a *both-and* within the cognitive, affective commitments to the interdependent experience of marriage. More than just a shared abode, more than just a shared set of activities, marriage is the psychological shift which moves one into the shared systems of marriage.

In this discussion I am attending to *marriage* rather than to less formally defined relationships. This does not mean I negate these or devalue them; it simply means I affirm that the two forms of relationship are different. My focus is on marriage because this union, this chosen system, has definitions of its own, and thus, a life of its own.

Marriage is a rite of passage, a statement in the eyes of one's culture that "I love this person and intend to commit myself until 'death do us part.'" Just because this commitment does not always work over time does not negate the commitment, for most couples who come to me believed at one time that their marriages were forever. Although sociologists and anthropologists have played with the concept of "serial monogomy" as a model of contemporary marriage — as though one could easily and unemotionally move through marital forms in sequential progression — the pain and the disruption that occur with divorce give clear evidence that such a pattern of relationship does not work very well. Believing this and also believing that the developmental concerns are different for a married couple than for live-in partners, I put all my attention here on marital therapy.

The languages and techniques I use here include all the cognitive developmental languages and techniques I have named and used thus far, but they are featured within contexts of the marital synergy. Particularly important are the vocabularies of *love and care*, for I place much emphasis on discovering how my couples interpret and live out those terms. This may seem obvious, yet the following report rather neatly illustrates how easy it is to forget these significant human dynamics in our scramble for technique:

Several months ago a medical school asked four different therapists to counsel a couple. Each therapist was a master at what he or she did. At the end of the last session, the couple was asked whether anything was missing.

"Nobody asked us whether we loved each other, or why we stayed together for 10 years," the couple replied. (Pincs, 1985)

As before, this is a health model which attends to the strengths and growths of each individual, which respects his or her uniqueness, and which does not approach therapy as though one or the other person is to blame. This is a systems model, therefore, which attends to interactive dynamics of both individual and marital systems, an attention which is joined with dialectical approaches and assumptions which declare that there is not *one* way of doing things or of looking at things, but a synergy of many ways.

Once again the tacit form for this therapy is that of the evolving, developmental processes of establishment, data gathering, pattern and process, and integrative conclusions which prepare one for the future.

Establishment and Data Gathering

I think here of a couple who came for the first time the other night. Bringing carefully detailed lists, they shared concerns of job hunting, career dissatisfaction and insecurity, the stresses of overwork, unfinished business with parents, learned patterns of fear and anger, sexual inhibitions trained by family belief systems, a love which sometimes seemed to disappear, and their great desire that their marriage would become more satisfying to both of them. What these people were bringing, therefore, was a complex set of issues requiring attention on both individual and couple levels.

Taking a deep breath I began to sort these problems with them as I probed history, current experiences, motivations, emotions, and commitment:

- How much do you love each other?
- Do you want to stay together?
- Are you willing to work hard on this?

As these questions were being asked I moved from one to the other, affirming, paraphrasing, alternately addressing questions of history and questions of the feelings and thoughts in the moment. My purpose in all that was to make each of them feel understood in his or her unique perceptions of the problems. At the end of that first hour they seemed reassured that I would be paying attention not only to their marriage but to their individual needs as well.

In empathic responsiveness is the offering of therapeutic care. Without that genuine offering the therapy will fail, for each partner has to trust that there is no collusion against him, that he is not being labeled as an identified patient, and that he is going to be understood and respected in his perceptions and descriptions of the marital problem. Here the therapist's skill is tested in providing a unique response to each person at the same time he or she starts negotiating the tasks of therapy.

The question "What are you feeling right now?" continues to be essential. Not only does it give me feedback as to whether I am on target in hearing problems and initiating early actions, but this question often also defuses hidden objections to the therapeutic process. In addition, it opens discussions in areas which I might not have considered. For example, with the couple I described above, it became apparent through this more subjective questioning that the husband was feeling a desperation about his job which needed priority attention. If I had not asked my feeling question, this might have been missed.

In these opening discussions I also check out needs for individual therapy vis-à-vis couple therapy as I explore the differing directions we can go. Usually clients want to leave these decisions up to me, but occasionally I get significant information from them which helps me to decide.

For example, consider the case of a wife who was still grieving the death of a young husband who had died of cancer. Although our couple therapy started out fairly successfully, it became quickly obvious that we were going nowhere until she did her grief work. So, I scheduled a few sessions where I could allow her private reflections on the meanings of her grief within the context of her new marriage. Time was also allowed for her emotional expressions of pain and loss. It was not long before she stated very clearly that she was "ready to be married again" and wanted to return to a couple format. Although I was scheduling the sessions with her, she was serving as her own intuitive guide in pacing her grieving and in indicating her readiness to move on.

CLASSES OF CONCERN

Establishment and data gathering are built upon the kinds of marital concern which are brought to the therapist. In sorting my cases I find three very generalized classes of these concerns: (1) enrichment, (2) career exploration, and (3) marital crisis and breakdown.

Enrichment. These cases can be very rewarding. Even though there may be serious difficulties in the marriage, the partners are usually committed and open to process, are still in love with each other, are motivated to improve their marriage, and frequently have enough perspective to stand outside the marriage and look in. These people recognize their difficulties, may not know what to do with them, but are not heavily caught in the emotional turmoil which characterizes marriages which are breaking apart. Generally, there is mutual respect and care and the communication is not characterized by name-calling and emotional abuse.

Sometimes these people are newly married (and very often these are second marriages), well aware that they have much to learn if their marriage is to continue to grow in a rich and rewarding fashion. Several times I have done this enrichment work with former clients who had previously worked through a divorce with me. Now they come with their new partner, knowing full well the pitfalls in this intimate relationship, and often well aware that they still carry some of the negative habits and emotional garbage which contributed to the breakup of their previous marriage. The task here is to bring the new partner into harmony with the relationship I have already established as I work to avoid emotional alignments.

Career Exploration. Candidates for this kind of therapy do not usually walk in the door with a request for marital career counseling and therapy. More typically this joint career search develops from individual work with clients whose marital concerns are affecting career decision-making, or from general marital therapy which begins to focus not only on individual work concerns, but upon the greater challenges of the couple's dual careers.

Every tool which I have described in my career development chapter is useful here: "Who am I?" exercises, interest testing, values clarification, creative listings of personal needs—and so on through the many possibilities for identity clarification. The joint self-search usually improves communication skills as each partner questions the other in a kind of therapeutic partnership. To facilitate this I frequently ask each partner to interview the other, using a yellow pad and asking the same kinds of questions that I ask during therapy. Often I illustrate this with my own experience with my husband, telling how one Sunday morning, during a leisurely brunch, I interviewed him in a way I had never done during our 37 years of marriage. After an hour, with the focus completely on him, we both felt much more aware of some hopes and fears which had never been expressed, and we felt much closer and more in tune with each other.

Marital Crisis. A third group of clients includes those whose marriages are in serious trouble. Often headed for separation and/or divorce, these people bring an intensity of grief, disappointment and mutual recrimination which makes these cases a very real challenge for the therapist. The very fact that they have come for therapy, however, is a hopeful sign. Even if the outcome is the dissolution of the marriage, the individuals involved will have had a chance to express their feelings and their interpretations of what has gone wrong.

Indeed, Robert S. Weiss (1975) feels that the creation of a meaningful narrative of the dying marriage is not only vital for successful closure, but significant as preparation for later, more satisfying relationships. To know what has gone wrong, to replace blame with the acknowledgment that this was a marriage which did not work out, and to come to some understanding of why that is so, is to put the marriage to rest. In Weiss' words:

The account is of major psychological importance to the separated, not only because it settles the issue of who was responsible for what, but also because it imposes on the confused marital events that preceded the separation a plot structure with a beginning, middle, and end and so organizes the events into a conceptually manageable unity. Once understood in this way, the events can be dealt with: They can be seen as outcomes of identifiable causes and, eventually, can be seen as past, over, and external to the individual's present self. Those who cannot construct accounts sometimes feel that their perplexity keeps them from detaching themselves from the distressing experiences. They may say, "If only I knew what happened, if only I could understand why . . . " (1975, p. 15)

William Bridges' (1980) description of *Transitions* adds a dimension of meaning here. Drawing on anthropological studies of rites of passage, he suggests that every transition consists of three stages: (1) endings, (2) the middle, "neutral" zone, and (3) new beginnings. The time of *endings* is the time when one works through losses as he or she leaves an experience, a place, a relationship. This is the time of making sense of what has happened (the narrative Weiss describes) and of grieving the loss of what went on before. All this is very important preparation for the new opportunity which *will* come.

In working with couples in crisis I do not generally encourage the escalation of anger in my office (although it may well happen!). There are enough battle scars already. What I do encourage is searching within the anger for the other feelings which are being protected—hurt, fear, disappointment, grief, for example. And I often begin teaching about anger, as I suggest books and models for communication. Lerner's *The Dance of Anger* has been especially helpful in this respect.

This is the time, then, of interrupting the bad habits which are tearing the couple apart. Here, too, is the detective work which identifies and plots negative cycles of argument and anger. Graphing the sequential patterns which have become established in the marital communication is often helpful. Once we have graphed and described a typical sequence, we are often well on our way towards more effective marital dialogue (see Figure 5).

To soften emotional extremes I continually offer support to both partners, while working to create a little breathing space for the transitional processes which are obviously underway. By adopting this exploratory role with my couples, by mixing individual meetings with conjoint sessions, I am often able to buy a kind of developmental time. In that way, if genuine transitional shifts are taking place, we have opportunity to *allow* them by slowing down the therapy process somewhat. This doesn't always work of course, and the choice for such marital therapy must come from the couple. They may well choose to move quickly towards separation and/or divorce, using therapy for their decision-making, their support, and their grieving.

But if I believe that the marriage is a "holding environment" for individual and marital developmental change, then I will do all that I can to reinforce and sustain it. And I will do this by making therapy a holding environment for the issues and processes which are asking for their own confirmations, continuities, and contradictions. Serving this role, therapy provides a forum for discussion and naming, and a context of caring during the upheavals of individual and couple change.

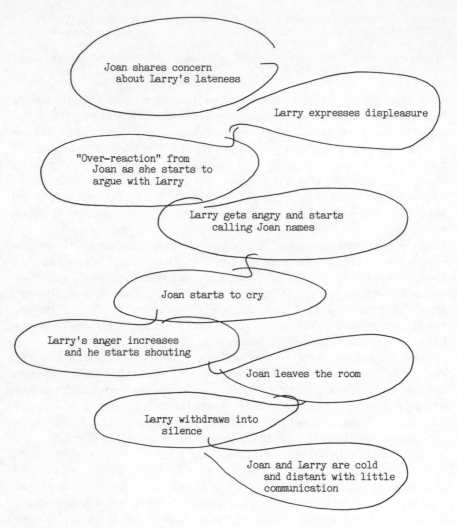

FIGURE 5 Argument sequence

Who are the couples most difficult to help? Certainly, those couples where the hurt has built such barriers that their love has died—without that spark to energize the process, it is unlikely that reconciliation can come about. Or the partners who have never really committed to the hard work of marriage, who want a successful relationship without that necessary hard work and commitment a marriage requires. And certainly, the couples where trust has been broken through infidelity or dishonesty. How does one re-build trust once it has been broken? That's a hard one. I'm not sure we can ever know whether shattered trust can be restored. But, once again, if we consider the "commitment to process" as a variable which holds individuals in marriage, there may be further, often unexpected, opportunity for the rebuilding of the trust which has been broken.

When couples have very differing needs or values, it may be difficult to restore the marriage. If one person needs much nurture and support and the other needs independence and freedom, we have a problem. Or if one person is oriented to spiritual values and the other totally rejects the metphysical, we have another kind of problem. With such differences we begin to tap some of the most difficult dilemmas in marital therapy: What do we do when partners have vastly differing needs? And what do we do if the individuals are at differing levels of development? When one partner is living the hedonistic, free life of the adolescent, and the other is at the committed, invested stage of intimacy development, for example? When one individual is reaching for forms of enmeshed intimacy while the other is out exploring the world? Or when one partner views the world through black/white, either/or lenses while the other partner has already moved into growing forms of dialectical thinking? And how does the therapist help the marital partners if they have not yet achieved a marital commitment which will support these differing growths?

These interrelated questions concerning individual/marital needs and individual/marital developments are central to a meaning-making therapy because we are working with the sequential, evolving processes of marriage which are shaped and formed by cognitive/affective construction. Let us move, then, to a consideration of these less tangible, less easily named, dynamics in marriage.

DEFINING MARITAL ISSUES

In *Marriage Contracts and Couple Therapy*, Clifford Sager has performed an impressive service by naming and ordering categories of marital issues. Using a theory of "marital contracts" to identify the differing kinds of "quid pro quo" marital agreements which couples create (and these can operate verbally, nonverbally, or unconsciously, he believes) he developed three taxonomies: (1) 16 parameters based on expectations of the marriage such as a "mate who will be loyal, devoted, and exclusive" or a marriage which provides "a constant support against the rest of the world"; (2) 13 parameters based on intrapsychic and biological needs which include the following:

- independence-dependence
- activity-passivity
- closeness-distance
- use-abuse of power
- dominance-submission
- fear of loneliness or abandonment

- need to possess and control
- level of anxiety
- mechanisms of defense
- gender identity
- characteristics desired in one's sex partner
- acceptance of self and other
- cognitive style

And, finally, a third category which includes 12 parameters of the more external foci of problems rooted in categories 1 and 2:

- communication
- life-style
- families of origin
- child rearing
- relationship with children
- family myths
- sex
- values
- friends
- roles
- money
- interests

If one begins to combine these variables, the permutations are enormous. And, even further, if one begins to consider differing interpretations, differing attitudes, differing contexts, differing stages of development, one gains rapid confirmation of the awesome complexity of the marital challenge.

Although all these variables and all these interactions are important in my considerations of the marital problem, I am particularly interested in the cognitive/affective dynamics as I ask questions and frame suggestions through the lenses of cognitive developmental theory. Statements of these marital dimensions have been slow in coming and the speculations and research are only now being formulated. But I have drawn on three sources in considering cognitive style and/or cognitive construction: (1) Sager (1976), (2) Myers (1980) and her associates, who have given us the Myers-Briggs typology, and (3) Robert Kegan, his students and colleagues, who are currently researching the interrelationships of developmental stage and marital dynamics.

COGNITIVE STYLE

Cognitive style is one of the parameters Sager named in his listing of intrapsychic concerns within a marriage. Believing that this is a dimension often ignored by therapists, he offered this definition:

Cognitive style may be defined as the characteristic way a person selects information to take in, how he processes it, and the way he communicates the outcome to others. . . . Spouses often approach and work on problems differently or view situations differently. They select or perceive a variety of data and may come up with very different conclusions; direct argument between them rarely resolves the difference. All too often they do not respect the value of the mate's style and of having two sets of perceptions or processes to work with. Difference in cognitive styles, which includes sensory intake differences and thought process differences, is the source of a great deal of marital conflict and unhappiness. (1976, pp. 15–16)

And what is unfortunate, he believes, is that few couples learn to name, appreciate, and capitalize on the positive aspects of these differences. The challenge and potential here, he suggests, are to celebrate the difference, as we teach couples to use their contrasting characteristics and styles as contradictory stimuli for an exciting and evolving marriage.

I find this business of cognitive style (and these terms blur into definitions of *cognitive construction*) one of the more interesting but often perplexing and defeating arenas of marital therapy. For example, how does one begin to work with couples whose perceptions of reality are as different as those of Jane and John who argued the view out my window:

"The sky is blue!"

"No, it's gray!"

"No, it's blue."

"How could you say such a stupid thing? You know the sky is gray!"

Or of Tim and Anne, who were caught in definitions of *hobby*, as Tim tried to label Anne "lazy, passive, unmotivated" because she did not have a "hobby." You might consider this a trivial concern, but for Tim it was a deeply serious matter as he tried to fathom a wife whose approaches to life were so different from his own. For him, to be "right" was to be like him, to follow his pronouncements, his interpretations of what a "hobby" was like.

Hoping to shake awarenesses towards an increased understanding and appreciation of personal differences, I started a free association exercise. Tim began as he named the words which came to mind when he thought of hobby:

- living out a set of challenges
- having aspirations
- mastering something
- doing something well
- being well-rounded, knowing, better able to communicate challenge, sharing, relaxing, space, stimulating, drawing conclusions.

Hobbies, then, were very important to Tim for they gave him a sense of achievement and meaning. Lack of hobby was to be a failure, to be lazy, to be without achievement, and those were the labels he was pinning on his wife.

Anne showed how different she was in cognitive style and in her interpretations of *hobby* by naming these associations:

- privacy
- being alone

- looking around
- being creative
- enjoyment

And, she added, "I simply don't need or want a hobby."

These were two people, then, caught in struggle over values, goals, time management, issues of achievement, and issues of perception. And they were people at differing levels of cognitive development. Tim couched his terms in black/white, authoritarian styles and seemed fixed in his definitions of the world. And he actively resisted any thought of change. Anne, on the other hand, seemed right in the middle of change, as she began to declare her needs and to protest Tim's tendency to dominate marital choices and interaction.

Because Tim was so resistant to any suggestion of change, or to the very idea of therapy, marital therapy did not last very long. But Anne continued to come to me for therapeutic work in stress management, assertiveness training, and self-identity. As her extreme stress subsided she also gained an ability to step outside her marital problems with new objectivity—an ability which helped her resolve her differences with Tim. At last report, she and Tim are still living together and doing fairly well.

In sorting cognitive style I frequently use the Myers-Briggs Type Indicator—both as an evaluative tool and as a teaching instrument for furthering respect for individual differences (see Chapter 7 for a full discussion of this instrument). In this therapy with couples I adopt the philosophy which Myers continually reinforces in *Gifts Differing*:

Differences in type between husband and wife may give rise to friction, but this can be diminished or eliminated when its origin is understood. Nothing in this chapter is intended to discourage anyone from marrying a person of largely opposite type, but such a marriage should be undertaken with full recognition that the other person *is* different and has a right to remain different, and with full willingness to concentrate on the virtues of the other's type rather than the defects. (1980, p. 127)

The Myers-Briggs typology adds further dimensions to understandings of this rather vague terminology called "cognitive style." What Myers describes is the "way people *prefer* to use their minds, specifically the way they perceive and the way they make judgments" (p. 1).

Perceiving is here understood to include the processes of becoming aware of things, people, occurrences, and ideas. *Judging* includes the processes of coming to conclusions about what has been perceived. Together, perception and judgment, which make up a large portion of people's total mental activity, govern much of their outer behavior, because perception—by definition—determines what people see in a situation and their judgment determines what they decide to do about it. Thus, it is reasonable that basic differences in perception or judgment should result in corresponding differences in behavior. (1980, pp. 1–2)

As we proceed you may well ask (as I have) what correlations exist between the Sager concepts of "cognitive style," the Myers-Briggs formulations of type, and the stage constructions defined by the cognitive developmental theorists. I don't think we have those answers yet, but this could be a fruitful area for research.

What seems most important here is that differences in cognitive style, in cognitive processing and judgment, and in construction, do bring critical questions into marital process, as well as real dilemmas as the therapist searches for ways to open an authoritarian, dualistic partner to another person's point of view, or to stimulate the person threatened by change or the growth of a partner to autonomous work on his own behalf. Marital therapy all too often breaks apart on the shoals of these differences.

Kegan has briefly addressed marital differences in *The Evolving Self*, as he points out the powerful challenge for a marriage when the individual or individuals in a marriage are moving from one way of making meaning to another—the time when they are standing on the brink between two ways of constructing the world. Using his metaphor of the "holding environment," he calls a marriage a "context for continued evolution" rather than a set contract for a particular point in time.

Building on Kegan's concept of the marital holding environment, two researchers have used his theoretical constructs and his *Subject/Object Interview* (among other research instruments) to initiate more formal study of the interactions between cognitive developmental stages and marital functioning. Though their samples are small and though they are among the first to explore these topics, Jane Jacobs (1984) and Steven Allison (1987 conversation regarding Ph.D. dissertation in process) are reporting findings which confirm the intuitions of some of us that developmental differences in marital partners contribute to some of the unique, contrasting interpretations of the marital world and its functions in the lives of the partners involved, and our further intuitions that those very contrasts are what contribute to marital tension and disruption.

But we also have to recognize that couples can support a relatively conflict-free marriage with such differences—in fact, couples often build the marital expectations and dynamics around their differing developmental needs and outlooks. Indeed, Jacobs (1984) determined that "partners recruit one another to enact a central role in their central psychic dramas"—in other words, to fulfill some important function in their respective growths and development. She further determined that how they view each other and interpret their respective processes is reflective of developmental stage.

In research complementary to Jacobs', Allison found that "Stage 3" partners (Kegan's "interpersonal" stage) wanted security and protection within their marriages and looked to their spouses for their safety. Because stability was so important to them, they feared and resisted change. "Stage

4" partners (the "institutional" stage) on the other hand, looked on change, conflict, growth and development, and transitional pain as normative, useful, valuable and necessary. Accepting the dynamics of process they also seemed able to acknowledge and accommodate their partner's needs.

According to these studies, then, individuals at "higher" levels of development seemed more willing to be "in process," to accept the fluctuations and discomforts of change, to compare and contrast their position with that of their partners, and to open themselves to developmental experience. All these qualities fit the dialectical forms of thinking which Basseches has delineated. Even more, these findings mesh with pieces of research coming from social psychologists who have discovered positive correlations between educational attainment and marital functioning.

. . . more educated respondents also differ from the less educated in two almost paradoxical ways. On the one hand, they are less likely to describe themselves upset about sex. On the other hand, they are less likely to deny certain bad feelings that come up about marriage: feeling irritated and resentful toward their spouse, feeling upset about sex, and feeling that divorce is sometimes the best solution for marital problems. Perhaps their alertness to problems in relationships makes the highly educated more able to manage conflicts when they do occur. Education can be thought of as effecting changes in people which allow them greater facility in relationships — facility in the open exchange in daily interaction which encourages a rich, rewarding relationship, greater skills with which to handle and resolve marital conflict when it develops.

. . . . the more educated see their marriages as a coalescence of two separate people and also express considerable happiness in marriage and a sense of open communication and understanding. This differentiation of experience evidently does not jeopardize happiness and adjustment in marriage or create stress since it seems to be combined with the capacity to communicate and work through conflicts. (Veroff, Douvan, & Kulka, 1981, pp. 188, 192)

These findings add support for my perspective on therapy as an education and training for dialectical thinking. But I would raise further question: If we hold normative standards for the love, care and wisdom which Erikson has suggested, would we find dialectical thinking related to more loving and compassionate relationship, to a wisdom which is concerned with an ethic of care? Perhaps we don't know this yet. But the ability to take another person's point of view would definitely seem to enhance more caring relationships with others. And the ability to risk and allow change would appear to contribute to the "safe harbor" of partnership which Rogers has described so effectively.

In this marital meaning-making therapy, then, I actively teach and facilitate the kinds of thinking and perception which will open people to each other. Within the space constraints of this chapter I share a few methods and models which I have found helpful in doing this.

MODELS FOR THERAPEUTIC PROCESS

The overlapping circles (see Figure 6). This systems model has proved useful in opening and widening couple understanding of the dynamics of self-process vis-à-vis couple process. I show each circle as the system of the

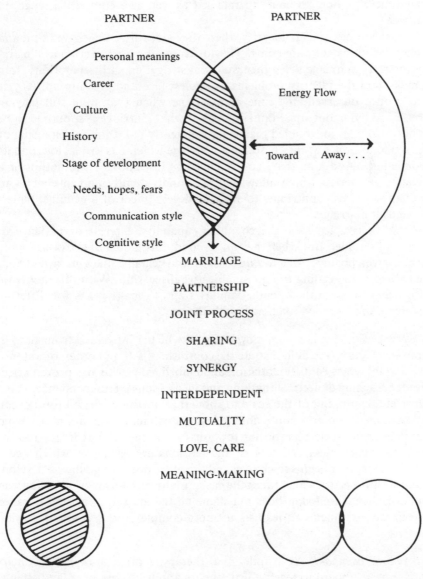

FIGURE 6 The overlapping circles

individual person and then I show the overlap of these circles which syner-
gistically integrates and transforms portions of the life, thought and action
of each person. This overlap can vary in the ways shown: The circles can
tightly overlap, as in an enmeshed marriage where one identity is frequently
subsumed within another. Or they can be so separate that there is little or no
overlap, as in a marriage which is more like a live-in arrangement of house-
mates. Or finally, the overlapping circles can create a balanced relationship
where there is room to be a separate self as well as a committed, engaged
partner.

Most couples quickly identify where they are, where they have been, and
where they think they are going. They often see the tight overlap as illustrative of early marriage when they were still struggling with separations from
families and the identity problems of adolescence and growing up. (Or, as
Vicky once observed, the time of marriage when they were still playing
house and living out some fantasy ideal of what marriage is supposed to be
about.) Couples in troubled marriages frequently point to the distancing of
the separate circles as they describe a marriage which has lost its love and its
momentum. And almost all couples become intrigued by the notion of a
balance of overlap which allows for both individuality and intimacy—an
overlap which can contribute to evolving development of a genuinely interdependent marriage.

Not all couples have the cognitive capability, interest or patience to
accept this model. But when they do respond, this model of the overlapping
circles gives positive fuel for discussion and usually takes us away from
anger and name-calling to a more objective discussion. With this model we
also begin to name therapeutic emphases and to make plans for differing
combinations of individual and couple therapy.

The scale. This is a very simple figure which I introduce from time to
time (see Figure 7) to demonstrate the contrasts of self and other, of autonomy and intimacy, of differentiation and embeddedness. It has proved effective for teaching dialectical thinking and ideas about interdependence. I also
illustrate the tipping of the scale to show that anything carried too far can
bring a distortion or a vulnerability. Using this model, we talk about what
happens if the scale tilts too far towards togetherness, or if it tilts too far
towards separateness. We talk of the tensions and struggles which occur
when one partner begins to change and the other does not—when a developmental shift occurs which takes the person into new forms of thinking and
outlook. This discussion does not name all the answers, but simply raises
the questions which can lead us to more complex thought about marital
process.

The helix model. As in individual therapy, I often draw Kegan's helix
model on the board to teach a little theory about how we grow and change

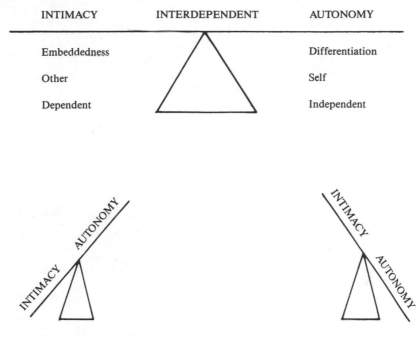

INTIMACY INTERDEPENDENT AUTONOMY

Embeddedness Differentiation

Other Self

Dependent Independent

FIGURE 7 The Scale

through life (see Figure 8). While I do this I feature once again his ideas of the "holding environment," and his concept that marriage can be a powerful source and support for the movements through developmental stages if it has its own strength and holding power through the processes of change.

(As I write this I remember a personal conversation with Kegan. When I happened to comment that I had been married for 37 years, he responded, "You have had many marriages." That provocative idea has been featured in a number of marital therapy sessions when I let people know that their "old marriage" can reform, making way for a new construction, a new formation of who and what they are as a couple; it is not a destruction of the old but a reconstruction which reconciles that which has been with that which is to come. Couples remember this idea and find it reassuring as they struggle through their crisis experience.)

A model for therapeutic process comes from the research of Meyer Friedman (1980), who has done basic research on the "Type A" personality. In his tripartite model (see Figure 9), therapy can be accessed through behavioral work, through factors in the psychological and interpersonal domains which induce stress, or through the cognitive/affective work of thought, attitude and emotion. He uses this model in working with hypertensive men and women and comments, "We can teach behavioral techniques like walk-

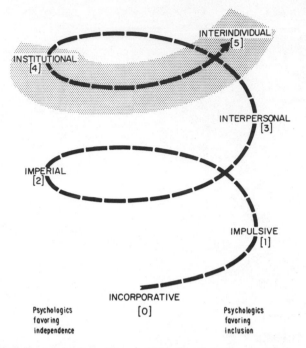

FIGURE 8 The helix model from Kegan, 1980. Reprinted by permission.

ing in a garden, breathing deeply, using biofeedback. We can work with stress management programs where we help people to lower their stress levels. But, we find it much harder to help people alter their attitudes and beliefs about life. Those are often the most necessary points of change — and the most difficult" (my paraphrase of his ideas).

I use this model to demonstrate that I will be entering the marital system in a number of differing ways, that shifts in behavior *can* bring shifts in attitudes, expectations, and feelings, and that shifts in thought, feeling and attitude can spin back onto the behaviors of marriage. Further, I emphasize that if psychological/emotional issues are contributing to an overload of stress or burdening the marriage by creating increased tension, we may have to start with that level of intervention. Obviously, we cannot separate one level of intervention from another, but the model has proved extremely useful in helping couples understand the differing ways we can approach the problem.

Thus, I often turn to behavioral assignments, believing they give a sense of direction to the couple at the same time they offer active practice for constructive change. Whether in the areas of sexual, sensual intimacy, in the

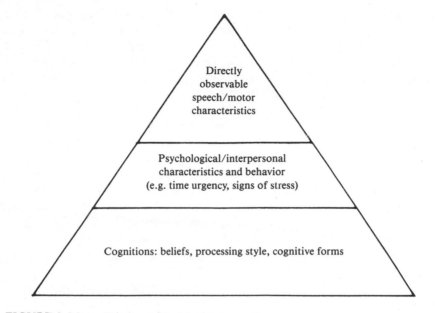

FIGURE 9 Meyer Friedman Model of Intervention

arenas of long-range financial planning, or in the defining of negative communication, such assignments are essential for taking therapeutic work out of the therapy room into the everyday experience of daily life. Within successive approximations of new marital behavior (and it is important to make the assignments simple and achievable so that couples will find some level of success), the marital partners can practice and then return for corrective inputs and reinforcement of what has been accomplished. (Rich resources for such assignment can be found in Lederer's *Creating a Good Relationship*.)

Sometimes I just share a book to be read. I also keep a number of handouts which I share with couples at the end of the hour – articles which deal with the presenting concern, whether it be communication, career questions, marital enrichment, violence, alcoholism, drug addiction, depression, time management, or sexual intimacy. A certain looseness is necessary to avoid making these assignments too definite. The last thing I want is one partner's parading of personal knowledge over the other's failure to invest in the process.

CLOSURE

Marital therapy is characterized by a great variety of closures, ranging from the nicely paced to the abrupt, from the clearly defined to the vague and ambiguous. Because of this I find it much more difficult to name closures as "successful" or complete. Indeed, I have been frequently fooled. I may send a couple along their way believing that their marriage is doomed to failure—and then, two years later, I meet them walking down the street hand-in-hand. Or, in contrast, I may say "goodbye" to a husband and wife, believing strongly that their differences are resolved, only to have them come to me a year later with all hell breaking loose. This is the marital version of the "revolving door" which swings open and shut according to the couple's need—the revolving door which honors the reality that what we are dealing with is "a set of *processes* which people engage in and you never know where they're going to go" (Rogers, 1972, p. 190).

And here I find myself frustrated! I have only lightly touched this subject of marital meaning-making (indeed, it will have to wait for a book of its own), raising questions, suggesting a few answers, and then stating there really is no way to know whether the work we have done is going to make a difference or not. But trusting in the concept that new learnings, new understandings and awarenesses, and new developmental movement can bring about increased potential for effective marital process, I continue to do this work. Once again I build on my belief that learning can open new ways to think and new ways to live both on an individual and partnership level.

Life is a terminal illness, of which age is a symptom. Memory—
the act of recalling the past—is man's spontaneous attempt to find
a cure.

—Robert N. Butler, 1971, p. 49

The past acquires meaning only in relation to the unfolding sense
of my life as a whole. Part of the significance of anything that
happens to me rests on that which does not yet exist. To fully
understand an episode in my story, I must wait for the "ending."

—Stuart Charme, 1984, p. 31

Perhaps the most important thing that has come out of life is the
discovery that if you prepare yourself at every point as well as you
can, with whatever means you may have, however meager they
may seem, you will be able to grasp the opportunity for broader
experience when it appears. Without preparation you cannot do
it. The fatal thing is rejection. Life was meant to be lived, and
curiosity must be kept alive. One must never, for whatever reason,
turn his back on life.

—Eleanor Roosevelt, 1961, p. xix

CHAPTER 13

Creative Aging

THE TERM "AGING" can be used in two ways: to describe the overarching
process of life from birth to death, and as the *stage* of life that brings the
person into and through the closing years of this process. Within the one are
all the passages of life which shape and form successive constructions of
personal meaning-making. Within the other are the symptoms and challenges of old age as each individual faces his or her dialogue with "integrity
versus despair."

These overlapping definitions place our considerations of aging within the
context of the whole of life. I agree with M. Powell Lawton (1986) that the
specialization of aging must not go so far that it loses the sense of the
dialectic—of endings and beginnings, of part and whole, of content and
process. By attending to these dialectical juxtapositions we attend to the
person as participant/meaning-maker in the the drama of life, as the individual who acts in, on, and with life, while seeking to make sense of personal
experience, to fulfill human needs and potential, to share with important

others, and to maintain some sort of hope and forward motion as a counter-balance to bitterness and despair.

Concepts of creativity widen the images of aging as they build upon the cognitive, dialectical, developmental perspectives which feature and encourage the following as essential to creative thought and process:

- free thinking with flexibility of thought and action;
- the catching of similarities in putting ideas and experiences together in new ways;
- dialectical forms of thinking which help the older individual to hold the negative and the positive aspects of aging in creative tension;
- the ability to play off the analytical/logical against the narrative/metaphorical without losing either;
- an openness to experience which captures the imaginative, the unexpected, the novel, and the possible;
- an attitude which honors and affirms the earned wisdom and integrity which comes with active, creative involvements in life as long as one lives.

These descriptions of creativity reinforce my strong bias that there *is* a *better way* built into the order of things: a better way to think, a better way to relate to one's friends and neighbors, a better way to fulfill oneself, a better way to order a world, a better way to grow older.

What also affirms my bias is continuing study of the kinds of developmental models featured in this book — models which encourage the personal growth of:

- wisdom and integrity over stupidity, ignorance, and despair;
- generativity and care over self-aggrandizement and narcissistic pre-occupation;
- open-mindedness over rigid, closed thinking;
- a willingness to entertain new ideas over opinionated self-righteousness;
- transcendent relationship over the extremes of either self or other.

And even more than that I am affirmed by models which identify capacities within older people which enable them to continue living as effectively as possible — those models which give attention to ways of "going right" over ways of "going wrong." This is an attention which sorts models of health which go beyond those of the average, the well-adjusted, or the reasonable to those which reflect an ideal of what human living is all about (Korchin, 1976, pp. ix-xiii).*

By opening our eyes to these models of the more positive potentials of aging we are more able to:

. . . consider the immense range of reactions to the aging process while at the same time focusing on some of the regularities of development manifested in the course of aging. Recognition of such diversity allows for appreciation of opportunities and potentials as well as the vulnerabilities of the later years. To the extent that older persons are viewed as able to transcend biological decline and progression toward inevitable death, an optimistic view of the later years may prevail. Similarly, to the degree that the older individual is seen as able to extricate him/herself from the presses and limited expectations of society, old age may be viewed as a period of positive potential. Ultimately it is the belief that the individual psyche can achieve mastery over both negative biological and societal influences which gives us the most potentially positive view of old age. (Kahana, 1982, pp. 885–886)

This is a therapeutic attitude and attention, therefore, which does not ignore the negative sides of aging (isn't that what Erikson's "integrity vs. despair" is all about?), but which advocates increased attention to positive preparation for aging, to human qualities of love, care and wisdom, to human emotion and "interior" experience, and to the facilitation and development of constructive altruism, openness to experience, and a sense of active involvement in life regardless of age.

In adopting these attitudes and ideals for aging we do not ignore the reality that many clients will be unable to go very far in realizing the ideal, whether because of lack of health or personal capability, or because their attitudes and beliefs lock them into negative patterns of life, or because they do not agree with these particular ideals. Rather, we affirm the potential within each of us to consider, internalize, and activate a set of possibilities and standards for more effective living in the later years.

In this chapter I first turn to models of the exceptional rather than the normative. For, as William James (1902) commented, "to study religion one should study the most religious man at his most religious moment." Thus, to study creative aging one must find the most creative persons in their most creative processes. And that is what I have set out to do.

Once I have offered these illustrations and suggestions for creative aging, I take you further into a discussion of human needs, of challenges and tasks in old age, and finally, into consideration of how these ideas can be incorpo-

---

*M. Powell Lawton, Robert Kastenbaum, Jurgis Karuza, Elizabeth Midlarsky, Boaz Kahana, and Eva Kahana, are among those gerontologists who call for a more balanced consideration of the healthful, the active, and the intentional in old age—a consideration that offers an important counterbalance to psychology's tendency to cast the psychological issues of aging in pathological terms. In the view of these theorists and researchers expectations for the elderly must be reframed within images of the proactive and the independent rather than left primarily within those which are reactive and dependent.

rated into the *doing* of therapy. That discussion will not be a simple statement of therapy with the "old" (however we would name such an entity!), but rather a statement of how the therapist is to interact with the contents, goals, and processes of aging and of what the therapeutic attitude must be in its focus on the tasks and needs of old age. What I emphasize is that no particular body of therapeutic technique can be separated out as belonging *only* or even *particularly* to the old. After all, whenever we do therapy we adapt our techniques to the needs of the person. But what can be continually stressed — and thus placed as a figure upon the ground of therapeutic effort — are the particular demands, concerns and synthesizing questions and reviews of the closing years of life.

To more fully understand an ideal for creative aging, I turn now to models of the exceptional.

Models of Creative Aging

I start with Florida Scott-Maxwell. After careers as actress, writer, wife, suffragette, she began training with Carl Jung for still another career as an analytical psychologist (this at the age of 50!). With this training she practiced psychology in Scotland and England until her retirement.

At 82 Scott-Maxwell felt impelled to write about her strong reactions to being old, and to the time in which she lived. To read her words is to find wisdom:

We who are old know that age is more than a disability. It is an intense and varied experience, almost beyond our capacity at times, but something to be carried high. If it is a long defeat it is also a victory, meaningful for the initiates of time, if not for those who have come less far. (1968, p. 5)

She also wrote about a passion which was not faltering but growing in its intensity:

Age puzzles me. I thought it was a quiet time. My seventies were interesting, and fairly serene, but my eighties are passionate. I grow more intense as I age. To my own surprise I burst out with hot conviction. Only a few years ago I enjoyed my tranquillity, now I am so disturbed by the outer world and by human quality in general, that I want to put things right as though I still owed a debt to life. I must calm down. I am far too frail to indulge in moral fervour. (pp. 13–14)

Her book takes us into realms of development not covered by our neatly diagrammed steps, helixes, and circles, to awareness that we don't know yet what aging is all about — what it is to be the "young-old," the "old," and the "old-old." Her observations are a remarkable commentary on a person's capacity to continue feeling and reacting, analyzing and comprehending, intuiting and creating into the very late years of life. Indeed, to read her book is to become humble before human potential and accomplishment.

Such themes of creativity and the growth of wisdom are developed in the studies of John A. B. McLeish (1976, 1983). In *The Ulyssean Adult* and *The Challenge of Aging,* he has collected the stories and experiences of fulfilled, healthy, older people, looking for the qualities which have helped them to age effectively and creatively. He sees his books as unique in "their *systematic* attacks on the myths of aging; their emphasis on sustained creative powers in the later years; and their identification and description of what are now becoming widely known as 'Ulyssean people'" (1983, p. ix)—those people who have maintained a *sense of quest* in their lives and who fit the creed of the "Ulyssean Society," which McLeish has spearheaded and organized:

As a Companion of *The Ulyssean Society* I am committed to the noble concept and the provable fact that men and women in the middle and later years can, if they choose to do so, richly maintain the powers to learn, produce, and create until the very last day of the life journey. (1983, pp. ix-x)

He describes these creative "Ulysseans" as adults incorporating a sense of control of personal standards, of going someplace to the end of life. With openness and flexibility they savor the complex as well as the simple, often coupling the primitive with the sophisticated in a willingness to be open to what life brings them. They carry the ability to see and to repond, to be puzzled by ideas and happenings, to let go and to flow with the abandon of a child, to savor momentary chaos while ordering the disorderly. They are people who demonstrate dialectical thinking as they maintain a capacity to hold two contradictory ideas at the same time, developing what the poet, Keats, called the "negative capability" without retreating into dogma, stereotype, or a quick search for the facts (McLeish, 1976).

McLeish's definition of the "Ulyssean" complements and illustrates the more abstract notions of Arieti, Kegan, Basseches, and Erikson, by demonstrating open, caring, generative relationships between people and people, and between people and their creative endeavors.

Abraham Maslow's (1968b) model of the self-actualizing person is pertinent to creative aging. Although he was not focusing on the later years, he was researching creative approaches to self-discovery and self-development. And he was also researching the intangibles of human health believing that the question was so important that "any leads, any suggestions, any bits of data" could be of value in developing new theories that emphasize individual quality and human potential. He searched for answers to these questions in the lives of contemporary and historical figures. He looked for people who had made or were making full use of their talents, capacities, and potentialities, who seemed to be fulfilling themselves in doing their best to live life well.

He gave these people the title "self-actualizers," saying they were creative in many ways—everything from creative homemaking or shoemaking to poetry, music, or art. These people seemed unusually sensitive to what was false or dishonest and looked at the world through fewer filters than did most people—filters of personal wishes, hopes, fears, anxieties, or limiting belief. Being relatively free of stereotypical thinking, they were more accepting of themselves, and therefore, more accepting of others. Maslow felt these people had transcended the "battle of the sexes," for example, finding their interactions with members of the other sex a delightful collaboration rather than a conflict. Although natural differences such as class, caste, role, religion, sex or age can be fertile breeding grounds for hostility, aggression or jealousy, these people demonstrated that they need not be.

Maslow has been criticized as offering a preoccupation with a "kind of psychological self-aggrandizement" which has contributed to narcissistic preoccupation in American culture (Basseches, 1984, p. 6). But I think Maslow would have argued with this. Indeed, if we study his writings in *Eupsychian Management* (1965) and in *Motivation and Personality* (1970), we find another perspective. He wrote that the "culture-individual dichotomy needs reexamination. There should be less exclusive stress on their antagonism and more on their possible collaboration and synergy" (1970, p. 102).

What Maslow offered must also be seen within the context of history, for when he wrote about self-actualization in the 1950s self-denial was the ethic of the time.* In challenging people to fulfill themselves, to work for "self-actualization," he was giving us a correction factor. And he did not neglect the problem of the dichotomy of selfishness and unselfishness noting that "highly developed, psychologically healthy people, self-actualizing people, whatever you choose to call them, you will find, if you try to rate them, that they are extraordinarily unselfish in some ways, and yet also they are extraordinarily selfish in other ways . . ." (Maslow, 1971, p. 43). Furthermore:

Somehow the polarity, the dichotomy, the assumption that more of one means less of the other, all this fades. They melt into each other and you now have a single concept for which we have no word yet. High synergy from this point of view can represent a transcending of the dichotomizing, a fusion of the opposites into a single concept. (1971, p. 210)

Another model for creative aging and health comes from psychologist Al Siebert (1983), who incorporated some of the ideas of Abraham Maslow into his study of a group of people whom he called "survivor personalities." These "survivors" represented the "small fraction of individuals made stronger by extreme circumstances and torturous conditions"—in other words, people who had survived crisis in a positive fashion. In looking back on their crisis experience these people showed:

- They had surmounted the crisis through personal effort.
- They emerged from the experience with previously unknown strengths and abilities.

---

*Yankelovich (1982) has characterized the ethic of the 1950s as self-denial and that of the 1960s and 1970s as self-fulfillment. He believes these both have failed because they are lacking in the sacred/expressive aspects of life. A new ethic of *commitment* seems to be emerging in the 1980s as people express a longing for "connectedness, commitment and creative expression" (p. 10).

• In retrospect, found value in their experience.

In studying these people Siebert asked:

• Is there a basic pattern of traits that survivors share? If so, what are the traits?
• What about their uniqueness? How can a person be similar to others and yet be a unique individual?
• What are survivors like when they aren't surviving?
• Is the survivor personality inborn or can it be learned? If it can be learned, what are the learning parameters?

In his research results he discovered that people with "survivor personalities" cope effectively with crises because they have biphasic, paradoxical personality traits. They combine such personality "opposites" as seriousness and playfulness, self-confidence and self-criticism, diligence and laziness, introversion and extraversion, thus contradicting traditional thinking in psychology, which conceptualizes personality traits as unidimensional. (I am reminded once again of Montaigne's whimsical description of himself: "All contradictions may be found in me . . . bashful, insolent; chaste, lascivious; talkative, taciturn; tough, delicate; clever, stupid; surly, affable; lying, truthful; learned, ignorant; liberal, miserly and prodigal." Aren't those exactly what Siebert has called "paradoxical" qualities?)

And what seems to happen is that survivor personalities develop a *repertoire of responses* to meet the varying situations in which they find themselves. This repertoire makes them more adaptable, more changeable, more able to approach or to retreat according to the needs of the crisis moment.

Siebert speculates that these people demonstrate particular kinds of neurological growth occurring as a result of spontaneous, self-motivated activities. He bases this speculation on the discoveries that these people use a variety of perceptual process which enables them to use subliminal perception as a valid, useful source of information. Thus, they are able to pick up on early clues about possible developments which need meaningful actions. These individuals also have the capacity to become comfortable in and even amused by ambiguous situations that might frighten others. Siebert hypothesizes that such indicators allow us to infer that self-motivated, self-managed learning can lead to advanced levels of neurological development. And from his research he hypothesizes that neurological maturation can continue in humans throughout their lives.

Siebert opens windows on aging by suggesting the important role of flexible repertoires of personal traits — traits which do not fit tight categories or predictive statistics. His model complements dialectical models which call for the transcendence of the either/ors of life and living, offering therapeutic parameters for therapists to consider in the teaching and facilitating of creative aging. Here is rich material, also, for considering the "dangerous opportunity" of the crisis experience. If crisis is the reaching of our limits of knowing—of a way of being—then the wider the repertoire for imagining life, for fitting life together, for solving dilemmas, for opening oneself to new experience, the greater the ability to handle one crisis effectively in preparation for the next.

But what do these idealized models (using Nadler's terminology, p. 31) have to offer the therapist? I see them as images of that which a person can become—images which can plant seeds of hope and intention even in the face of physical loss and the times of despair which are so much a part of growing older. To hold these models is to counteract the long held myths of aging which name this as a period of inevitable decline.

If anything, then, studying positive models can help the therapist to face biases, stereotypes, repressed feelings, negative attitudes, in order to be more effective in the service of creative aging. These models can also make us much more aware of the need to *prepare* people early in life to meet the challenges which will inevitably be theirs. And to study these models is to find much illustration of dialectical thinking, of intergenerational love and care, of the power of generative activity, and of the important dynamics of relationship and culture. In the stories of these creative people is food for thought, goals to consider, and personal traits to be encouraged and developed.

Human Needs

With these models joining our tacit knowledge as an influence on what we do, let us consider another area important to the therapist who works in creative aging. This is the therapeutic task of helping people to fulfill their needs. But first we need to consider these dimensions of need.

Everyone has noted the astonishing sources of energy that seem available to those who enjoy what they are doing or find meaning in what they are doing. The self-renewing man [or woman] knows that if he has no great conviction about what he is doing he had better find something that he can have great conviction about. . . . Everyone . . . should be doing *something* about which he cares deeply. And if he is to escape the prison of self, it must be something not essentially egocentric in nature. (Gardner, 1961, pp. 16–17)

I have long savored these words of John Gardner as a powerful statement of basic human need. Therefore, I use them to introduce this discussion of need fulfillment as an important part of creative aging. If the fulfillment of needs fires us, satisfies us, comforts us, and completes us, then needs are extremely important in any consideration of creative aging. And this consideration is one way to alert us as therapists to the tragedy of *uncreative* aging, when the environments, contexts, or negative learnings of aging deny people fulfillment of such basic needs.

And just what are these needs?

Though there are varying taxonomies in psychological literature, I have created my own:

Identity Needs

- to be perceived and respected for one's uniqueness
- to find creative outlets for that uniqueness
- to continue to grow in the meaning of that uniqueness

Participation Needs

- to actively participate in success
- to create and complete personal goals
- to find rewards valued by one's culture and by oneself

Partnership and Intimacy Needs

- to blend self with another, independence with dependence, autonomy with intimacy.

I was alerted to such needs in 1972 when I did a study (reported in Carlsen, 1973) of women undergraduates, 35 years and older. In an open-ended question I asked them what their late-life educational experience contributed to feelings of self-fulfillment. In response, they offered thoughtful, poignant responses which grouped themselves into clusters of expressive human needs. These women felt that their educational experience — an act of direct participation — showed them how important it is to:

- give
- be an active part of life
- view the world with a widening perspective
- complete difficult goals
- build a balance between creative learning and creative vocation
- find monetary success in a world that honors money
- find a feeling of self-identity

In their answers they named process verbs which helped them to fulfill these needs: contribute, achieve, partake, earn, challenge, exert, compete, explore, prove, and succeed. And they noted the qualities which they had discovered through the striving for new learning — flexibility, awareness, self-confidence, self-possession, expression, capability — all spin-offs of dynamic involvement in new learning experience.

To quote a few of these women undergraduates:

As I have said, it [the college experience] returned to me the knowledge that I can.

For the first time I feel confident that I am equal to meeting the challenges of living that occur outside the shelter of a protected housewife situation.

[I am] no longer just a recipient of "TV" ads, of built-in conveniences, of husband's income. Now [I] partake and give.

Growth in self-confidence increased these women's participation in life. They experienced a greater openness to risk as well as a greater trust of the ambiguities and paradoxes of life. They appeared to accept the fact of *being in process*—an acceptance that seems to come to people who work through subjective problems to greater objectivity about themselves. Several of their statements give evidence of this new attitude about themselves and about life process:

The knowledge that education is not confined to the first few years of life but can continue forever makes life much more challenging and much more eventful and much more rewarding.

I am less afraid of voicing my opinion, of entering into controversial exchanges, and am willing to recognize other points of view not as threats but as part of the learning experience.

I would never have been satisfied to only fulfill my sex role in life although it was the most present and necessary for my well being.

In these women's reporting was evidence that growing self-acceptance, self-knowledge, and self-understanding helped them to relinquish fixed standards and protective structures. Becoming more independent in decision-making and more tolerant of personal liabilities and limitations, they illustrated increasing belief in themselves. Although many of the women suffered physical and emotional strain through the intensity of the learning experience, and although some of the women found their emerging learning and growth threatening to a partner or a spouse, over half of the women in this survey found enrichment of their intimate relationships. Thus did their self-development—their "self-actualization" as it were—become translated into a synergy of relationship with family and friends. What they also seemed to be touching was underlying human needs which are of a universal sort, which have no basis in gender.

These women have offered models for lifelong learning, for the capacity to *be in process,* for continuing exploration, for the ability to compare and contrast where one has been with where one is going, for some sort of transcendence of the dicohotomies of self and other, for a dialectic of self development and other development. And they have demonstrated quite dramatically the motivating power of need fulfillment and the resulting growth and development which can come with the fulfillment of those needs.*

---

*Compare these findings with those of Belenky, Clinchy, Golberger, and Tarule (1986) and those of William Perry (1970, 1981). I speculate that out of these emerging pieces of research on cognitive process we may come to fuller understanding of the interactions between our far-reaching gender programmings and our cognitive developmental processes.

Within the contexts of developmental process another body of needs must be considered — what Angyal calls our "neededness":

We ourselves want to be needed. We not only have needs, we are also strongly motivated by *neededness*. To be of no use to anything or anybody would make life intolerable. What is the main problem of old people? Some of them are well provided for and do not suffer from the insecurity that arises out of losing one's earning power and thus the satisfaction of one's "needs." But they are not happy. They suffer from the diminution of their usefulness, from the feeling that they cannot be of help to anybody any more. This would not make any sense if the human being were merely an egocentric organization complete within itself. We are restless when we are not needed, because we feel "unfinished," "incomplete," and we can only get completed in and through these relationships. (1965, p. 20)

From a developmental standpoint the need to be needed is closely involved in the processes and virtues of love, care, and wisdom — the virtues which Erikson has defined as the unique tasks of the middle and later years. Jurgis Karuza (1986) directs us to the valuable contributions elderly adults can make interpersonally and intergenerationally, and emphasizes that the "study of altruism in later life may provide an important piece of the puzzle of successful aging, one that may be especially timely." Elizabeth Midlarsky and Eva Kahana (1986) address this same concern as they report research findings which show that helping may be an "important route to meaningful participation by the elderly." With a frequently untapped wealth of competencies and experiences, older people have much to give. This fact, coupled with fewer requirements for their time, gives them unique opportunity to assume special kinds of helping roles. By assuming such roles "individuals active in providing for the welfare of others may become deeply involved in a process which results in an expansion and enrichment of their sense of self, and may enjoy one or a series of peak experiences" (p. 5).

Although this "need to be needed" may seem rather obvious, those of us in the helping profession would do well to remind ourselves frequently of this particular need as we address its meaning and facilitate its fulfillment in the lives of the people who come seeking our help.

Hans Selye, who drew on his biological research to postulate a model for human health and development, suggests a means for the fulfillment of the needs which I have named above. Selye acknowledges that he has "strayed from simply reporting my investigations into the biochemical or histological details of stress," as he mixes philosophy with science, often treading where he "doesn't belong." But he counters by saying "my attempt to develop a new philosophy of life is only the logical development of my work, since my aim has always been to discover how we can live with stress and make it work for us" (1978, p. 70).

The challenge of living with stress brought Selye to his postulation of "altruistic egoism" as a synergistic model for life. In formulating this he was concerned with the extremes of either altruism or egotism. On the one hand, he believed that "altruism carried to an extreme—constantly putting other people's good before your own—violates our nature, the biological basis of life, and leads, in all cases I've seen, to constant, if not always conscious, stressful frustration and resentment." On the other hand, extreme egotism—"the ruthless and exclusive pursuit of one's own ends . . . creates antagonism and enemies around you. One of the most striking things I've noticed through life is how frighteningly quickly rank, fortune, and power can be lost. Pity the poor men and women who, having clawed their way to the top, have created so much ill will around them that they desperately have to remain there—or else" (Selye in an interview with Cherry, 1978.

Specifically, Selye's "altruistic egoism" is a recipe which he calls an antidote to the stresses of life. In this he challenges us to honor our "egoism"—our need to look after ourselves—and to avoid the opposite quality of "egotism," a ruthless pursuit of our own ends.

And so, little by little, drawing on my own experience and scientific work, I was able to make a kind of recipe for the best antidote to the stresses of life. The first ingredient . . . is to seek your own stress level, to decide whether you're a racehorse or a turtle and to live your life accordingly. [And this has great pertinence to retirement planning.] The second is to choose your goals and make sure they're really your own, and not imposed on you by an overhelpful mother or teacher. . . And the third ingredient in this recipe is altruistic egoism—looking out for oneself by being necessary to others, and thus earning their goodwill. (Cherry, 1978, p. 70)

Selye acknowledges that most of us cannot make the contributions of an Einstein, a da Vinci, or a Mozart, but that every one of us can find something to give which gives us meaning in the eyes of others, and which thus can give us meaning in our own. He believes that "striving to make yourself ever more useful and necessary is an aim you can safely pursue throughout your life, and one that will protect you from the worst of all modern social stresses, purposelessness. I think the response to this idea from people all over the world indicates how great a need there is for this kind of direction to our lives" (Cherry, 1978, p. 70).

The processes of lifelong meaning-making suggest one final need for this discussion: the need to create the view down the mountain as one orders and makes sense of life. Indeed, here lies the task of "integrity versus despair" as the aging individual considers the meanings of his or her life not only within the contexts of the immediate and the personal, but within those dimensions which can be called spiritual and universal. Erikson summarizes the challenge and need in this manner:

It is through this last stage that the life cycle weaves back on itself in its entirety, ultimately integrating maturing forms of hope, will, purpose, competence, fidelity, love, and care, into a comprehensive sense of wisdom. Throughout life, the individual has, on some level, anticipated the finality of old age, experiencing an existential dread of "not-being" alongside an ever-present process of integrating those behaviors and restraints, those choices and rejections, those essential strengths and weaknesses over time that constitute what we have called the sense of "I" in the world. In old age this tension reaches its ascendancy. The elder is challenged to draw on a life cycle that is far more nearly completed than yet to be lived, to consolidate a sense of wisdom with which to live out the future, to place him- or herself in perspective among those generations now living, and to accept his or her place in an infinite historical progression. (Erikson, Erikson, & Kivnick, 1986, pp. 55–56)

The activity of *life review* can translate the abstract needs described above into the meaning-making of old age. Robert Butler is one of those who affirms the power and importance of this activity:

The life review, a looking-back process that one sets in motion by anticipating death, can be a major step in personality development. Memory serves our sense of identity: it provides continuity, wisdom and serenity. Goethe noted that "he is the happiest man who can see the connection between the end and the beginning of his life." The act of recall can renew our awareness of the present and restore our sense of wonder. (1971, p. 51)

Furthermore:

A continuing life-long identity crisis seems to be a sign of good health. Such vaguely defined features of the personality as flexibility, resilience and self-awareness all seem to be factors in the way an older person experiences life. They also influence the way he faces death. The most positive uses of the life review, and of the self-controlled identity crisis, occur in the creative works of the aged. (1971, p. 51)

The therapist can do a great deal in encouraging the kinds of altruistic activities suggested here, and by stimulating the aging client to pull together the experiences of life into a meaningful, understandable whole. This is the time when the therapist must walk beside his or her clients within their continuing developmental meaning-makings.

As I close this discussion of needs significant for creative aging, I add a caveat that no simplistic listing can ever cover the complex motivations of human beings. Indeed, needs are idiosyncratic, giving clues to the particular sources of meaning and purpose which bring fulfillment and comfort to the person. Accepting the structure as only suggestive, therefore, I emphasize that helping our clients to find central purpose, central contributions, central structures for ordering meaning, is one way we translate concepts of basic needs into strategies for creative aging.

CHALLENGES IN THE LATER YEARS

Adult development theorist Bernice Neugarten (1968) has combined some of the more global, abstract challenges of the later years into what she calls the "salient issues" of adulthood:

(1) The use of experience.
(2) The structuring of the social environment.
(3) Dealing with perspectives of time.

(4) Examining ways to shape the major themes of love, time and death.

(5) Coming to terms with changes in self-concept, and changes in identity as one faces success, contingencies of marriage and relationship, parenting, career development and decline, retirement, widowhood, illness and personal death. (p. 139)

Neugarten also speaks of the "executive" processes of personality in adulthood, which provide the skills for solving the issues named above. These include "self-awareness, selectivity, manipulation and control of one's environment, personal mastery, and competence" (1968, p. 139) These processes give both the means and the challenge for the adult to keep growing as long as he or she lives.

Another set of challenges for therapist and client to address together include those found in *Enjoy Old Age* by B.F. Skinner and M.E. Vaughan. To read their chapter titles is to find an insightful outline of what this business of aging is about:

- Doing Something about Old Age
- Keeping in Touch with the World
- Keeping in Touch with the Past
- Thinking Clearly
- Keeping Busy
- Having a Good Day
- Getting Along with People
- Feeling Better
- "A Necessary End"
- Playing Old Person
- A Great Performance

Skinner and Vaughan remind us that older people have fewer new things to be learned, and thus tend to fall back on old routines. But because some problems cannot be solved in old ways (and boredom is one of them), it becomes important to stimulate new activity and new interest. Novelty, deliberate change, and new learning are essential for the older person. The challenge is to keep creatively busy.

But one of the disappointments for the older person is losing some of the pleasurable things he or she once had: a job, for example, or a sport, or a musical skill. Skinner and Vaughn say this is:

. . . rather like the depression we experience when we move from one city to another. Things we did in the old city can no longer be done in the new. We cannot go to the same supermarket, walk to the same neighbor's house, say hello to the same postman, take the dog for a walk on the same streets. A great many of the things we once enjoyed are no longer feasible. The resulting depression is also like missing someone who has died; everything we enjoyed doing with that person can no longer be done. *When retired, we miss our job as we miss a city or an old friend.* (1983, p. 81)

An antidote to this is to teach people to fully engage the present — to counter what Alfred North Whitehead calls our "human style," which is "to mourn the past and worry about the future, while all the time the Sacred Present is passing us by, half-used, half-enjoyed" (cited in McLeish, 1983, p. 37). This "sacred present" is what people often discover for the first time when they recover from a near-death experience. Seeing life for the first time in all its sensual intensity, they report finding a vividness in their surroundings never seen before. The use of this "present" is found in the work of a woman novelist whom McLeish describes: "She sets to work, sitting at her desk, and writes steadily day by day, week by week, not fretting over time lost or invisible obstacles that may lie ahead — living and working in 'the Sacred Present'" (1983, p. 37). Can we as therapists teach this attitude to our clients?*

To face the present is also to acknowledge the "double-edged nature of aging." Atchley (1983) writes:

The double-edged nature of aging can be found in the current literature on aging. Some researchers emphasize the negative aspects of aging. They focus on sickness, poverty, isolation, and demoralization. The theories they develop seek to explain how people arrive at such an unhappy state. And they tend to see aging as a social problem. Other researchers emphasize the positive. They look at the elderly and see that most have good health, frequent contact with family members, adequate incomes, and a high degree of satisfaction with life. The theories they develop try to explain how aging can have such positive outcomes. They see the social problems of aging as applying to only a minority of the elderly. Because aging can have both positive and negative outcomes, neither side is wrong. Certainly both kinds of outcomes exist, and understanding both outcomes is important. (p. 10)

Erik Erikson's developmental ladder is an excellent representation of the "double-edged nature of aging" as he names the psychosocial tasks of middle age and aging as "generativity vs. stagnation," and "integrity vs. despair." In Tables 4 and 5 I have charted these opposing forces to name some of the alternative choices and results which can occur with the facing of these issues. The therapist can use these tables in various ways for teaching, for entering a particular issue in a more focused way — the vocational, for example — with full awareness that this attention to one facet of aging must be widened at a later time if the complex, overlapping problems of aging are to be fully addressed.

Another representation of the tasks of aging (Table 6) comes from Bessie Robinson, a nurse who offered a presentation at one of the workshops on aging which I facilitated. Her ideas take us closer to some of the day-by-day, here-and-now problems which the older person must consider. I find Robinson's model a helpful complement to the more abstract models above.

And finally (Figures 10, 11), Helen Ansley rather pointedly dares the

---

*Turn again to the material on career development in Chapter 11. Much of that material is very pertinent to the maintenance of a meaningful "sacred present" in late life careers and activities.

TABLE 4 Erikson Concept: Generativity vs. stagnation

Stagnation	Generativity
Boredom	Energy, motivation
Mental decline	Mental growth
Self-absorbed	Other-absorbed
Obsessive pseudo-intimacy	The establishment of the next
Narcissistic self-indulgence	generation through the production
	and care of offspring, or through
	other altruistic and creative acts

Relationships

1. Deteriorating	1. Growing
2. Selfish	2. Selfless
3. Taking	3. Giving
	4. Involved in community, children, others

Mind

1. Closed	1. Open
2. Rigid	2. Flexible
3. Stuck	3. Growing
	4. Creative

Physical

1. Unrealistic body image	1. Realistic body image
2. Imbalance	2. Balance

Vocation

1. Disillusionment	1. Sense of being needed
2. Boredom	2. Ongoing exploration, discovery
3. No sense of contribution to others	3. Contribution to society, children
4. Stagnation	4. Generativity

helping professional to look with fresh eyes at the influences foisted upon the older person, and at the reforming of old models of ascent and decline. In her eighties, Helen brings excellent credentials to the study of aging. Courageous in her ongoing confrontation of the aging process, she has forged unique wisdom and understanding in a demonstration of what creative aging is about. She knows the "double-edged sword of aging," for she has often felt the despair of growing older. But as an advocate for older people, as a teacher of both seniors and gerontologists, as a person who has struggled with integrity versus despair, and as a person not yet ready to die (and she says she maintains that choice), she points to one of the biggest challenges, which is to shift and redirect physical prowess and energy into

TABLE 5 Erikson Concept: Integrity versus despair

Despair	Integrity
Arousal/anxiety/blocking	Serenity
Pulling in from life	Continuity, openness to life
Decline of perceptual acuity	Growth or maintenance of perceptual acuity

Relationships, Family

1. Loneliness	1. Ability to be alone
2. Excessive dependency	2. Solution of problems presented by others: aging parents, children, spouse
3. No support system	3. Maintenance of support systems

Mind

1. Decline in mental functioning	1. Continuing study: adult education
2. Boredom	2. Artistic expressions
3. Self-absorbed	3. Service to others

Physical

1. Repression of fears of physical decline	1. Realistic evaluation and acceptance of losses
2. Rejection of aging peers	2. Acceptance of aging peers
3. Development of invalid role	3. Perceptual awareness
4. Preoccupation with illness	4. Satisfactory resolution of illness experience

Vocation/meaning

1. Disillusionment	1. A sense of being needed
2. Boredom	2. Continuing shaping of personal meaning
3. Stimulus deprivation	3. Effort to find novelty
4. No investment of meaning	4. Something to be committed to
5. Negative outcome	5. Use of personal abilities in interesting, challenging activity

mental and spiritual development which can continue to grow and expand until the time of death.

What is interesting to me in all these models, in all these statements of needs and challenge, is their flavor of consistency, of overlap, of echoing the same themes, which gives credence to the concept of a universal program for life which helps people to find greater serenity, unity, and contentment in their old age. These models also point with consistency to an intensification of becoming as one grows older; to the challenge of putting one's personal

TABLE 6 Guide for retirement growth: From gaps to goals. Prepared by Bessie
Rice Robinson December 7, 1976

BASIC NEEDS of all	My age NOW ____	Plan of Action Between NOW AND THEN→ ____years	My age** "THEN" ____
HEALTH Food Shelter Activity	*		
LOVE Family Friends Animals			
SOCIAL Religion Education Groups			
SECURITY Work Budget Assets			
LEGAL Protection Provisions Wills, etc			
TIME Habits Hobbies Priorities			

*Check each block heading: (1) excellent (2) good (3) poor
**Your own estimate of life expectancy

house in order while sorting the viewpoints down the mountain and struggling aginst the disappointments and losses which can not help but come
with old age.

BUT WHAT ARE OUR THERAPEUTIC TASKS?

Perhaps our first and greatest task is to treat the older client in the same
manner as we would treat any client. Although attending to the unique tasks
and challenges of old age, this cognitive developmental therapy uses all the

NEW IMAGE OF AGING
BECOMING A WHOLE PERSON

We're the target — being pulled apart by the people who are trying to help us

Taking responsibility for ourselves — Reaching a balance

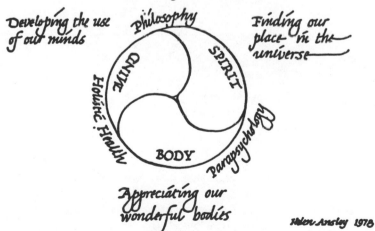

FIGURE 10 New image of aging

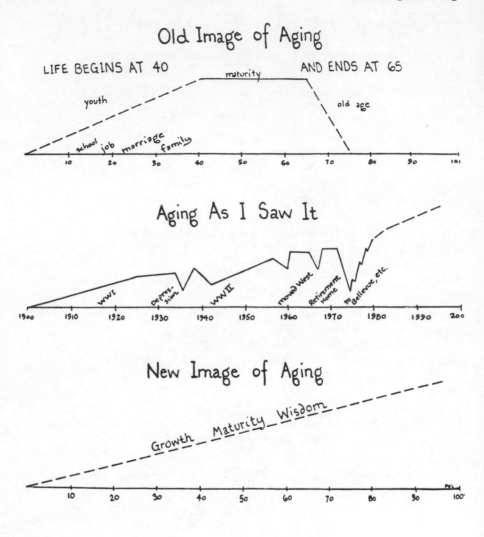

Old Image of Aging

LIFE BEGINS AT 40   AND ENDS AT 65

maturity

youth   old age

school job marriage family

10   20   30   40   50   60   70   80   90   10(

Aging As I Saw It

WWI   depres-   WWII   moved West   Retirement   to Bellevue, etc.
        sion   Home

1900 1910 1920 1930 1940 1950 1960 1970 1980 1990 200

New Image of Aging

Growth — Maturity — Wisdom

10   20   30   40   50   60   70   80   90   100

HELEN ANSLEY   SEPT. 1980

FIGURE 11 Images of aging

techniques and approaches suggested in this book as it continues to cultivate healing through genuine dialogue and through the establishment, data gathering, patterning, and reconciliation processes of meaning-making. This therapeutic approach recognizes that all the developmental tasks and questions of earlier years may arise again with new urgency and dimension. Here the therapist must understand not only the physiological processes of aging, but the larger concerns of the person who is still a "being-in-the-process-of-becoming." We need to counteract psychology's tendency to ignore the global aspects of human *being* — what Lawton (1973) calls the "interior" of the older person. He has pointedly asked: "Can there not be a psychodiagnostic based partly upon feelings, attitudes, self-perceptions, *Weltanschaung*? Unless we ask the older person how he feels, we shall not really know how best to administer treatment, whether through reassurance, behavior therapy, occupational therapy, or group activity" (1973, p. 342). Robert Kastenbaum (1973) also calls for attention to the "sleeping, dreaming, imaging, fantasizing, meditating, creating, loving, grieving, dying" of the older person (p. 699).

Joan heightened my awarenesses of all these issues when she came at 69 to work on a recurrent depression. Alert and highly intelligent Joan held no college degrees but showed a sensitivity and openness to continuing learning and growth as she discussed insights coming from some of the books she was reading. She also showed a remarkable dialectical capability as she compared and contrasted old and new beliefs which were undergoing renewed questionings as she struggled with her religious faith, her relationship to her husband, and her current challenge of long-held assumptions. With a major developmental disequilibrium shaking her forms of thought and relationship, Joan's therapy was as exciting in its momentum as any that I encounter. Here was a woman poised between two worlds and courageous enough to risk the leap into new forms of thinking, feeling and being.

The only therapeutic accommodation that I made to Joan's age was in the choice of chairs. Because she had a back problem which made it difficult to sit for extended periods of time, I made special physical arrangements to ease her discomfort. What I couldn't do was say this was "therapy with an old person" — because she wasn't old, because she was engaged in all the tasks of lifelong development, and because it would have been an insult to her uniqueness to classify her simplistically according to age. In working with her I learned a great deal as I found many of my own stereotypes surfacing and tumbling as we met together. What was remarkable was that this therapy went *fast* as Joan put together scattered pieces of meaning and sorted and adjusted her patterns of life. What came was an enriched sense of her integrity as she gained further insight into early relationships with her mother, her husband, and an identification with the little girl who had struggled into and through adulthood in a search for a genuine "knowing that I am somebody." As Joan put it, "This is the little girl I have been grieving over all these years."

Joan also began to come to terms with a long-term cognitive habit of dwelling on the past, paying attention to unhappiness, tending to remember the negative things, and tending to bring up a tragedy . . . I'm just beginning to be aware." Those last words speak to the remarkable ability of the person to find new awareness regardless of age, and to take the new awarenesses into new approaches to thought and feeling.

Out of my work with Joan and others like her, out of my study of the needs and challenges of old age, and out of my belief in the developmental models which I have discussed in this book, I name the following tasks as important in working with older people (and note how many of these refer to the attitudes and tacit assumptions of the therapist):

- To see both the negatives and positives of aging.
- To come to terms with stereotype and bias.
- To appreciate the challenges and losses inherent in the aging process.
- To explore and facilitate second careers in reframing retirement as possibility rather than withdrawal.
- To identify and teach models for creative aging.
- To facilitate the fulfillment of personal needs.
- To encourage and develop dialectical thinking, intergenerational love and care, and a transcendence of the dichotomies of self and other, of the communal and the autonomous.
- To support exploration and review of personal history in order to create a narrative of life.

And further, as I have already suggested above, a vital therapeutic task is to help the client come to terms with the griefs of old age. To effectively do this the helping professional must be sensitive not only to the loss experiences, but to the inherent challenge present in the crisis experience. Here, certainly, is much of the raw material for emergent wisdom. In fact, Parkes (1972) reports that his research shows a new identity emerges from a major loss of the magnitude of bereavement. Within the stocktaking, the establishment of a new life style, relationships, reactions from friends, neighbors, the individual has to establish a fresh place. Included can be the destruction of old assumptions, reassessment of personal power and possessions, and the working-through of shifts in self-esteem. All this can bring a major shift in self-identity.

Other therapeutic tasks include the life review discussed above, proactive preventive medicine, and family therapy which deals with shifting parent/child roles and patterns of independence and dependence. But a central task, according to gerontologist Carl Eisdorfer (1974), is to help the older person "put it all together and to put it all together in advance of the breakdown of the system, rather than to come back in after it's broken down and run around with a series of band-aids trying to contain it before it oozes out at the seams." And, in doing this, the helping professional must be able to step back as he or she teaches, facilitates, and supports the older person:

. . . our role is to optimize or maximize the adaptive capacity of the individual by providing assistance and support where necessary, and gradually and appropriately withdrawing those supports in order to help the person retain control over his or her own life to the greatest extent possible. (Eisdorfer, 1974, p. 69)

This is to counter the tendency of the mental health professional to intervene in crisis, to want to do something about it, to act in some way. Eisdorfer comments, "it may be that we professionals are not as needed as we would like to think we are. In dealing with a crisis, our role may be to prepare people and then not attempt to provide them with a crutch so that they will become dependent on us" (p. 62).

So one of the key elements is helping our clients to find a way to put their challenges together ahead of time with a wisdom that sees the negatives but also sees the continuing potential for genuine growth and development. In our helping role we can serve as supporters, arbiters, advocates, facilitators, and teachers as we treat the older client with dignity and respect, without a stereotyping which pins them to the great mass called "elderly" or "senior." And we may increasingly realize what Eisdorfer has further suggested—that older people are geting brighter and brighter, wiser and wiser, and they are simply not going to stand for the "kind of nonsense that the aged had to contend with 10 years ago." As we redefine successful aging we will come to respect older people in new and increasing ways, not because they are old but "because they are valuable, because there is a role that's crucial to the development and continuity and identity of the individuals in the tribe. Because in a sense the old are the glue that's keeping the tribe together" (Eisdorfer, 1974, p. 67).

On that note of sensitive challenge I close this chapter as I leave this book. Indeed, it seems appropriate that I bow out of this discussion after considering creative endings for the meaning-makings of life.

REFERENCES

Adams, James (1974). *Conceptual blockbusting*. San Francisco: W.H. Freeman and Company.

Adler, Alfred (1958). *What life should mean to you*. New York: Capricorn Books.

Adler, Alfred (1959). *Understanding human nature*. New York: Premier Books.

Adler, Alfred (1969). *The science of living*. New York: Doubleday Anchor Books.

Allman, L. R. & Jaffe, D. T. (Eds.). (1977). *Readings in adult psychology: Contemporary perspectives* (1977–1978 Edition). New York: Harper & Row.

Allport, Gordon W. (1962). Psychological models for guidance. *Harvard Educational Review*, *32*(4), 373–381.

Allport, Gordon W. (1968). *The person in psychology*. Boston: Beacon Press.

Allport, Gordon W. (1979). *The nature of prejudice*. Menlo Park, CA: Addison Wesley.

Anastasi, Anne (1976). *Psychological testing* (4th ed.). New York: Macmillan.

Angyal, Andras. (1941). *Foundations for a science of personality*. New York: Commonwealth Fund.

Angyal, Andras (1948).The holistic approach in psychiatry. *American Journal of Psychiatry*, *105*, 178–182.

Angyal, Andras. (1965). *Neurosis and treatment: A holistic theory*. (Eugenia Hanfmann & Richard M. Jones, Eds.). New York: Viking.

Angyal, Andras (1969). A logic of systems. In F. E. Emery (Ed.), *Systems thinking*. Harmondsworth, Middlesex, England: Penguin.

Antonovsky, Anton. (1979). *Health, stress, and coping*. San Francisco: Jossey-Bass.

Arieti, Silvano (1976). *Creativity: The magic synthesis*. New York: Basic Books.

Arnett, Ronald C. (1982). The inevitable conflict and confronting in dialogue. In John Stewart (Ed.), *Bridges Not Walls* (3rd ed.). Reading, MA: Addison-Wesley.

Atchley, Robert (1983). *Aging: Continuity and change*. Belmont, CA.: Wadsworth.

Baltes, Paul B., & Brim, Orville, G. (1982). *Life-span development and behavior*. New York: Academic Press.

Barnlund, Dean (1982). Toward a meaning-centered philosophy of communication. In J. Stewart (Ed.), *Bridges not walls* (3rd ed.) Reading, MA: Addison-Wesley.

251

Basseches, Michael (1984). *Dialectical thinking and adult development*. Norwood, NJ: Ablex.

Bateson, Gregory (1958). *Naven* (2nd. ed.). Stanford: Stanford University Press.

Bateson, Gregory (1972). *Steps to an ecology of mind*. New York: Chandler.

Bateson, Gregory (1978). Breaking out of the double bind [Interview by Daniel Goleman]. *Psychology Today*, *12*(3), 42–51.

Bateson, Gregory (1979). *Mind and nature: A necessary unity*. New York: Bantam Books.

Baxter, Neale (1982). The joy of classifying: A counselor's guide to taxonomies and crosswalks. *Occupational Outlook Quarterly*, *26*(4), 13–20.

Bedrosian, Richard C., & Beck, Aaron T. (1980). Principles of cognitive therapy. Chapter 5 in Michael Mahoney (Ed.). *Psychotherapy Process*. New York: Plenum Press.

Belenky, M. F., Clinchy, B. M., Goldberger, N. R., & Tarule, J. M. (1986). *Women's ways of knowing: The development of self, voice, and mind*. New York: Basic Books.

Bellah, R. N., Madsen, R., Sullivan, W. M., Swidler, A., & Tipton, S. M. (1985). *Habits of the heart: Individualism and commitment in American life*. Berkeley, CA: University of California Press.

Blank, Thomas O. (1982). *A social psychology of developing adults*. New York: John Wiley.

Bolles, Richard N. (1979). *The quick job-hunting map*. Berkeley, CA: Ten Speed Press.

Bolles, Richard N. (1981). *What color is your parachute?* Berkeley, CA: Ten Speed Press.

Boulding, Kenneth E. (1985). *The world as a total system*. Beverly Hills, CA: Sage.

Bowlby, J. (1977). The making and breaking of affectional bonds: II. Some principles of psychotherapy. *British Journal of Psychiatry*, *130*, 421–431.

Bridges, William (1980). *Transitions: Making sense of life changes*. Menlo Park, CA: Addison-Wesley.

Brown, Duane & Brooks, Linda (Eds.) (1984). *Career choice and development*. San Francisco: Jossey-Bass.

Bruner, Jerome (1986). *Actual minds, possible worlds*. Cambridge, MA: Harvard University Press.

Buber, Martin (1965). *The knowledge of man* (M. Friedman & R. G. Smith, Trans.). London: George Allen & Unwin.

Buber, M., Rogers, C., & Friedman, M. (1965). Dialogue between Martin Buber and Carl Rogers. In M. Buber, *The knowledge of man* (M. Friedman, Ed.). New York: Harper & Row.

Buber, Martin (1970). *I and thou* (W. Kaufmann, Trans.). New York: Charles Scribner's Sons. (Original work published 1957).

Bugental, James (1967). *Challenges of humanistic psychology*. New York: McGraw-Hill.

Buhler, C. & Massirik, F. (Eds.). (1968). *The course of human life: A study in the humanistic perspective*. New York: Springer.

Buhler, Charlotte (1977). Meaningfulness of the biographical approach. In Lawrence Allman & Dennis Jaffe (Eds.), *Readings in adult psychology: Contemporary perspectives*. New York: Harper & Row.

Butler, Robert (1971). Age: The life review. *Psychology Today*, *5*(7), pp. 49, 51, 89.

Butler, Robert (1975). *Why survive? Being old in America*. New York: Harper & Row.

Butler, R. N., & Lewis, M. I. (1976). *Love and sex after sixty*. New York: Harper & Row.

Carlsen, Mary L. B. (1973). A four-year retrospective view of the educational experience of a group of mature women undergraduate students. Doctoral dissertation, University of Washington. *Dissertations abstracts international*. *35*(1), 153A.

Cavan, Ruth (1965). *Marriage and family in the modern world*. 2nd edition. New York: Thomas Y. Crowell.

Charme, Stuart L. (1984). *Meaning and myth in the study of lives: A Sartrean perspective*. Philadelphia: University of Pennsylvania Press.

Cherry, C. (1961). *On human communication*. New York: Science Editions.

Cherry, L. (1978). On the real benefits of eustress. [Interview with Hans Selye]. *Psychology Today*, March, 60–70.

Clayton, Vivian (1975). Erikson's theory of human development as it applies to the aged: Wisdom as contradictive cognition. *Human development*, *18*, 119–128.

Colarusso, C. A. & Nemiroff, R. A. (1981). *Adult development: A new dimension in psychodynamic theory and practice*. New York: Plenum Press.

Coles, Robert, M. D. (1971, Oct.). On the meaning of work. *Atlantic Monthly*, 103–4.

Creelman, Marjorie (1966). *The experimental investigation of meaning*. New York: Springer.

Crystal, J. & Bolles, R. N. (1974). *Where do I go from here with my life?* Berkeley: Ten speed Press.

Cunningham, S. (1985). Rollo May: the case for love, beauty and the humanities. *APA Monitor*, *16*(5).

Douglass, B. G. & Moustakas, C. (1985). Heuristic inquiry: The internal search to know. *Journal of Humanistic Psychology*, *25*(3), 39–55.

Downs, H. & Roll, R. J. (1981). *The best years book: How to plan for fulfillment, security, and happiness in the retirement years*. New York: Delacorte Press/Eleanor Friede.

Dryden, Windy (1984). Rational-emotive therapy and cognitive therapy. In M. Reda & M. Mahoney (Eds.), *Cognitive psychotherapies: Recent developments in theory, research, and practice*. Cambridge, MA: Ballinger.

Duvall, Evelyn M. (1967). *Family development* (3rd ed.). New York: Lippincott.

Eisdorfer, Carl (1974). The role of the psychiatrist in successful aging. In Pfeiffer, Eric (1974). *Successful aging*. Durham, NC.: Center for the Study of Aging and Human Development, Duke University.

Eisdorfer, C. & Lawton, M. P. (Eds.). (1973). *The psychology of adult development and aging*. Washington D.C.: American Psychological Association.

Emery, F. E. (Ed.). (1969). *Systems thinking*. New York: Penguin Books.

Erikson, E. H. (1964). *Childhood and society*. (Rev. ed.). New York: W. W. Norton.

Erikson, Erik H. (1966). Reading #3. Developmental themes of the mature years. In L. D. Kleinsasser & D. B. Harris (Eds.), *The middle years: Development and adjustment*. State College, PA: State University, Center for Continuing Liberal Education.

Erikson, Erik H. (1968). *Identity, youth and crisis*. New York: W. W. Norton & Company.

Erickson, Erik H. (1974). *Dimensions of new identity*. New York: W. W. Norton.

Erikson, Erik H. (1978a). *Adulthood*. New York: W. W. Norton and Co.

Erikson, Erik H. (1978b). Reflections on Dr. Borg's life cycle. In E. H. Erikson (Ed.), *Adulthood*. New York: W. W. Norton.

Erikson, Erik H. (1981). On generativity and identity: From a conversation with Erik and Joan Erikson. *Havard Educational Review*, *51*(2), 249–269.

Erikson, Erik H. (1982). *The life cycle completed*. New York: W. W. Norton.

Erikson, E., Erikson, J., & Kivnick, H. (1986). *Vital involvement in old age*. New York: W. W. Norton.

Feldman, David (1980). *Universals in cognitive development*. Norwood, NJ: Ablex Publishing Corporation.

Ferguson, Marilyn (1982). Karl Pribram's changing reality. In Ken Wilber (Ed.), *The holographic paradigm and other paradoxes*. Boulder, Colorado: Shambhala.

Fingarette, H. (1963). *The self in transformation*. New York: Harper & Row.

Fowler, James W. (1981). *Stages of faith: The psychology of human development and the quest for meaning*. San Francisco: Harper and Row.

Fowler, J. (1984). *Becoming adult, becoming Christian*. San Francisco: Harper & Row.

Fowler, J. and Keen, S. (1979). *Life maps: conversations on the journey of faith*. Waco, TX: Work Books.

Frame, Donald. M. (Trans.). (1968). *The complete essays of Montaigne*. Palo Alto, CA: Stanford University Press.

Frankl, Viktor (1963). *Man's search for meaning: An introduction to logotherapy*. New York: Washington Square Press.

Frankl, Viktor (1966/Fall). Self-transcendence as a human phenomenon. *Journal of Humanistic Psychology*, *6*(2), pp. 97–106.

Freud, Sigmund (1937). *Analysis terminable and interminable*. Standard edition 23:216. New York: W. W. Norton.

Friedman, Maurice S. (1965/1960). *Martin Buber: The life of dialogue*. New York: Harper Torchbooks, The Cloister Library, Harper & Row.

Friedman, Maurice S. (1985a). Healing through meeting and the problematic of mutuality. *Journal of Humanistic Psychology*, *25*(1), 7–40.

Friedman, Maurice S. (1985b). Healing dialogue. Selections from *The healing dialogue in psychotherapy* (1985) in *AHP Perspective*, December.

Friedman, Maurice S. (1985c).*The healing dialogue in psychotherapy*. New York: Jason Aronson.

Friedman, Meyer (1980). May 3, Lecture, "Type A" behavior and stress-related disease, Portland, Oregon.

Fuller, R. B. (1978). *Operating manual for spaceship earth*. New York: Dutton.

Gardner, John W. (1961). *Excellence*. New York: Harper & Row.

Gilligan, Carol (1982). *In a different voice: Psychological theory and women's development.* Cambridge, MA: Harvard University Press.

Ginzberg, Eli (1972). Toward a theory of occupational choice: A restatement. *The Vocational Guidance Quarterly, 20*(3), 169–176.

Ginzberg, Eli (1984). Career development. In D. Brown & L. Brooks (Eds.), *Career choice and development* (pp. 169–191). San Francisco: Jossey-Bass.

Glaser, Robert (1984). Education and thinking: The role of knowledge. *American Psychologist, 39*(2), 93–104.

Goleman, Daniel (1978). Breaking out of the double bind. Interview with Gregory Bateson in *Psychology today, 12* (3), 42–51.

Gould, Roger L. (1978). *Transformations: Growth and change in adult life.* New York: Simon and Schuster.

Graubard, S. R. (1978). Preface. In E. H. Erikson (Ed.), *Adulthood.* New York: W. W. Norton.

Greer, Frank (1980). Toward a developmental view of adult crisis: A re-examination of crisis theory. *Journal of humanistic psychology, 20*(4), pp. 17–29.

Gruber, Howard (1974). *Darwin on man: A psychological study of scientific creativity.* New York: Dutton.

Gruber, Howard (1981). Breakaway minds. [Interview by H. Gardner]. *Psychology Today, 15*(7), 64–73.

Gruber, Howard (1984). Preface. In M. Basseches, *Dialectical thinking and adult development.* Norwood, NJ: Ablex.

Gubrium, J., & Buckholdt, D. (1977). *Toward maturity.* San Francisco: Jossey-Bass.

Guidano, V. F., & Liotti, G. (1983). *Cognitive processes and emotional disorders: A structural approach to psychotherapy.* New York: Guilford.

Haldane, Bernard (1974). *Career satisfaction and success: A guide to job freedom.* New York: AMACOM.

Hampden-Turner, Charles (1981). *Maps of the mind.* New York: Macmillan.

Harper dictionary of modern thought. (1977). New York: Harper & Row.

Havighurst, R. J. (1972). *Developmental tasks and education.* (3rd ed.). New York: McKay.

Hayek, F. A. (1952). *The sensory order.* Chicago: University of Chicago Press.

Hayward, Jeremy W. (1984). *Perceiving ordinary magic: Science and intuitive wisdom.* Boulder, CO: New Science Library, Shambhala.

Hegel, G. W. F. (1967). *The phenomenology of mind.* (Translated by J.B. Baillie.) New York: Harper & Row.

Holland, J. L. (1973). *Making vocational choices: A theory of careers.* Englewood Cliffs, NJ: Prentice-Hall.

Holland, J. L. (1979). *The self-directed search professional manual.* Palo Alto, CA: Consulting Psychologists Press.

Holland, J. L. (1983). In C. Minor & F. Burtnett (Producers). *Career development: Linking theory with practice* [Videotape]. Arlington, VA: American Association for Counseling and Development.

Holland, J. L. (1985). *Making vocational choices: A theory of vocational personalities and work environments* (2nd ed.). Englewood Cliffs, NJ: Prentice-Hall.

Horowitz, F. D., & O'Brien, M. (Eds.). (1985). *The gifted and talented: Developmental perspectives.* Washington, DC: American Psychological Association.

Jackson, Michael R. (1984). *Self-esteem and meaning.* Albany: State University of New York Press.

Jackson, Tom (1978). *Guerrilla tactics in the job market: A practical manual.* New York: Bantam Books.

Jacobs, Jane (1984). Holding environments and developmental stages: A study of marriage. *Dissertation Abstracts International, 45*(6), 21188B.

James, William (1902). *The varieties of religious experience.* New York: Longmans.

Janis, Irving L. (1969/1971). *Stress and frustration.* New York: Harcourt Brace Jovanovich.

Janis, I., & Wheeler, D. (1978). Thinking clearly about career choices. *Psychology today, 11*(12), 67–76, 121, 122.

Jung, Carl G. (1957). *The undiscovered self.* New York: New American Library.

Kagan, Jerome (1984). *The nature of the child.* New York: Basic Books.

Kahana, Boaz (1982). Social behavior and aging. In B. Wolman, G. Stricter, S. Ellman, P. Keith-Spiegel, & D. Palermo (Eds.). *Handbook of developmental psychology* (pp. 871–889), Englewood Cliffs, NJ: Prentice-Hall.

Kakar, Sudhir (Ed.) (1979). *Identity and adulthood*. Delhi, India: Oxford University Press.

Kakar, Sudhir (1968). *Philosophy east and west*. [Reprinted as Chapter I, Setting the stage. In Sudhir Kahar, (1979), *Identity and adulthood*.]

Karuza, Jurgis, Jr. (1986). Psycho-social issues in successful aging: A change in focus. *Adult Development and Aging News, 13*(3).

Kastenbaum, Robert J. (1973). Epilogue: Loving, dying, and other gerontologic addenda. In Carl Eisdorfer & M. Powell Lawton (Eds.), *The psychology of adult development and aging*, Washington, DC: American Psychological Association.

Keen, Sam (1983). *The passionate life: Stages of loving*. New York: Harper & Row.

Keen, S., & Fox, A. V. (1974). *Telling your story: A guide to who you are and who you can be*. New York: Signet.

Keeney, Bradford P. (1983). *The aesthetics of change*. New York: Guilford.

Kegan, Robert G. (1977). *Ego and truth*. Unpublished doctoral dissertation, Harvard University.

Kegan, Robert G. (1980). There the dance is: Religious dimensions of a developmental framework. In *Toward moral and religious maturity*. Report on the First International Conference on Moral and Religious Development. Morristown, NJ: Silver Burdett Company.

Kegan, Robert G. (1982). *The evolving self: Problem and process in human development*. Cambridge, MA: Harvard University Press.

Kegan, Robert G. (1983, June). Lecture presented at the Lifespan Clinical-Developmental Institute at Harvard University.

Kegan, R. G., Noam, G. G., & Rogers, L. (1982). The psychologic of emotion: A neo-Piagetian view. In D. Cicchetti & P. Pogge-Hesse (Eds.), *New directions for child development: Emotional development*. San Francisco: Jossey-Bass.

Keirsey, D., & Bates, M. (1978). *Please understand me: An essay on temperament styles*. Del Mar, CA: Prometheus Nemesis Books.

Kelly, George A. (1955). *A theory of personality: The psychology of personal constructs*. New York: W. W. Norton.

Kleinsasser, L. D., & Harris, D. B. (1966). *The middle years: Development and adjustment*. State College, PA.: The Pennsylvania State University, Center for Continuing Liberal Education.

Klinger, Eric (1977). *Meaning and void: Inner experiences and the incentives in people's lives*. Minneapolis: University of Minnesota Press.

Koestler, Arthur (1970). *The act of creation*. London: Pan Books.

Koestler, Arthur (1978). *Janus*. New York: Random House.

Kohlberg, Lawrence (1984). *The psychology of moral development* (Vol. 2 of *Essays on moral development*). San Francisco: Harper & Row.

Korchin, Sheldon J. (1976). *Modern clinical psychology*. New York: Basic Books.

Kramer, N. J. T. A., & de Smit, J. (1977). *Systems thinking*. Leiden, Netherlands: Martinus Hijhoff Social Sciences Division.

Krech, D. (1949). Notes toward a psychological theory. *Journal of Personality, 18*, 66–87.

Kreitler, H., & Kreitler, S. (1976). *Cognitive orientation and behavior*. New York: Springer.

Lakoff, G., & Johnson, M. (1980). *Metaphors we live by*. Chicago: University of Chicago Press.

Langer, Suzanne (1967). *Mind: An essay on human feeling* (Vol. 1). Baltimore, MD: Johns Hopkins University Press.

Lasker, H., & Moore, J. (1980). *Adult development and approaches to learning*. Washington, DC: U.S. Government Printing Office.

Lawton, M. Powell, (1973) Clinical psychology? In C. Eisdorfer & M. P. Lawton, (Eds.). *The psychology of adult development and aging*. Washington, DC: American Psychological Association.

Lawton, M. Powell (1986). In K. Fisher, Demographics beckon young to maturing field. *APA Monitor*, January, 18–19.

Lazarus, Arnold A. (1971). *Behavior therapy and beyond*. New York: McGraw-Hill.

Lazarus, Arnold A. (1976). *Multimodal behavior therapy*. New York: Springer.

Lazarus, Arnold A. (Ed.) (1985). *Casebook of multimodal therapy*. New York: Guilford.

Lazarus, Richard (1982). Contribution to article, "Understanding psychological man." In *Psychology today, 16*, (5), 43–44.

Lazarus, R. S. & Folkman, S. (1984). *Stress, appraisal, and coping*. New York: Springer.

Lederer, William J. (1984). *Creating a good relationship.* W. W. Norton.
Leibowitz, Zandy & Lea Daniel (Eds.) (1986). *Adult career development: Concepts, issues and practices.* Silver Spring, MD: National Career Development Association.
Lee, B., & Noam, G. (Eds.). (1983). *Developmental approaches to the self.* New York: Plenum.
L'Engle, Madeleine (1980). *Walking on water: Reflections on faith and art.* Wheaton, IL: Harold Shaw.
Lerner, Harriet (1985).*The dance of anger: A woman's guide to changing the patterns of intimate relationships.* New York: Harper & Row.
LeShan, L. (1974). *How to meditate: A guide to self-discovery.* New York: Bantam Books.
LeShan, L., & Margenau, H. (1983). *Einstein's space and Van Gogh's sky: Physical reality and beyond.* New York: Macmillan.
Levinson, Daniel J., et al. (1978). *The seasons of a man's life.* New York: Knopf.
Levinson, Daniel J. (1986). A conception of adult development. *American Psychologist, 41*(1), 3–13.
Loder, J. E. (1981). *The transforming moment.* San Francisco: Harper & Row.
Loevinger, Jane (1982). *Ego development.* San Francisco: Jossey-Bass.
Mahoney, Michael J. (Ed.) (1980). *Psychotherapy process: Current issues and future directions.* New York: Plenum.
Mahoney, Michael J. (1982). Psychotherapy and human change processes. In J. H. Harvey & M. M. Parks (Eds.), *The master lecture series* (Vol. 1, pp. 73–122). Washington, DC: American Psychological Association.
Mahoney, M. J., & Freeman, A. (Eds.). (1985). *Cognition and psychotherapy.* New York: Plenum.
Maslow, Abraham H. (1961). Health as transcendence of environment. *Journal of Humanistic Psychology, 1*(1), 1–7.
Maslow, Abraham H. (1965). *Eupsychian management.* Homewood, IL: Richard D. Irwin.
Maslow, Abraham H. (1968a). Human potentialities and the healthy society. In H. A. Otto (Ed.), *Human potentialities: The challenge and the promise* (Chapt. V, pp. 64–79), St. Louis, MO: Warren H. Green, Inc.
Maslow, Abraham H. (1968b). *Toward a psychology of being.* (Second ed.). Princeton, NJ: Van Nostrand.
Maslow, Abraham H. (1970). *Motivation and personality* (2nd ed.). New York: Harper & Row.
Maslow, Abraham H. (1971). *The farther reaches of human nature.* New York: Viking.
May, Rollo (1953). *Man's search for himself.* New York: W. W.Norton.
May, Rollo (1975). *The courage to create.* New York: W. W. Norton.
May, Rollo (1979). *Psychology and the human dilemma.* New York: W. W. Norton.
May, Rollo (1981). *Freedom and destiny.* New York: W. W. Norton.
McCrae, Robert R., & Costa, Paul T. (1982). Aging, the life course, and models of personality. In T. Field, A. Huston, H. C. Quay, L. Troll, & G. Finley (Eds.), *Review of human development.* New York: Wiley.
McGoldrick, M. & Gerson, R. (1985). *Genograms in family assessment.* New York: W. W. Norton.
McLeish, John A. B. (1976). *The Ulyssean adult: Creativity in the middle and latter years.* New York: McGraw-Hill Ryerson.
McLeish, John A. B. (1983). *The challenge of aging: Ulyssean paths to creative living.* Vancouver, BC: Douglas and McIntyre.
Merrill, John E. (1894). *Ideals and institutions: Their parallel development.* Hartford, CT: Hartford Seminary Press.
Midlarsky, E., & Kahana, E. (1986). Altruism, meaningfulness, and the sense of mastery in late life. *Adult Development and Aging News, 13*(3), 5–6.
Minor, Carole W. (1986). Career development: Theories and issues. In Zandy Leibowitz & Daniel Lea (Eds.), *Adult career development: Concepts, issues and practices* (Chapt. 2). Silver Spring, MD: National Career Development Association.
Minsky, M. & Papert, S. (1974). *Artificial intelligence.* Eugene, OR: Oregon State System of Higher Education.
Mitchell, Arnold (1983). *Nine American lifestyles: How our values, beliefs, drives, and needs will combine with social trends to shape our future.* New York: Warner Books.
Montaigne. (1968). *The complete essays of Montaigne.* (Frame, Donald. M., Trans.) Palo Alto, CA: Stanford University Press.
Montalvo, B. (1976). Observations of two natural amnesias. *Family Process, 15*, 333–342.

Mosak, Harold H. (1979). Adlerian psychotherapy. In Raymond J. Corsini (Ed.), *Current psychotherapies* (Chapt. II, 2nd ed.). Itasca, IL: Peacock.

Myers, Isabel B. (1980). *Gifts differing*. Palo Alto, CA: Consulting Psychologists Press.

Nadler, Gerald (1967). *Work systems design: The ideals concept*. Homewood, IL: Richard D. Irwin, Inc.

Nagel, Paul C. (1983). *Descent from glory*. New York: Oxford University Press.

Neugarten, Bernice L. (Ed.) (1968). *Middle age and aging: A reader in social psychology*. Chicago: University of Chicago Press.

Neugarten, Bernice L. (1971). Grow old along with me! The best is yet to be. *Psychology today, 5*(7), 45-48, 79-81.

Neugarten, Bernice L. (1977). Adult personality: Toward a psychology of the life-cycle. In Lawrence Allman & Dennis Jaffe (Eds.), *Readings in adult psychology: Contemporary perspectives*. New York: Harper & Row.

Noam, G., & Kegan, R. (1982). Social cognition and psychodynamics: Towards a clinical developmental psychology. In W. Edelstein & M. Keller (Eds.), *Perspektivitat und interpretations*. Frankfurt: Suhrkamp.

Noddings, Nell (1984). *Caring: A feminist approach to ethics and moral education*. Berkeley, CA: University of California Press.

Offer, D., & Sabshin, M. (1984). *Normality and the life cycle*. New York: Basic Books.

Parkes, C. Murray (1971). Psycho-social transitions. *Social Science and Medicine, 5*, 101-115.

Parkes, C. M. (1972). *Bereavement: Studies of grief in adult life*. New York: International Universities Press.

Paul, H. & Paul, M. (1983). *Do I have to give up me to be loved by you*? Minneapolis: CompCare Publications.

Peck, M. Scott (1978). *The road less traveled*. New York: Simon & Schuster.

Perry, W. G., Jr. (1970). *Forms of intellectual and ethical development in the college years*. New York: Holt, Rinehart & Winston.

Perry, W. G. (1981). Cognitive and ethical growth: The making of meaning. In A. Chickering (Ed.), *The modern American college* (pp.76-116). San Francisco: Jossey-Bass.

Pfeiffer, Eric (1974). *Successful aging: A conference report*. Durham, NC: Center for the Study of Aging and Human Development, Duke University.

Pines, Ayala (1985, November). In C. Turkington, Finding what's good in marriage. *APA Monitor, 16*(11).

Polanyi, Michael (1975). *Meaning*. Chicago: University of Chicago Press.

Pribram, Karl (1971).*Languages of the brain*. Englewood Cliffs, NJ: Prentice-Hall.

Pribram, Karl (1986).The cognitive revolution and mind/brain issues. *American Psychologist, 41*(5), 507-520.

Prigogine, Ilya (1984).*Order out of chaos*. New York: Bantam Books.

Riegel, Klaus F. (1975). Toward a dialectical theory of development, *Human Development, 18*, 50-64.

Riegel, Klaus F. (1978). *Psychology mon amour*. Boston: Houghton Mifflin.

Ringer, R. (1978). *Looking out for number one*. New York: Fawcett.

Rogers, Carl R. (1951). *Client-centered therapy: Its current practice, implications, and theory*. Boston: Houghton Mifflin.

Rogers, Carl R. (1961). *On becoming a person: A therapist's view of psychotherapy*. Boston: Houghton Mifflin.

Rogers, Carl R. (1972). *Becoming partners: Marriage and its alternatives*. New York: Delacorte.

Roosevelt, Eleanor (1961). *The autobiography of Eleanor Roosevelt*. New York: Harper & Row.

Sager, Clifford J. (1976). *Marriage contracts and couple therapy*. New York: Brunner/Mazel.

Sanders, Lawrence (1983). *The tenth commandment*. New York: Berkeley Publishing Group.

Savary, Louis (1967). *Man, his world and his work*. New York: Paulist Press.

Schlossberg, Nancy K. (1984). *Counseling adults in transition: Linking practice to theory*. New York: Springer.

Schoen, Stephen (1982). Bateson, Gregory: In remembrance. *AHP Newsletter*, February, pp. 3-6.

Schumacher, E. F. (1977). *A guide for the perplexed*. New York: Harper & Row.

Scott-Maxwell, Florida (1968). *The measure of my days*. New York: Knopf.

Selman, Robert L. (1969). Role taking ability and the development of moral judgment. *Dissertation Abstracts International, 30*(5), 2154A.

Selye, Hans (1978). *The stress of life* (revised edition). New York: McGraw-Hill.

Siebert, A. (1983, August). *The survivor personality*. Revised paperbased on presentation to the Western Psychological Association Convention, San Francisco, April 1983.

Skinner, B. F., & Vaughn, M. E. (1983). *Enjoy old age: A program of self-management*. New York: W. W. Norton.

Smith, Huston (1985). The sacred unconscious, with footnotes on self-actualization and evil. *Journal of Humanistic Psychology, 25*(3), 65–80.

Smith, Huston (1965). *Condemned to meaning*. New York: Harper & Row.

Standley, Nancy V. (1971). Kierkegaard and man's vocation. *Vocational Guidance Quarterly, 20*(2), 119–122.

Stewart, John (1982). *Bridges not walls* (3rd ed.). Reading, MA: Addison-Wesley.

Super, Donald E. (1957). *The preliminary appraisal in vocational counseling. Personnel and Guidance Journal, 36,* 3, 154–161.

Super, Donald E. (1976). *Career education and the meanings of work*. Washington, DC: U.S. Government Printing Office.

Super, Donald E. (1981).A developmental theory: Implementing a self concept. In D. H. Montross & C. J. Shinkman (Eds.), *Career development in the 1980s: Theory and practice*. Springfield, IL: Thomas.

Super, Donald E. (1984). Career and life development. In D. Brown & L. Brooks (Eds.), *Career choice and development* (pp. 192–234). San Francisco: Jossey-Bass.

Super, D., et al. (1963). *Career development: Self-concept theory*. New York: College Entrance Exam Board.

Tavris, Carol (1982). *Anger: The misunderstood emotion*. New York: Simon & Schuster.

Terkel, Studs (1974). *Working*. New York: Avon Books.

The Society for Projective Techniques and Rorschach Institute, Inc. Early recollections as a projective technique. (1958). *Journal of projective techniques, 22*(3).

Tillich, Paul (1952). *The courage to be*. New Haven, CT: Yale University Press.

Tolman, Charles (1983). Further comments on the meaning of "dialectic." *Human Development 26,* (320–324).

Trüb, Hans (1952). Healing through meeting. *(Heilung aus der Begegnung.) Stuttgart: ErnstKlett Verlag. Selections tranlated by William Hallo for M. Friedman (1964), Worlds of existentialism*. New York: Random House, p. 500.

Tu Wei-ming (1978). The Confucian perception of adulthood. In Erik H. Erikson (Ed.), *Adulthood* (pp. 113–127). New York: W. W. Norton

Turkington, Carol (1985,November). Finding what's good in marriage. *APA Monitor*, 16(11).

Tyler, Leona E. (1978). *Individuality: Human possibilities and personal choice in the psychological development of men and women*. San Francisco, CA: Jossey-Bass.

Tyler, Leona E. (1983). *Thinking creatively*. San Francisco: Jossey-Bass.

Vaillant, George E. (1977). *Adaptation to life: How the best and the brightest came of age*. Boston: Little, Brown.

Veroff, J., Douvan, E., & Kulka, R.A. (1981). *The inner American: A self-portrait from 1957 to 1976*. New York: Basic Books.

Viscott, David (1976). *The language of feelings*. New York: Priam Books.

Von Oech, Roger (1983). *A whack on the side of the head*. New York: Warner Books.

Walton, Richard (1969). *Interpersonal peacemaking: Confrontations and third party consultation*. Reading, MA: Addison-Wesley.

Watson, James B. (1925). *Behaviorism*. New York: W. W. Norton.

Weil, Simone (1952). *The need for roots*. New York: Putnam.

Weiss, Robert S. (1975). *Marital separation*. New York: Basic Books.

Wheelis, Allen (1958). *The quest for identity*. New York: W. W. Norton.

Wheelis, Allen (1973). *How people change*. New York: Harper & Row.

Wilber, Ken (Ed.). (1982). *The Holographic paradigm and other paradoxes*. Boulder, CO: Shambhala.

Winnicott, Donald W. (1965). *The maturational process and the facilitating environment: Studies in the theory of emotional development*. New York: International Universities Press.

Wittig, Michele A. (1985). Metatheoretical dilemmas in the psychology of gender. *American Psychologist, 40*(7), 800–811.

Yankelovich, Daniel (1982). *New rules: Searching for self-fulfillment in a world turned upside down*. New York: Bantam Books.

INDEX